French
vocabulary handbook

Kate Dobson

**Berlitz Publishing / APA Publications GmbH & Co. Verlag KG,
Singapore Branch, Singapore**

French Vocabulary Handbook

Contacting the Editors

Every effort has been made to provide accurate information in this publication, but changes are inevitable. The publisher cannot be responsible for any resulting loss, inconvenience or injury. We would appreciate it if readers would call our attention to any errors or outdated information by contacting Berlitz Publishing, 193 Morris Avenue, Springfield, NJ 07081, USA. Fax: 1-908-206-1103. email: comments@berlitzbooks.com

Cover photo © PunchStock/Medioimages

Printed in Singapore by Insight Print Services (Pte) Ltd., February 2008.

The Author:
Kate Dobson is an experienced teacher at the primary school, high school, and adult level.

The Series Editor:
Christopher Wightwick is a former UK representative on the Council of Europe Modern Languages Project and principal Inspector of Modern Languages for England.

CONTENTS

How to use this Handbook

This Handbook is a carefully ordered work of reference covering all areas of French vocabulary and phrasing. It is based on the thesaurus structure of the Council of Europe's Threshold Level, expanded to include other major topics, especially in the fields of business, information technology, and education. Unlike a dictionary, it brings together words and phrases in related groups. It also illustrates their usage with contextualized example sentences, often in dialogue form. This enables learners and users of the language to:

- refresh and expand their general knowledge of vocabulary;
- revise systematically for public examinations, using the word groups to test their knowledge from French to English and vice versa;
- extend their knowledge of authentically French ways of saying things by studying the example sentences;
- support their speaking and writing on a given topic, when the logical arrangement of the sections will often prompt new ideas as well as supplying the means of expressing them.

THE STRUCTURE OF THE HANDBOOK

The Handbook is divided into four parts:

A Introduction

This section includes a concise account of the ways in which French creates compound words and phrases in order to express more complex ideas, together with a brief survey of nouns, adjectives and verbs in French. (For a more extensive treatment of these topics, see the *Berlitz French Grammar Handbook*.)

B Vocabulary topics

This section includes 96 vocabularies, grouped under 27 major areas of experience. Many vocabularies are divided into a number of sections, so that words and phrases are gathered together into closely related groups. Almost all sections contain example sentences showing the vocabulary in use. Wherever it makes sense to do so, these sentences are linked together to form short narratives or dialogues that help to fix them in the memory.

In some vocabularies the lists of words and phrases are both extensive and more independent of context, so that the role of the example sentences is reduced.

C Appendixes

This section includes lists of specific terms such as the names of countries or musical instruments. These would simply clutter up the main vocabularies, but they are linked to them by clear cross-references.

D Subject Index

This section has an alphabetical index of topics and themes, enabling you to locate the area you are interested in quickly.

LOCATING THE RIGHT SECTION

The Handbook can be approached in two main ways.

•   If you are not sure which topic will be best suited to your needs, start with the Table of Contents. This will give you a general picture of the areas covered. You can then browse through the sections until you find the one you want.

•   Alternatively, if you have a specific topic in mind, look it up in the *Subject Index* at the end of the book. This will take you directly to the relevant vocabulary or appendix. To help you find what you are looking for, topics are often listed more than once, under different headings. Within most sections there are cross-references to other related areas.

A
INTRODUCTION

Vocabulary & structure in the French language

Conventions used in this Handbook

The vocabulary of the French language

Similar features of French and English

Within the very large group of Indo-European languages, French and English could be regarded as second cousins. Although some of the structures of French are different from English patterns, because of the overriding influence of its Latin origin, a very large number of individual words are easily recognizable from one language to the other.

Related words

The Norman Conquest brought a number of Norman French words into English, and the Renaissance and the Modern Age have created a large number of scientific, abstract, and technical words common to many European languages. In addition, culinary and artistic terms have been borrowed from French into English. Some English words have been borrowed, somewhat uncomfortably, into French. It is useful for the student of French to identify this common ground and exploit it. Some words are spelled as in English, while some are not quite the same, and of course, adjectives and verbs undergo pronunciation and spelling changes in use.

These are some examples; many more could be cited.

English	*French*
Nouns	
Television; telephone	**Télévision; téléphone**
feast, beast, forest; tempest; crest	**fête; bête; forêt; tempête; crête**

The circumflex accent in French often shows that an "s" has been lost along the way.

liberty; beauty; quality; variety	**liberté; beauté; qualité; variété**
doctor; professor; actor	**docteur; professeur; acteur**
interpreter; minister	**interprète; ministre**
racism; communism; Buddhism	**racisme; communisme; Bouddisme**
mystery; ministry	**mystère; ministère**
glory; victory; memory	**gloire; victoire; mémoire**
harmony; (political) party	**harmonie; parti (politique)**
movement; government	**mouvement; gouvernement**
soufflé; flambé; café	**soufflé; flambé; café**

Adjectives

rare; imprudent	**rare; imprudent**
dramatic; comic; domestic	**dramatique; comique; domestique**
socialist; racist;	**socialiste; raciste**
realistic; simplistic	**réaliste; simpliste**
social; national	**social; national**
official; individual	**officiel; individuel**
possible; impossible	**possible; impossible**
capable; probable	**capable; probable**
popular; military	**populaire; militaire**
glorious; precious; pretentious	**glorieux; précieux; prétentieux**

Verbs

to respect; to interpret; to cede	**respecter; interpréter; céder**
to contemplate; to cultivate	**contempler; cultiver**
to film; to sponsor	**filmer; sponsoriser**

False friends

The learner also needs to be aware that there exist a number of words that look similar but have different meanings. These are often called "false friends" or **faux-amis**.

French	*English*
actuel	contemporary/of the present time
assister (à)	to attend, be present at
contrôler	to check, test
une fabrique	factory
une intoxication	poisoning
large	wide
la métropole	France (as opposed to its overseas territories)
malicieux	mischievous
sensible	sensitive
un stage	short course, period of training
un store	(window) blind

There are also words that have the meaning you anticipate, but that, in certain contexts, they may have a different sense.

une action	action; also a share (finance)
une chaîne	chain; also TV channel
l'édition	edition; also publishing
un parent	parent; also any relative
ignorer	to ignore; also (originally) not to know

Recent borrowings from English

Finally, we should mention the many words in French that have been borrowed from English, and still persist despite the attempts of *Académiciens* and others to eradicate them.

le bulldozer, le bungalow, le week-end, le meeting, le parking, le living (living room), **le shopping, le jogging, le basket** (sneaker), **le sweat-shirt** (often abbreviated to **le sweat**), **le hit-parade, le hamburger, la star** (in entertainment), **le hovercraft, le car-ferry**

And many more!

For a good number of such words, a French equivalent exists, but fails to suppress the use of the English word. Hence the term *franglais*, to describe these hybrids.

A few notes on French structures

(i)   *Nouns*

(A) Gender

All nouns in French are masculine or feminine in gender. The gender needs to be learned with the word itself, as it affects the use of articles, adjectives, pronouns, and some verb forms.

It is not generally possible to predict the gender of a noun from its meaning. If in doubt, check in a dictionary. However:

• Most nouns for male persons are masculine and female persons are feminine.

le père; le frère   la mère; la soeur

Confusion arises where women exercise professions where previously only men were found.

un docteur; un ministre; un ingénieur; un professeur (all masculine words, even if applied to women)

Nowadays forms such as **une professeur, une ministre** are also increasingly found. Otherwise, the feminine form is **une femme ingénieur.**

Some words can be either masculine or feminine:

le/la dentiste; le/la collègue

Jobs done by men and women often have a masculine and a feminine form:

le boulanger/la boulangère
le coiffeur/la coiffeuse
l'infirmier/l'infirmière

le fermier/la fermière
l'instituteur/l'institutrice

A few words are always feminine, even when they refer to men:

une personne, une victime, une star/vedette (de cinéma)

• All languages, days of the week, months, seasons and colors are masculine; as are most trees and shrubs and those fruits and flowers not ending in **-e.**

The majority of abstract nouns, most countries, all the continents, and all fruits and flowers ending in **-e** are feminine.

Almost all nouns adopted into French from English are masculine (**le club; le bungalow,** but **la star**). Nouns taken from other languages tend to keep their original gender (**la vodka; la pizza**).

• Some noun endings denote gender, and it may be helpful to memorize the more common of these. (There are occasional exceptions)

-et; -eau ; -isme; -oir; -al; -ail; -ent are masculine endings

-ise; -té; -tion; -ance; -ence; -oire are feminine endings.

• In this Handbook the definite or indefinite article is given before the noun, to show the gender:

| Masculine | **le béton** | **un téléphone** |
| Feminine | **la fabrication** | **une taxe** |

Where a noun is preceded by the articles **l'** or **les/des**, the gender is given after the noun:

l'échafaudage (*m*) **les affaires** (*f*)

(B) Plural of nouns

• Most French nouns form the plural by adding **-s.**

une voiture **deux voitures** **un croissant** **des croissants**

However, this **-s** is not pronounced. The listener understands the plural from the expression that precedes the noun: **les ... des ... deux ... quelques ... beaucoup de ...** etc.

• Some nouns have irregular plurals. For instance, those ending in **-al** form the plural in **-aux;** this also applies to some nouns ending in **-ail.**

un cheval **des chevaux** **le travail** **les travaux**
(road work)

Other plurals in **-x** include:

un bijou	des bijoux
un œil	les yeux
le ciel	les cieux

(C) Compound nouns

Compound nouns in French are formed in a variety of ways. There are noun-noun and verb-noun combinations, linked with a hyphen; various combinations linked by prepositions **à**, **de**, or **en**; and noun-adjective phrases (without hyphenation). It is not possible to predict with accuracy; each compound noun needs to be learnt or checked. (➤ *Berlitz French Grammar Handbook*, chapter 3.)

noun-noun	**un timbre-poste**
verb-noun	**un lave-vaisselle**
noun + **à** +noun	**un verre à vin** (*denotes usage*)
noun + **à** + verb	**une machine à écrire** (*denotes usage*)
noun+ **de** + noun	**une auberge de jeunesse**
noun + adjective	**une année scolaire**
preposition + noun	**un hors-d'oeuvre**

Verb-noun and preposition + noun compounds are generally invariable, though some of the former add **-s**.

un hors-d'oeuvre	**des hors-d'oeuvre**
un porte-monnaie	**des porte-monnaie**

but

un tire-bouchon	**des tire-bouchons**

Plurals of other compound nouns vary according to the elements in the compound.

un timbre-poste	**des timbres-poste**
un lave-vaisselle	**des lave-vaisselle**
un verre à vin	**des verres à vin**
une machine à écrire	**des machines à écrire**
une auberge de jeunesse	**des auberges de jeunesse**
une année scolaire	**deux années scolaires**

Consult the *Berlitz French Grammar Handbook* (➤ 18e) or a dictionary for further information on all these forms.

(ii) Adjectives

(A) Agreement

Adjectives alter their form according to what or who is being described. There may be as many as four forms: masculine singular, masculine plural, feminine singular, and feminine plural.

Possessives (**mon, ma, mes,** etc.) and demonstratives (**ce, cet, cette, ces**) and their usages need to be learned by heart.

• The majority of adjectives make their agreements with the noun as follows:

Masculine singular	as in the dictionary
Feminine singular	add **-e** (unless the masculine already ends in **-e**)
Masculine plural	add **-s** to singular (unless it already
Feminine plural	ends in **-s**)

un chapeau noir et jaune	**deux chapeaux noirs et jaunes**
une robe noire et jaune	**des robes noires et jaunes**

It should be noted that these added letters are frequently unheard, as in the example above, where all forms of **noir** and **jaune** have the same pronunciation.

When an adjective ends in a silent consonant in the masculine singular, the feminine agreement will cause the consonant to be pronounced, but the **-s** of the plural will still be unheard.

un chat gris	**une souris grise** (the **-se** is pronounced **-z**)

• Some adjectives have other slight changes from masculine to feminine. The most common are:

Doubling final consonant + **-e**

gentil, cruel	**gentille, cruelle**
parisien, italien	**parisienne, italienne**
gras, gros	**grasse, grosse**

-eux/euse, oux/-ouse

heureux, paresseux	**heureuse, paresseuse**
jaloux	**jalouse**

-er/-ère

cher, premier	**chère, première**

• Some common adjectives have an irregular feminine form:

blanc	**blanche**	**doux**	**douce**
frais	**fraîche**	**long**	**longue**
public	**publique**		

• Most adjectives ending in **-al** in the masculine singular end in **-aux** in the masculine plural:

un problème social   **des problèmes sociaux**

(B) Position of adjectives

• Most adjectives follow the noun in French.
• A few very common adjectives precede the noun:

bon, mauvais, beau, grand, gros, petit, vieux, jeune, nouveau, joli, premier

• A number of adjectives change their meaning according to the position:

une maison *ancienne* (*old*)   **un** *ancien* **élève** (*former*)

Consult the *Berlitz French Grammar Handbook* for a full treatment.

(iii)   Verbs

In this Handbook, most verbs are entered in the first-person singular of the present tense.

(A) Verbs ending in **-e** in the vocabulary lists belong to the **-er** conjugation, the largest group in French.

j'accuse   Infinitive: **accuser**   to accuse

The infinitive is included alongside the entry for otherwise regular **-er** verbs which undergo minor spelling changes.

il aboie   Infinitive: **aboyer**   to bark
je jette   infinitive: **jeter**   to throw
je me lève   Infinitive: **se lever**   to get up

(B) Verbs ending in **-is** (except irregular verbs, whose infinitives are given) belong to the **-ir** conjugation.

j'établis   Infinitive: **établir**   to establish
je finis   Infinitive: **finir**   to finish

(C) Verbs ending in **-ds** belong to the **-re** conjugation

je réponds   Infinitive: **répondre**   to answer
je vends   Infinitive: **vendre**   to sell

(D) All irregular verbs apart from **être, avoir, aller,** and **faire** have the infinitive shown alongside the entry.

je dis *(dire)*   **j'éteins** *(éteindre)*

Conventions used in this book

Nouns

Nouns are given in the singular form, generally preceded by the definite article. The plural form is included if irregular.

le/un indicates masculine gender
la/une indicates feminine gender
l' could apply to either gender for nouns beginning wth a vowel, so the correct gender is given in parentheses.

Verbs

Verbs are entered in the first-person singular of the present tense. Where this is inappropriate, the entry is in the third-person singular, for convenience, **il** is employed.

The infinitive of irregular verbs and verbs that undergo spelling changes follow the entry. Conjugations of all regular and regular verbs are found in the *Berlitz French Verb Handbook*, under the infinitive heading, along with explanations of usage and tenses.

Adjectives

Adjectives are in the masculine singular form. Irregular feminine forms are indicated in parentheses.

Abbreviations

acc	accusative	inf	infinitive
adj	adjective	intr	intransitive
adv	adverb	invar	invariable
conj	conjunction	m	masculine
dat	dative	pl	plural
f	feminine	subj	subjunctive
fam	familiar usage	tr	transitive

Symbols

( )   a part of a translation that is optional: **le repas (léger)**

/   alternative word: **la chambre double/pour deux personnes** – **la chambre double** or **la chambre pour deux personnes.**

,   an alternative translation

[ ]   feminine adjectival ending, included when it is not **-** or **-e**

( )   the infinitive of an irregular verb, or verb with a minor spelling change

➤   a cross-reference to a vocabulary or chapter

B

VOCABULARY TOPICS

1 Function words

Articles

a	**un/une**
the	**le/la/les/l'**
some	**des**

Demonstrative adjectives/pronouns

this/that	**ce/cet/cette**
these	**ces**
this one	**celui-ci/celle-ci**
that one	**celui-là/celle-là**
those (ones)	**ceux-là/celles-là**
the red one	**le/la rouge**

Personal pronouns (subject)

I	**je**
you	**tu /vous/on**
he	**il**
she	**elle**
it	**il/elle**
we	**nous/on**
they	**ils/elles**
one	**on**
them	**ils/elles**

Personal pronouns (accusative and dative)

me	**me**
you	**te/vous**
him	**le** *(acc)*, **lui** *(dat)*
her	**la** *(acc)*, **lui** *(dat)*
it	**le/la**
us	**nous**
them	**les** *(acc)*, **leur** *(dat)*
one	**vous**

Reflexive pronouns

myself	**me**
yourself	**te/vous**
himself	**se**
herself	**se**

itself	**se**
ourselves	**nous**
themselves	**se**
oneself	**se**
each other	**se**

Stressed pronouns

it's me	**c'est moi**
me	**moi**
you	**toi/vous**
him	**lui**
her	**elle**
it	**(ça)**
us	**nous**
them	**eux/elles**

Possessive adjectives

my	**mon/ma/mes**
your	**ton/ta/tes, votre/vos**
his	**son/sa/ses**
her	**son/sa/ses**
its	**son/sa/ses**
our	**notre/nos**
their	**leur/leurs**
one's	**son/sa/ses**

Possessive pronouns

mine	**le mien/la mienne/les miens/les miennes**
your	**le tien/etc., le vôtre/la vôtre, les vôtres**
his/hers	**le sien/etc.**
ours	**le nôtre/la nôtre/les nôtres**
theirs	**le leur/la leur/les leurs**
this is mine!	**celui-ci est à moi!**

Relative pronouns

who	**qui/que**
which	**qui/que**
that	**qui/que**
of which/whose	**dont**

12

what   **ce qui/ce que/ce dont**

Indefinite pronouns

somebody/one   **on, quelqu'un**
no one   **personne (ne...)**
anybody   **n'importe qui**
not ... anybody   **ne ... personne**
anyone   **n'importe qui**
not ... anyone   **ne ... personne**
nobody   **personne ...**
each (one)   **chacun/chacune**
everybody/one   **tout le monde**
something   **quelque chose**
anything   **n'importe quoi**
not ... anything   **ne ... rien**
nothing   **rien/ne ... rien**
everything   **tout**
all (of them)   **tous/toutes**
both (of them)   **tous les
    deux/toutes les deux**
some (of them)   **quelques-uns**

Questions

when?   **quand?**
where?   **où?**
how?   **comment?**
how far?   **à quelle distance?**
how much?   **combien?**
how long?   **pendant combien de
    temps?**
how hot?   **à quelle température?**
why?   **pourquoi?**
who?   **qui?**
whom?   **qui?**
to whom?   **à qui?**
whose?   **à qui?**
what?   **que? qu'est-ce que?**
which bus/car?   **quel bus?/quelle
    voiture?**
which buses/cars?   **quels bus?/
    quelles voitures?**
which one?   **lequel/laquelle?**
which ones?   **lesquels/lesquelles?**

*Common prepositions and
    conjunctions*

after he had bought sth.   **après
    qu'il eut acheté quelque chose**
after lunch   **après le déjeuner**
also   **aussi**
although   **bien que/quoique**
    (+ subj)
and   **et**
as (since)   **comme**
as if   **comme si**
as well as   **aussi bien que**
because   **parce que**
before he reads it   **avant qu'il le
    lise** (+ subj)
both ... and   **et ... et**
but   **mais**
even though/if   **même si**
except   **sauf**
however   **cependant**
if   **si**
(in order to) to   **pour, afin de** (+ inf)
not ... either   **ni ... ni**
on condition that   **à condition que**
    (+ subj)
only   **seulement/ne...que**
or   **ou**
provided that   **pourvu que** (+ subj)
since *(causal)*   **puisque**
since   *(time)* **depuis**
so   **donc**
so that   **afin que/pour que** (+ subj)
then   **puis, ensuite**
therefore, consequently   **par
    conséquent**
too   **aussi**
unless   **à moins que ... ne** (+ subj)
until he arrives   **jusqu'à ce qu'l
    arrive** (+ subj)
until she writes   **jusqu'à ce qu'elle
    écrive** (+ subj)
when   **quand, lorsque**
while *(time)*   **pendant que**
while/whereas   **tandis que**
with   **avec**
without   **sans**

2 Where? Position and movement

2a Position

about **environ**
above **au-dessus de**
above *(adv)* **au-dessus**
across **à travers**
after **après**
against **contre**
ahead **en avant**
ahead of **à l'avance, en avance**
along **le long de**
among **parmi**
anywhere **quelque part**
around *(adv)* **autour**
    around the house **autour de la maison, dans la maison**
as far as **jusqu'à**
at **à**
    at home **à la maison**
    at school **à l'école**
    at work **au travail**
back **l'arrière**
    at the back of **à l'arrière de**
    to the back **vers l'arrière**
backward **en arrière**
behind **derrière**
    behind *(adv)* **en arrière**
below **sous, au-dessous de**
    below *(adv)* **en bas, en dessous**

beside **à côté de**
between **entre**
beyond **au-delà de**
bottom **le fond**
    at the bottom (of) **au fond (de)**
center **le centre**
    in the center **au centre**
direction **la direction, le sens**
    in the direction of Dijon **en direction de Dijon**
distance **la distance**
    in the distance **au loin**
distant **distant**
down here/there **ici/là en bas**
downstairs **en bas**
edge **le bord**
    at the edge **au bord**
end **le bout**
    at the end of **au bout de**
everywhere **partout**
far **loin**
    far away (from) **loin (de)**
first **le premier**
    first (of all) **(tout) d'abord**
    I am first **je suis le premier**
forward **en avant**
from **à partir de**
front **le devant**

Over there in the distance is the river. It's not far away – about 1 km from our house.

Là-bas, au loin, se trouve la rivière. Ce n'est pas loin d'ici – à environ 1 km de notre maison.

Opposite the houses is the church and nearby are the shops/stores.

En face des maisons, il y a l'église et tout près d'ici, les magasins.

I am in front *(in the lead)* **je mène**
  in front of **devant**
  to the front **à l'avant**
here **ici**
  here and there **çà et là**
in **dans**
  in there **là-dedans**
inside **à l'intérieur de**
  inside *(adv)* **dedans**
into **dans**
last **le dernier**
  last of all **le tout dernier**
  last of all *(adv)* **en tout dernier**
  I am last **je suis le dernier**
left **gauche**
  on the left **à gauche**
  to the left **sur la gauche**
middle **le milieu**
  in the middle (of) **au milieu (de)**
I move **je bouge**
movement **le mouvement**
near **près de**
near(by) **près d'ici, tout près**
neigborhood **les alentours**
  in the neigborhood of **aux alentours de**
next **prochain**
  next *(adv)* **après**
  next to **auprès de, près de**
nowhere **nulle part**
on the way **en route**
onto **sur**
opposite **en face de**
out of **en dehors de**
  out there **là-bas**

outside **l'exterieur**
  outside *(adv)* **dehors, à l'extérieur**
over **(par-)dessus**
  over there **là-bas**
past **plus loin que**
position **la position**
right **droite**
  on the right **à droite**
  to the right **sur la droite**
round/around **autour**
  round/around the tree **autour de l'arbre**
side **le côté**
  at the side **au côté**
  at both sides of **des deux côtés de**
somewhere **quelque part**
straight ahead **tout droit**
there **là**
to **à**
top **le haut**
  top (of mountain) **le sommet (de la montagne)**
  at the top **en haut/au sommet**
  on top **dessus**
toward **vers**
under **sous**
up **haut**
  up here/there **ici/là en haut**
upstairs **en haut**
where? **où?**
where from? **d'où?**
where to? **vers où?**
with **avec**

At the top of the hill is a farm and in the middle of the village is the post office.

En haut de la colline, il y a une ferme et au milieu du village se trouve la poste.

The first house in the high street is near the river. Our house is the last. The next village is about five kilometers away.

La première maison de la rue principale est près de la rivière. Notre maison est la dernière. Le prochain village est à environ cinq kilomètres.

2b Directions and location

Points of the compass

atlas   l'atlas (m)
east   l'est (m)
   in the east   dans l'est
   to the east (of)   à l'est (de)
   east wind   le vent d'est
   on the east side   du côté est
   eastern France   l'est de la France
compass   la boussole
latitude   la latitude
location   l'emplacement (m)
longitude   la longitude

map   la carte
north   le nord
   in the north   dans le nord
   to the north (of)   au nord (de)
   north wind   le vent du nord
   north coast   la côte nord
   in northern France   dans le nord de la France
northeast   le nord-est
north-northeast   le nord-nord-est
northwest   le nord-ouest
north-northwest   le nord-nord-ouest

Nantes is north of La Rochelle. Right in the north is Lille. I prefer the north of France to the south.

Nantes est au nord de la Rochelle. Dans le nord, se trouve Lille. Je préfère le nord de la France au sud.

Look on the map. You go north.

Regarde sur la carte. Tu vas vers le nord.

To the south of the wood you can see the church spire.

Au sud du bois, tu peux voir le clocher de l'église.

The town lies at a longitude of 32°.

La ville se trouve par 32° de longitude.

– Are you lost?
– Yes. Can you tell me the quickest way to the post office?

– Etes-vous perdu?
– Oui. Pouvez-vous m'indiquer le chemin le plus court pour aller à la poste?

– It's down there on the left.

– C'est là-bas à gauche.

– How do I get to Antibes?

– Pour aller à Antibes, s'il vous plaît?

– Go straight on to the second intersection. Turn right at the lights and take the road to Nice. It's 25 kilometers from here.

– Continuez tout droit jusqu'au deuxième carrefour. Tournez à droite aux feux et prenez la route de Nice. C'est à 25 kilomètres d'ici.

point of the compass **le point cardinal**
south **le sud** *(see also* north*)*
  in the south **dans le sud**
  to the south (of) **au sud (de)**
southeast **le sud-est**
south-southeast **le sud-sud-est**
southwest **le sud-ouest**
south-southwest **le sud-sud-ouest**
west **l'ouest** *(see also* east*)*
  in the west **dans l'ouest**
  to the west (of) **à l'ouest (de)**

Location & existence

I am **je suis** *(étre)*
  there is **il y a**
  there isn't (any) **il n'y a pas de**
I become **je deviens** *(devenir)*
I exist **j'existe**
existence **l'existence** *(f)*
it lies **il se trouve**
I have got/I have **j'ai** *(avoir)*
I possess **je possède** *(posséder)*
possession **la possession**
present **présent**
  I am present **je suis présent**
  I am present at/I attend **j'assiste à**
I am situated **je me trouve**

– Is there a bank nearby?
– There is one behind the supermarket.
– Where is the tourist office?

– Opposite the town hall.

– Who's that? – It's me.

– How many children are present?

– There are 25. Five of them are at home.

– Is there any cake? Are there any cookies left?
– I am sorry, there is no cake, but there are some sandwiches.

I have been to London. I was present at a concert.

– **Y a-t-il une banque près d'ici?**
– **Il y en a une derrière le supermarché.**
– **Où se trouve l'office du tourisme?**

– **En face de la mairie.**

– **Qui est là? – C'est moi.**

– **Combien d'enfants sont présents?**

– **Il y en a 25. Cinq d'entre eux sont à la maison.**

– **Y a-t-il du gâteau? Est-ce qu'il y a encore des biscuits?**
– **Je suis désolé, il n'y a pas de gâteau, mais il y a des sandwiches.**

Je suis allé à Londres. J'ai assiste' à un concert.

2c Movement

I arrive	**j'arrive**
I bring	**j'apporte**
by car	**en voiture**
I carry	**je porte**
I climb *(intr)*	**je monte**
I climb *(tr)*	**je grimpe**
I come	**je viens** *(venir)*
I come back (home)	**je rentre à la maison**
I come down	**je descends**
I come in	**j'entre**
I come out	**je sors** *(sortir)*
I come up	**je monte**
I creep	**je rampe**
I drive	**je conduis** *(conduire)*
I drive on the right	**je roule à droite**
I fall	**je tombe**
I fall down	**je tombe par terre**
I follow	**je suis**
I get in	**j'entre**
I get out	**je sors** *(sortir)*
I get up	**je me lève** *(se lever)*
I go	**je vais**
I go down	**je descends**
I go for a walk	**je vais me promener**
I go in	**j'entre**
I go out	**je sors** *(sortir)*
I go around	**je fais le tour**
I go up	**je monte**
I go (by vehicle)	**je pars** *(partir)* **(en véhicule)**
I hike/go (by foot)	**je vais à pied** *(aller)*
I hitchhike	**je fais du stop** *(faire)*
I hurry (up)	**je me dépêche**
I jump	**je saute**
I leave	**je pars** *(partir)*
I leave *(place, person)*	**je quitte**
I leave *(something)*	**je laisse**
I lie down	**je m'allonge**
I march	**je marche**
I move	**je bouge**
on foot	**à pied**
I pass	**je passe** *(devant)*
I pass (in a car)	**je double, je dépasse**
I pull	**je tire**
I push	**je pousse**
I put	**je mets** *(mettre)*
I ride	**je monte**
I ride (a horse)	**je monte (à cheval)**
I run	**je cours** *(courir)*

Put the picnic in the car! Don't forget your umbrella.	**Mets le pique-nique dans la voiture! N'oublie pas ton parapluie.**
I will take you as far as the river. Then you must get out and walk.	**Je t'emmènerai jusqu'à la rivière. Ensuite tu devras sortir et marcher.**
Keep to the left. Be careful not to fall into the river.	**Tenez la gauche. Faites attention de ne pas tomber dans la rivière.**
We go down the hill, along the river, and then turn left toward the woods. We pass a farm.	**Nous descendons la colline, le long de la rivière, et ensuite, nous tournons à gauche en direction du bois. Nous passons devant une ferme.**

I run away   **je pars *(partir)* en courant**

I rush   **je me précipite**

I sit down   **je m'assieds *(s'asseoir)***

I sit up   **je me redresse**

I slip   **je glisse**

I stand   **je me tiens *(se tenir)* debout**

  I stand still   **je reste debout**

  I stand up   **je me mets *(se mettre)* debout**

I step   **je marche**

I stop   **je m'arrête**

straight   **droit**

  straight ahead   **tout droit**

I stroll   **je me promène *(se promener)***

I take   **je prends *(prendre)***

I turn   **je tourne**

  I turn left   **je tourne à gauche**

walk   **la promenade, la marche**

I walk   **je marche, je me promène *(se promener)***

I wander   **j'erre**

way   **le chemin**

Here and there

Come here!   **Viens *(venir)* ici!**

I go there   **je vais là-bas *(aller)***

I rush there   **je me précipite là-bas**

I travel there   **je voyage là-bas**

Up and down

I climb the mountain   **je fais l'ascension de la montagne**

I climb up the mountain   **j'escalade la montagne**

I climb the stairs (staircase)   **je monte les escaliers *(l'escalier)***

I climb the wall   **j'escalade le mur**

I fall down   **je tombe *(par terre)***

I go down the path   **je descends le chemin *(descendre)***

I lie down   **je m'allonge**

Do sit down!   **Mais assieds-toi! *(s'asseoir)***

Stand up!   **Mets-toi *(se mettre)* debout!**

Round

I go around the town   **je fais le tour de la ville *(faire)***

I run around the tree   **je cours *(courir)* autour de l'arbre**

I run here and there   **je cours *(courir)* ça et là**

I turn around   **je fais demi-tour, je me retourne**

– Where are you going? – To town. Are you coming?

– No, I am going to my mother's.

– Which direction is that?

– I take the first road on the left, then straight ahead up to the marketplace, then I turn right.

– I will follow you as far as the market.

– I am going by car but some of us will go on foot. John is going by motorbike.

– **Où vas-tu? – En ville. Tu viens?**

– **Non, je vais chez ma mère.**

– **C'est dans quelle direction?**

– **Je prends la première rue à gauche, puis je vais tout droit jusqu'à la place du marché et je tourne à droite.**

– **Je te suivrai jusqu'au marché.**

– **Je pars en voiture mais certains d'entre nous iront à pied. John va en moto.**

3 When? Expressions of time

3a Past, present, and future

about **environ**
after **après**
  after *(conj)* **après (que)**
  afterward **après, ensuite**
again **encore**
  again and again **à plusieurs reprises**
ago **il y a**
  a short time ago **il y a peu de temps**
already **déjà**
always **toujours**
anniversary **l'anniversaire** *(m)*
annual **annuel[le]**
as long as *(conj)* **tant que**
as soon as *(conj)* **dès que**
at once **immédiatement , tout de suite**
before **avant**
  before *(conj)* **avant (que)**
  before leaving **avant de partir**
  before, beforehand **auparavant**
I begin **je commence**
beginning **le début**
birthday **l'anniversaire** *(m)*
brief **bref [-ève]**
briefly **brièvement**

by (next month) **avant (le mois prochain)**
calendar **le calendrier**
centenary **le centenaire**
century **le siècle**
  in the twentieth century **au vingtième siècle**
continuous **continuel[le]**
daily **quotidien[ne], tous les jours**
date **la date**
dawn **l'aube** *(f)*
  at dawn **à l'aube**
day **le jour, la journée**
  by day **pendant la journée**
  every day **tous les jours**
  one day (when) **un jour (où)**
  the days of the week **les jours de la semaine**
decade **la décennie**
delay **le retard**
  delayed **retardé**
during **pendant**
early **tôt**
  I am early **je suis en avance**
end **la fin**
  I end *(something)* **je termine**

– Hello Peter, John Brown here/speaking. I have been working on the project for a few days. Have you finished yours yet? Call me this afternoon. We must get together sometime, what about the first of March?

– Allô Peter, c'est John Brown à l'appareil. Ça fait plusieurs jours que je travaille sur ce projet. Avez-vous terminé le vôtre? Appelez-moi cet après-midi. On devrait se retrouver un de ces jours, est-ce que le premier mars vous irait?

---

it ends **il se termine**
ever **jamais**
every **chaque**
  every time **chaque fois**
exactly **exactement**
fast **rapide**
  my watch is fast **ma montre avance**
finally **finalement**
I finish (reading) **je finis (ma lecture)**
first **premier [-ère]**
  at first **au début, d'abord**
first of all **pour commencer**
for **pour, pendant, depuis**
for a day (duration) **pendant une journée**
  (future) **pour une journée**
for good/ever **pour toujours, à jamais**
formerly **autrefois, jadis**
frequent **fréquent**
frequently **fréquemment**
from **de**
  from now on **à partir d'aujourd'hui, désormais**
I go on (reading) **je continue à (lire)**

half **la moitié, un demi**
  half **demi**
  one and a half hours **une heure et demie**
it happens **ce sont des choses qui arrivent, c'est la vie**
hence forth **dorénavant**
holiday/vacation **les vacances** (f)
hurry **la hâte**
  I am in a hurry **je suis pressé**
I hurry up **je me dépêche**
instant **instantané**
just **juste, justement**
  just now **à l'instant**
last/final **dernier [-ère], final**
  last night **hier soir**
  last/previous **dernier [-ère], précédent**
late **tard, en retard**
  I am late **je suis en retard**
  it's late **il est tard**
  lately **ces derniers temps**
  later (on) **plus tard**
long **long[ue]**
  long term **à long terme**
  in the long term **à long terme**
  a long time **longtemps**
many **plusieurs, de nombreux**

– Hello, John, Peter here/speaking. Thank you for yesterday's call. Sorry I couldn't call back sooner. I only got back from London a quarter of an hour ago.
After getting back I spent a long time with Anna; she thinks the project will take all month. We should start on the work at the beginning of June, before the summer vacations start. We can then get it done in good time.

– **Allô, John, c'est Peter à l'appareil. Merci pour votre appel d'hier, désolé de ne pas y avoir répondu plus tôt. Je viens de rentrer de Londres il y a tout juste un quart d'heure.**
Après mon retour j'ai passé un long moment avec Anna; elle pense que le projet prendra tout le mois. On devrait commencer le travail début juin, juste avant les grandes vacances. On aura alors amplement le temps de le terminer.

WHEN? EXPRESSIONS OF TIME

[-ses]
many times   **plusieurs fois**
meanwhile   **pendant ce temps**
   in the meanwhile   **en attendant**
middle   **le milieu**
moment   **le moment**
   at the moment   **en ce moment**
   at this moment *(right now)*   **à l'instant**
   at this moment   **en ce moment**
   at that moment   **à ce moment**
   in a moment   **dans un instant**
month   **le mois**
   monthly   **par mois, mensuel[le]**
much   **beaucoup**
never   **ne ... jamais**
next   **suivant**
   next *(adv)*   **puis, ensuite**
not till/until   **pas avant**
now   **maintenant**
nowadays   **de nos jours, actuellement**
occasionally   **de temps en temps, occasionnellement**
it occurs   **il arrive (que)**
often   **souvent**
on and off   **parfois**

once   **une fois**
   once upon a time   **il était une fois**
   once in a while   **une fois de temps en temps**
   once a day   **une fois par jour**
one day (when)   **un jour (où)**
only   **seulement**
past   **le passé**
per (day)   **par (jour)**
present   **le présent**
   present *(adj)*   **présent**
   presently   **tout de suite**
   at present   **en ce moment**
previous   **précédent**
prompt   **à l'heure**
   promptly at (two)   **(à deux heures) pile, précises**
rare(ly)   **rare(ment)**
recent   **récent**
recently   **récemment**
regular   **régulier [-ère]**
I remain   **je reste**
right away   **tout de suite**
season   **la saison**
seldom   **rarement**
several   **plusieurs**
   several times   **plusieurs fois**

– Last Friday the train was late and you didn't arrive till a quarter to/before three.
– I'll make it by three at the latest. How long does your bus take?

– Half an hour.
– If I'm late you can have a coffee till I get there.

– I don't want to spend all afternoon drinking coffee. Then there will be no time left for shopping.

– **Vendredi dernier, le train avait du retard et tu n'es pas arrivé avant trois heures moins le quart.**
– **J'arriverai à trois heures au plus tard. Combien de temps met le bus?**

– **Une demi-heure.**
– **Si je suis en retard, vous pouvez prendre un café en m'attendant.**

– **Je ne veux pas passer toute l'après-midi à boire du café. Il ne me restera plus assez de temps pour faire les courses.**

short **court**
  (in the) short term **à court terme**
  shortly **bientôt**
since **depuis**
slow **lent, qui retarde**
  my watch is slow **ma montre retarde**
sometimes **parfois, quelquefois**
soon **bientôt**
  sooner or later **un jour ou l'autre**
  the sooner the better **le plus tôt sera le mieux**
I stay **je reste**
still **encore, toujours**
I stop (doing) **j'arrête (de faire)**
suddenly **soudain, tout à coup**
sunrise **le lever du soleil**
sunset **le coucher du soleil**
I take (an hour) **je mets** *(mettre)* **(une heure)**
  it takes (an hour) **ça prend (une heure)**
then *(next)* **puis**
  then *(at that time)* **alors**
till **jusqu'à ce que**
time *(in general)* **le temps**

time *(occasion)* **une fois**
  at any time **n'importe quand**
  at that time **en ce temps-là, à ce moment-là**
  at the same time **au même moment, en même temps**
  from time to time **de temps en temps**
  the whole time **tout le temps**
time zone **le fuseau horaire**
twice **deux fois**
two weeks **quinze jours**
until **jusqu'à ce que**
usually **d'habitude**
I wait **j'attends**
week **la semaine**
  weekly **hebdomadaire**
  weekday **le jour ouvrable**
  weekend **le week-end**
when **quand**
whenever **chaque fois que**
while *(conj)* **pendant que**
year **l'an** *(m)*, **l'année** *(f)*
  yearly **par an**
yet **encore**
  not yet **pas encore**

– You're sometimes late too.

– Vous êtes parfois en retard vous aussi.

– Only in winter or in bad weather.

– Uniquement en hiver ou quand il fait mauvais.

– Last month I had to wait for twenty minutes.

– Le mois dernier, j'ai dû attendre vingt minutes.

– Oh dear, what a pity! I've just remembered that I haven't yet finished painting the kitchen.

– Oh la la, quel dommage! Je viens de me souvenir que je n'ai pas encore fini de peindre la cuisine.

– Perhaps it would be better to meet another time. I'll call next week.

– Peut-être vaudrait-il mieux se rencontrer une autre fois. Je rappellerai la semaine prochaine.

WHEN? EXPRESSIONS OF TIME

3b The time, days, and date

The time of day

a.m.   **du matin**
morning   **le matin, la matinée**
   in the morning   **le matin, dans la matinée**
   in the mornings   **le matin**
   early in the morning   **tôt le matin**
noon   **midi**
at noon   **à midi**
afternoon   **l'après-midi** *(m/f)*
   in the afternoon   **dans l'après-midi**
   in the afternoons   **l'après-midi**
p.m.   **de l'après-midi, du soir**
evening   **le soir, la soirée**
   in the evening(s)   **le soir, dans la soirée**
night   **la nuit**
   at night   **le soir, la nuit**
midnight   **minuit**
   at midnight   **à minuit**
today   **aujourd'hui**
   a week from today   **dans une semaine**
tomorrow   **demain**
   tomorrow morning/evening **demain matin/soir**
   the day after tomorrow   **après-demain**
tonight   **ce soir**
yesterday   **hier**
   yesterday morning   **hier matin**
   yesterday evening   **hier soir**

the day before yesterday
avant-hier

Telling the time

second   **la seconde**
minute   **la minute**
hour   **une heure**
   half an hour   **une demi-heure**
   in an hour's time   **dans une heure**
   hourly   **toutes les heures**
quarter   **un quart**
   quarter of an hour   **un quart d'heure**
   three-quarters of an hour   **trois-quarts d'heure**
   quarter past/after (two)   **(deux) heures et quart**
   quarter to/of (two)   **(deux) heures moins le quart**
half past (two)   **(deux) heures et demie**
half past twelve   **midi/minuit et demi**
17:45   **dix-sept heures quarante-cinq**
five past/after six   **six heures cinq**
two a.m.   **deux heures du matin**
two p.m.   **deux heures de l'après-midi**
eight p.m.   **huit heures du soir**
12:00 noon   **midi**
12:00 midnight   **minuit**

– What's the date today?

– The twenty-first of January.

– And what's the time, please?

– Ten past/after ten.

– **On est le combien aujourd'hui?**

– **Nous sommes le vingt et un janvier.**

– **Et quelle heure est-il, s'il vous plaît?**

– **Dix heures dix.**

*The days of the week**

Monday	**lundi**
Tuesday	**mardi**
Wednesday	**mercredi**
Thursday	**jeudi**
Friday	**vendredi**
Saturday	**samedi**
Sunday	**dimanche**

*The months**

January	**janvier**
February	**février**
March	**mars**
April	**avril**
May	**mai**
June	**juin**
July	**juillet**
August	**août**
September	**septembre**
October	**octobre**
November	**novembre**
December	**décembre**

The seasons

spring	**le printemps**
summer	**l'été** *(m)*
autumn/fall	**l'automne** *(m)*

winter **l'hiver** *(m)*
in spring **au printemps**
in summer/autumn(fall)/winter **en été/automne, hiver**

The date

last Friday **vendredi dernier**
on Tuesday **mardi**
on Tuesdays **le mardi**
by Friday **avant vendredi**
(on) the first of January **le premier janvier**
in (the year) 2000 **en (l'an) deux mille**
1st January/January 1st, 1994 **le premier janvier dix-neuf cent quatre-vingt-quatorze**
at the end of 1999 **à la fin de l'année dix-neuf cent quatre-vingt-dix neuf**
at the beginning (of July) **au début du mois (de juillet)**
in December **en décembre**
in mid/the middle of January **à la mi-janvier**
at the end of March **à la fin du mois de mars**

– What time does the film/movie start this evening?
– At eight o'clock.

– **A quelle heure le film commence-t-il ce soir?**
– **À vingt heures (à huit heures du soir)**

– How long does it last?
– One and a half hours. It will be over by nine-thirty.

– **Combien de temps dure-t-il?**
– **Une heure et demie. Il sera terminé avant vingt et une heures trente (neuf heures et demie du soir).**

We're going on vacation next week. In three days we'll be in Spain.
In 1993 we had to wait a long time at the airport. We got there three hours late.

Nous partons en vacances la semaine prochaine. Dans trois jours nous serons en Espagne.
En dix-neuf cent quatre-vingt-treize, il nous a fallu attendre longtemps à l'aéroport. Nous sommes arrivés avec trois heures de retard.

* All days and months in French are masculine.

4 How much? Expressions of quantity

4a Length and shape

angle	l'angle *(m)*	narrow	étroit
area	l'aire *(f)*	parallel	la parallèle
bent	courbé	perpendicular	perpendiculaire
big	grand	point	le point
center	le centre	room *(space)*	la place
concave	concave	round	rond
convex	convexe	ruler	la règle
curved	arrondi	shape	la forme
deep	profond	short	court
degree	le degré	size	la taille
depth	la profondeur	small	petit
diagonal	la diagonale	space	l'espace *(m)*
dimensions	les dimensions *(f)*	straight	droit
distance	la distance	surface area	la surface
I draw	je dessine	tall *(person)*	grand
height	la hauteur	tall *(thing)*	haut
high	haut	thick	épais[se]
horizontal	l'horizontale *(f)*	thin	mince
large	gros[se]	wide	large
length	la longueur	width	la largeur
line	la ligne		
long	long[ue]	*Shapes*	
low	bas[se]	circle	le cercle
it measures	il mesure	circular	circulaire

You need a straight ruler and pencil. Measure the space and then draw a plan.

Tu as besoin d'une règle et d'un crayon. Mesure l'espace et ensuite dessine un plan.

Don't make the lawn too wide. Leave room for some vegetables. The distance from the house to the fence is 12 meters. The garden is not wide enough for a pool.

Ne fais pas la pelouse trop large. Laisse de la place pour les légumes. La distance entre la maison et la palissade est de douze mètres. Le jardin n'est pas assez large pour une piscine.

– How high is the tree? – About 5 meters.

– Quelle est la hauteur de l'arbre? – Environ cinq mètres.

cube **le cube**
   cubic **cubique**
cylinder **le cylindre**
pyramid **la pyramide**
rectangle **le rectangle**
   rectangular **rectangulaire**
sphere **la sphère**
   spherical **sphérique**
square **le carré**
   square *(adj)* **carré**
triangle **le triangle**
   triangular **triangulaire**

Units of length

centimeter **le centimètre**
foot **le pied**
inch **le pouce**
kilometer **le kilomètre**
meter **le mètre**
mile **le mile**
millimeter **le millimètre**
unit of length **l'unité** *(f)* **de longueur**
yard **le yard**

Expressions of quantity

about **environ**
almost **presque**
approximate **approximatif [-ve]**
approximately **à peu près**
as much as **autant de ... que**

at least **au moins**
capacity **la capacité**
it contains **il contient** *(contenir)*
cubic capacity **le volume**
it decreases **il diminue**
difference **la différence**
empty **vide**
I empty **je vide**
enough **assez**
I fill **je remplis**
full (of) **rempli, plein (de)**
growth **la croissance, la pousse**
hardly **à peine**
increase **l'augmentation** *(f)*
it increases **il augmente**
little **peu**
   a little **un peu**
   little by little **peu à peu**
a lot (of) **beaucoup (de)**
I measure **je mesure**
measuring tape **le mètre ruban**
   folding measuring tape **le mètre pliant**
more **plus**
nearly **presque**
number **le nombre**
part **la partie**
quantity **la quantité**
sufficient **suffisant**
too much **trop**
volume **le volume**

The shed will be at an angle of about 40 degrees to the house, diagonally across from the gate.

L'abri sera à un angle d'environ quarante degrés de la maison, en diagonale depuis la porte.

The area of our garden is 100 square meters. It is 10 meters long and 10 wide, so it is a square.

La surface de notre jardin est de cent mètres carrés. Il fait dix mètres de long sur dix mètres de large, c'est donc un carré.

We put a round pond in, only 80 to 100 centimeters deep.

Nous avons creusé un bassin rond, de quatre-vingt à cent centimètres de profondeur seulement.

HOW MUCH? EXPRESSIONS OF QUANTITY

4b Measuring

whole   l'ensemble *(m)*
　　whole *(adj)*   tout, entier [-ère]

Expressions of volume

bag   le sac
bar (of gold)   la barre (d'or)
bottle   la bouteille
box   la boîte
container   le conteneur, le récipient
cup   la tasse
gallon   le gallon
glass   le verre
hectare   l'hectare *(m)*
liter   le litre
　　centiliter   le centilitre

centiliter   le millilitre
pack   le paquet
pair   la paire
piece   le morceau
　　a piece of cake   un morceau de
　　gâteau
pint   la pinte
portion   la portion
pot   le pot
sack   le sac
tube   le tube

Temperature

it boils   il bout *(bouillir)*
I chill   je mets *(mettre)* au frais

– How many centiliters are there in the bottle?
– 75, but you can also get it in liter bottles.

– Combien y a-t-il de centilitres dans la bouteille?
– soixante-quinze, mais tu peux aussi l'avoir en bouteilles d'un litre.

Could I have two packets of tissues and a bottle of aspirin, please?

Pourrais-je avoir deux paquets de Kleenex® et un tube d'aspirine, s'il vous plaît?

I need a little flour and a lot of sugar.

J'ai besoin d'un peu de farine et de beaucoup de sucre.

– What is the volume of water in the swimming pool?
– 10,000 gallons, which is about 45,000 liters.

– Quel est le volume d'eau dans la piscine?
– 10.000 gallons, ce qui représente environ 45.000 litres.

– How much wood do you want? – Enough for the whole fence. I must not buy too much. Yes, that should be sufficient. Give me a bag of cement too.

– Quelle quantité de bois voulez-vous? – Assez pour toute la palissade. Je ne dois pas en acheter de trop. Oui, ça devrait être suffisant. Donnez-moi un sac de ciment aussi.

– How many cubic meters of concrete do you need? – About two.

– Combien de mètres cubes de ciment avez-vous besoin? – Environ deux.

cold **le froid**
  cold **froid**
cool **frais [fraîche]**
  I cool it down **je le fais refroidir**
degree **le degré**
it's freezing **il gèle** *(geler)*
heat **la chaleur**
  I heat **je fais chauffer**
  I heat (the house) **je chauffe (la maison)**
hot **chaud**
temperature **la température**
warm **(assez) chaud**
  warmth **la chaleur**
I warm it (up) **je le fais réchauffer**

Weight & density

dense **dense**
density **la densité**
gram **le gramme**
heavy **lourd**
kilo **le kilo**
light **léger [-ère]**
mass **la masse**
ounce **l'once** *(f)*
pound *(lb)* **la livre**
scales **la balance**
ton **la tonne**
I weigh **je pèse** *(peser)*
weight **le poids**

– It's so hot! What's the temperature? It must be nearly 30 degrees. I am too hot.

– Would you like a cup of tea? – No, I would prefer a glass of water.

– In winter it's cold here. We all freeze in this house and have to put the heating on in September. When the temperature reaches zero we have to light two fires.

Can you warm some water? The vegetables are still frozen. The water is boiling now. Warm up the pizza in the oven. Have you chilled the wine?

– Can you weigh out the ingredients? – How many grams of sugar do we need?
  – I want a pound — that must be about 500 grams.

– Il fait si chaud! Quelle est la température? Il doit faire environ trente degrés. J'ai trop chaud.

– Aimerais-tu une tasse de thé?
– Non, je préférerais un verre d'eau.

– En hiver, il fait froid ici. Nous tous gelons dans cette maison et nous devons mettre le chauffage en septembre. Quand la température descend à zéro, nous devons allumer deux feux.

Peux-tu faire chauffer de l'eau? Les légumes sont encore gelés. L'eau bout maintenant. Fais réchauffer la pizza dans le four. As-tu mis le vin au frais?

– Peux-tu peser les ingrédients?
– De combien de grammes de sucre avons-nous besoin? –
J'en veux une livre. Cela doit faire environ cinq cent grammes.

HOW MUCH? EXPRESSIONS OF QUANTITY

4c Numbers

Cardinal numbers

zero	**zéro**
one	**un**
two	**deux**
three	**trois**
four	**quatre**
five	**cinq**
six	**six**
seven	**sept**
eight	**huit**
nine	**neuf**
ten	**dix**
eleven	**onze**
twelve	**douze**
thirteen	**treize**
fourteen	**quatorze**
fifteen	**quinze**
sixteen	**seize**
seventeen	**dix-sept**
eighteen	**dix-huit**
nineteen	**dix-neuf**
twenty	**vingt**
twenty-one	**vingt et un**
twenty-two	**vingt-deux**
twenty-nine	**vingt-neuf**

thirty **trente**
thirty-one **trente et un**
forty **quarante**
fifty **cinquante**
sixty **soixante**
seventy **soixante-dix, septante** *(Bel, Switz*)*
seventy-one **soixante-onze, septante et un** *(Bel, Switz)*
eighty **quatre-vingt, huitante** *(Switz)*
eighty-one **quatre-vingt-un, huitante-un** *(Switz)*
ninety **quatre-vingt-dix, nonante** *(Bel, Switz)*
ninety-two **quatre-vingt-douze, nonante-deux** *(Bel, Switz)*
a hundred **cent**
a hundred and one **cent un**
two hundred **deux cents**
a thousand **mille**
two thousand **deux mille**
million **un million**
two million **deux millions**
billion **un milliard**

Half of the house belongs to my brother. We divided it between us. However, he only pays a quarter of the costs as I let my half out in summer.

La moitié de la maison appartient à mon frère. Nous l'avons partagée entre nous. Cependant, il ne paie qu'un quart des dépenses car je loue ma moitié pendant l'été.

---

* *Bel, Switz* indicate variants used in Belgium and Switzerland.

Ordinal numbers

first	**premier**
second	**deuxième**
third	**troisième**
fourth	**quatrième**
nineteenth	**dix-neuvième**
twentieth	**vingtième**
twenty-first	**vingt-et-unième**
hundredth	**centième**

Nouns

one **un**
   units **les unités** *(f)*
ten **dix**
   tens **les dizaines** *(f)*
dozen **la douzaine**
about twenty **une vingtaine**
hundred **cent**
   hundreds of **des centaines de**
   about one hundred **une centaine**
thousands of **des milliers de**

Writing numerals

1,000	**1.000**
1,500	**1.500**
1st	**1er**
2nd	**2e, 2ème**
1.56	**1,56 (un virgule cinquante-six)**
.05	**0,05 (zéro virgule zéro cinq)**

Fractions

half **la moitié**
   a half **la moitié**
   one and a half **un et demi**
   two and a half **deux et demi**
quarter **le quart**
a quarter **un quart**
   three-quarters **trois-quarts**
third **le tiers**
fifth **le cinquième**
sixth **le sixième**
   five and five sixths **cinq et cinq sixièmes**
tenth **le dixième**
hundredth **le centième**
thousandth **le millième**

– You cannot all have half a bar of chocolate.

– Vous ne pouvez pas tous avoir la moitié d'une barre de chocolat.

There is only enough for a quarter each.

Il y en a seulement assez pour un quart chacun.

And a quarter of a liter of apple juice.

Et un quart de litre de jus de pomme.

– I don't want a quarter, I want a half.

– Je n'en veux pas le quart, j'en veux la moitié.

4d Calculations

addition **l'addition** *(f)*
  I add **j'additionne**
average **la moyenne**
  I average out **je fais la moyenne**
  on average **en moyenne**
I calculate **je calcule**
  calculation **le calcul**
  calculator **la calculatrice**
correct **juste**
I count **je compte**
data **les données** *(f)*
  piece of data **la donnée**
decimal **la décimale**
  decimal point **la virgule**
diameter **le diamètre**
digit **le chiffre**
  two digits **deux chiffres**
I double **je double**
division **la division**
  I divide by **je divise par**
  six divided by two **six divisé par deux**

equal **égal**
  three times four equals twelve **trois fois quatre font douze**
equation **l'équation** *(f)*
  it is equivalent to **cela équivaut** *(équivaloir)* **à**
I estimate **j'estime**
even **pair**
figure **le chiffre**
fraction **la fraction**
graph **le graphe, le graphique**
is greater than **est plus grand que**
is less than **est moins que**
is smaller than **est moins grand que, est plus petit que**
maximum **le maximum**
  maximum *(adj)* **maximum**
  up to a maximum of **jusqu'à un maximum de**
medium **le milieu**
  medium *(adj)* **moyen[ne]**
minimum **le minimum**
  minimum **minimum**

An inch is the same as 2.54 cm, and there are 12 inches in a foot, 36 in a yard. A mile is 1,760 yards. A kilometer is 1,000 meters.

Un pouce est égal à 2,54 cm; il y a 12 pouces dans un pied et 36 dans un yard. Un mile représente 1.760 yards. 1.000 mètres font un kilomètre.

What is 14 plus 8? It equals 22. Did you get the right result?

Combien font 14 plus 8? Ça fait 22. Est-ce que tu as répondu juste?

20 minus 5 is 15, 20 divided by 5 equals 4.

20 moins 5 font 15, 20 divisé par 5 font 4.

Work out 12 times 22. That is an easy sum.

Résous 12 fois 22. C'est une somme facile.

2 to the power of 3 is 8. Three squared equals 9.

2 à la puissance 3 égal 8. Trois au carré égal 9.

minus **moins**
mistake/error **la faute**
multiplication **la multiplication**
   I multiply **je multiplie**
   three times two **trois fois deux**
negative **négatif [-ve]**
number **le nombre**
   cardinal numbers **les nombres**
   (m) **cardinaux**
   ordinal numbers **les nombres**
   (m) **ordinaux**
numeral **le numéral**
odd **impair**
percent **pour cent**
   by 10% **de 10%**
   percentage **le pourcentage**
plus **plus**
   two plus two **deux plus deux**
positive **positif [-ve]**
power **la puissance**
   to the power of 5 **puissance**
   cinq
problem **le problème**
quantity **la quantité**

ratio **le rapport**
   a ratio of 100:1 **un rapport de**
   cent contre un
result **le résultat**
similar **identique**
solution **la solution**
   I solve **je résous** *(résoudre)*
square **le carré**
square root **la racine carrée**
   three squared **trois au carré**
statistic **la statistique**
statistics **les statistiques** *(f)*
statistical **statistique**
sum **la somme**
subtraction **la soustraction**
I subtract/take away **je soustrais**
   (soustraire)
symbol **le symbole**
total **le total**
   in total **au total**
I triple **je triple**
triple **le triple**
I work out **je résous** *(résoudre)*
wrong **faux [-se]**

– I estimate that we have some 500 visitors a year.
– What percentage of visitors are local? – 20% (percent).

– **J'estime que nous recevons environ 500 visiteurs par an.**
– **Quel est le pourcentage de gens du quartier? – 20% (pour cent).**

A snail travels at an average speed of 0.041 kilometers per hour.

Un escargot se déplace à une vitesse moyenne de 0,041 kilomètres par heure.

– In this game you add up your score over the week.
– What was the total score?
– I have a total of 500 points.
– To calculate the average you add up the totals and divide by the number of games

– **Dans ce jeu, tu additionnes ton score de la semaine.**
– **Quel était le résultat final?**
– **J'ai un total de 500 points.**
– **Pour calculer la moyenne, tu additionnes et tu divises par le nombre de jeux.**

5 What sort of? Descriptions and judgments

5a Describing people

appearance	**l'apparence** (f)
attractive	**séduisant**
average	**la moyenne**
bald	**chauve**
beard	**la barbe**
bearded	**barbu**
beautiful	**beau [belle]**
beauty	**la beauté**
blond	**blond**
broad	**large**
build	**la carrure**
chic	**chic**
clean-shaven	**rasé de près**
clumsy	**maladroit**
complexion	**le teint**
curly	**bouclé**
dark	**foncé**
I describe	**je décris** (décrire)
description	**la description**
different (from)	**différent (de)**
elegant	**élégant**
energy	**l'énergie** (f)
expression	**l'expression** (f)
fat	**gras[se]**
features	**les traits** (m) **du visage**
female, woman	**la femme**
feminine	**féminin**
figure	**la ligne**

fit	**en forme**
I frown	**je fronce**
glasses	**les lunettes** (f)
good-looking	**beau [belle]**
I grow	**je grandis**
hair	**les cheveux** (m)
hairstyle	**la coupe de cheveux**
handsome	**attrayant**
heavy	**lourd**
height	**la hauteur**
large	**gros[se]**
I laugh	**je ris** (rire)
laugh	**le rire**
I am left/right-handed	**je suis gaucher [-ère]/droitier [-ère]**
light	**léger [-ère]**
long-sighted	**presbyte**
I look like	**je ressemble à**
I look well	**j'ai bonne mine**
male, man	**l'homme** (m)
masculine	**masculin**
moustache	**la moustache**
neat	**soigné**
neatness	**la propreté, l'ordre** (m)
obese	**obèse**
overweight	**trop gros[se]**
part of body	**la partie du corps**
paunch	**le ventre**

adolescence	**l'adolescence** (f)
adolescent/teenager	**un adolescent, une adolescente**
age	**l'âge** (m)
elderly	**une personne âgée**
grown up (adj)	**adulte**
grown up	**un/une adulte**
middle-aged	**d'un certain âge**

old	**vieux [vieille]**
older/elder	**aîné**
old man	**un vieillard**
young	**jeune**
young person	**un/une jeune**
young people	**les jeunes** (m/f)
youth	**la jeunesse**
youthful	**jeune**

physical **physique**	spotty **boutonneux [-se]**
plump **grassouillet[te]**	stocky **trapu**
pretty **joli**	strength **la force**
red-haired **roux [rousse]**	striking **frappant**
I scowl **je fronce les sourcils**	strong **fort**
sex/gender **le sexe**	tall **grand**
short **petit**	thin **maigre**
short-sighted **myope**	tiny **minuscule**
similar (to) **pareil[le] (à)**	trendy **dans le vent**
similarity **la ressemblance**	ugliness **la laideur**
size **la taille**	ugly **laid**
slim/slender **mince**	walk **la marche**
small **petit**	wavy **ondulé**
I smile **je souris *(sourire)***	I weigh **je pèse *(peser)***
smile **le sourire**	weight **le poids**
spot **le bouton**	

I get fat **je grossis**	I lose weight **je perds du poids**
I get fit **je me mets *(se mettre)* en forme**	I put on my make up **je me maquille**
	I put on weight **je grossis**
I get thin **je maigris**	I diet **je suis au régime**

– What a wonderful family photo! What's your uncle like? Can you describe him?
– He looks very much like my father, but he wears glasses.
– Look, who's that tall fellow with the beard? – That's my brother. He's obsessive about keeping fit.

– What a pretty girl! Is that your cousin? – Yes, she's blond with blue eyes. She's very slim, with a good figure and a beautiful smile.

– Little Ben now has dark hair and is about 1 meter tall. – He looks very well, but he's very thin.

– Yes, he only weighs 16 kilos.

– **Quelle merveilleuse photo de famille! A quoi ressemble ton oncle? Peux-tu me le décrire?**
– **Il ressemble beaucoup à mon père, mais il porte des lunettes.**
– **Regarde, qui est ce grand type à barbe? – C'est mon frère. Il est obsédé par son maintien en forme.**

– **Quelle jolie fille! C'est ta cousine? – Oui, elle est blonde aux yeux bleus. Elle est très mince, bien faite, et elle a un beau sourire.**

– **Le petit Ben a maintenant les cheveux noirs et il mesure environ un mètre. Il a bonne mine, mais il est très maigre.**
– **Oui, il ne pèse que seize kilos.**

WHAT SORT OF? DESCRIPTIONS AND JUDGMENTS

5b The senses

bitter **amer [-ère]**
bright **clair**
bright (lively) **vif [-ve]**
cold **le froid**
   cold **froid**
dark **foncé**
dark blue **bleu foncé** *(inv)*
delicious **délicieux [-se]**
disgusting **dégoûtant**
dull **terne**
I feel . . . **je sens** *(sentir)*
   it feels **il semble**
I hear **j'entends**
heat **la chaleur**
hot **chaud**
light *(color)* **clair**
   light gray **gris clair** *(inv)*
I listen **j'écoute**
I look (at) **je regarde**
loud **fort**
noise **le bruit**
noisy **bruyant**
odor **l'odeur** *(f)*
opaque **opaque**
perfume **le parfum**
perfumed **parfumé**

quiet **calme**
rough **dur**
salty **salé**
I see **je vois** *(voir)*
sense **le sens**
shade *(color)* **la nuance, le ton**
shadow/shade **l'ombre** *(f)*
shrill **criard**
silence **le silence**
silent **silencieux [-se]**
smell **l'odeur** *(f)*, **la senteur**
I smell **je sens** *(sentir)*
   it smells (of onion) **il sent
   (l'oignon)**
   smelly **malodorant**
soft *(texture)* **soyeux [-se], lisse**
   soft *(sound)* **doux [-ce]**
sound **le son**
it sounds **il semble**
   it sounds like **il ressemble à**
sour **acide**
sticky **collant**
   it is sticky **il est collant**
sweet **sucré**
taste **le goût**
I taste **je goûte**

– What color is your new coat? –
Well, it's sort of red.
– Dark or light red? – It is more
mauve.

**– Quelle est la couleur de ton
nouveau manteau? – Eh bien,
c'est une sorte de rouge.
– Rouge clair ou foncé? – Un
rouge qui tire sur le mauve.**

– What a beautiful smell! – Yes,
that's the flowers.

**– Que ça sent bon! – Oui, ce
sont les fleurs.**

The jam tastes of fruit but is very
bitter.

**La confiture a un goût de fruits,
mais elle est très amère.**

Don't touch that book, your hands
are all sticky.

**Ne touche pas à ce livre, tes
mains sont toutes collantes.**

it tastes (of)   **il a un goût (de)**
tepid   **tiède**
I touch   **je touche**
transparent   **transparent**
visible (in-)   **(in)visible**
warm   **chaud**
warmth   **la chaleur**

Common parts of the body

arm   **le bras**
back   **le dos**
body   **le corps**
  part of the body   **la partie du corps**

chest   **la poitrine**
ear   **l'oreille** *(f)*
eye   **l'œil** *(m)* *(pl* **les yeux)**
face   **le visage**
hand   **la main**
head   **la tête**
leg   **la jambe**
mouth   **la bouche**
neck   **le cou**
nose   **le nez**
shoulder   **l'épaule** *(m)*
stomach   **l'estomac** *(m)*
tooth   **la dent**

Colors

beige   **beige**
black   **noir**
blue   **bleu**
brown   **brun, marron**
brownish   **brunâtre**
color   **la couleur**
cream   **crème**
gold   **or**
green   **vert**
gray   **gris**

mauve   **mauve**
orange   **orange**
pink   **rose**
purple   **pourpre, violet, mauve**
red   **rouge**
scarlet   **écarlate**
silver   **argent**
turquoise   **turquoise**
violet   **violet**
white   **blanc**
yellow   **jaune**

– What's in that bag? It feels hard.

– Let me feel. It's a bottle. What's in it?

– I don't know. It looks like orange juice. I'll taste it. It's disgusting! It tastes of oranges but it's too sweet.

– Have you seen my new perfume?
– What does it look like?
– It's a small, pink bottle.

– **Qu'est-ce qu'il y a dans ce sac? Ça a l'air dur.**

– **Laisse-moi toucher. C'est une bouteille. Qu'est-ce qu'il y a dedans?**

– **Je ne sais pas. Cela ressemble à du jus d'orange. Je vais goûter. C'est dégoûtant! Ça a un goût d'orange mais c'est trop sucré.**

– **As-tu vu mon nouveau parfum?**
– **A quoi ressemble-t-il?**
– **C'est une petite bouteille rose.**

5c Describing things

big	**grand**	genuine, real	**vrai**
something big	**quelque chose**	hard	**dur**
de grand		height	**la hauteur**
broad	**large**	kind	**gentil[le]**
broken	**cassé**	large	**gros[se]**
appearance	**l'apparence** *(f)*	liquid	**liquide**
clean	**propre**	little	**petit**
closed	**fermé**	long	**long[ue]**
color	**la couleur**	it looks like	**il ressemble à**
colorful	**coloré**	low	**bas[se]**
colored	**en couleur, coloré**	main	**principal**
damp	**humide**	material	**le tissu**
deep	**profond**	they match	**il vont bien ensemble**
depth	**la profondeur**	matter	**la matière**
dirt	**la saleté**	moist	**moite**
dirty	**sale**	moldy	**moisi**
dry	**sec [sèche]**	narrow	**étroit**
empty	**vide**	natural	**naturel[le]**
enormous	**énorme**	new	**nouveau, neuf [-ve]**
fashionable	**à la mode**	open	**ouvert**
fat	**gros[se]**	out of date	**démodé**
fatty *(food)*	**gras[se]**	painted	**peint**
firm	**ferme**	pale	**pâle**
flat	**plat**	pattern	**le motif**
flexible	**souple**	patterned	**à motifs**
fresh	**frais [fraîche]**	plump	**rembourré**
full (of)	**plein (de)**	resistant	**résistant**

– What's that over there?
– That thing there? It's a new kind of bottle opener.
– Does it work? – Yes indeed. It's the best there is.

– I'm looking for something big to stand on.

– Will anything do?

– Well, it must be something solid.
– What about this?
– Is there nothing bigger?

– Qu'est-ce qu'il y a là-bas?
– Cette chose-là? Une nouvelle sorte d'ouvre-bouteille.
– Ça marche? – Bien sûr. C'est ce qu'il ya de mieux.

– Je cherche quelque chose de grand pour me mettre debout dessus.

– Est-ce que n'importe quoi fera l'affaire?

– Et bien, il faut que ce soit solide.
– Que dis-tu de cela?
– Il n'y a rien de plus grand?

rotten **pourri**
shade **la nuance**
shallow **peu profond**
shiny **brillant**
short **court**
shut **fermé**
small **petit**
smooth **lisse, soyeux [-se]**
soft (texture) **doux [-ce]**
solid **solide**
soluble **soluble**
sort **la sorte**
spot **le pois**
spotted **à pois**
stain **la tache**
stained **taché**

stripe **la rayure**
striped **à rayures**
subsidiary **subsidiaire**
substance **la substance**
such **tel[le]**
synthetic **synthétique**
thick **épais[se]**
thing **la chose**
thingamajig **le truc**
tint **la teinte**
varied **varié**
waterproof **imperméable**
wet **mouillé**
wide **large**

Ten questions

What's that thingamajig? **Qu'est-ce que c'est que ce truc?**
What's it for? **Ça sert à quoi?**
What do you use it for? **Tu l'utilises pour quoi faire?**
Can you see it? **Tu peux le voir?**
What's it like? **C'est comment?**

What does it look like? **A quoi ça ressemble?**
What does it sound like? **De quoi ça a l'air?**
What does it smell of? **Ça sent quoi?**
What color is it? **C'est de quelle couleur?**
What exactly is it? **C'est quoi, exactement?**

– Stand on the chair.
– It's too soft.
– All the other chairs are too low.

– **Monte sur la chaise.**
– **C'est trop mou.**
– **Toutes les autres chaises sont trop basses.**

– Get a ladder.
– Which one? This one?
– No, that one there.

– **Va me chercher une échelle.**
– **Laquelle? Celle-ci?**
– **Non, celle-là là-bas.**

– I am looking for a striped material, something to match my coat.

– **Je cherche un tissu à rayures, quelque chose qui va avec mon manteau.**

The fridge/refrigerator is empty and the sink is full of water.

Le frigo est vide et l'évier est plein d'eau.

5d Evaluating things

abnormal **anormal**
I adore **j'adore**
all right **d'accord, bon**
it is all right **c'est d'accord/bon**
appalling **effroyable**
bad **mauvais**
beautiful **beau [belle]**
better/best **meilleur/le meilleur**
cheap **bon marché** *(invar)*
correct **exact**
it costs **il coûte**
delicious **délicieux [-se]**
I detest **je déteste**
difficulty **la difficulté**
difficult, hard **difficile**
disgusting **dégoûtant**
I dislike **je n'aime pas**

I enjoy **j'aime**
easy **facile**
essential **essentiel[le]**
excellent **excellent**
expensive **cher [-ère]**
I fail **j'échoue**
failure **l'échec** *(m)*
false **faux [-sse]**
fine **bon[ne]**
good **bon[ne]**
good value **un bon rapport**
  qualité-prix
great, terrific **génial, formidable**
I hate **je déteste**
high **haut**
important (un-) **(pas) important**
incorrect **inexact**

---

a bit **un peu**
enough **assez**
extremely **extrêmement**
fairly **plutôt**
hardly at all **presque pas du tout**
litte **peu**
  a little **un peu de**
a lot **beaucoup**

much (better) **bien mieux**
not at all **pas du tout**
particularly **surtout**
quite **assez**
rather **plutôt**
really **vraiment**
so **tellement, si**
too (good) **trop (bon[ne])**
very **très**

I tried to call you yesterday, but the telephones were out of order.

– J'ai essayé de t'appeler hier, mais les téléphones étaient en dérangement.

– Would you like to try this wine?
– Thank you, it is quite delicious.

– Voudriez-vous goûter ce vin?
– Merci, il est vraiment délicieux.

– Do you enjoy going to the movies?
– Yes, I particularly enjoyed last week's film.

– Vous aimez aller au cinéma?

– Oui, j'ai surtout aimé le film de la semaine dernière.

inessential **superflu**
interesting (un-) **(in)intéressant**
I like **j'aime**
mediocre **médiocre**
necessary (un-) **(pas) nécessaire, (in)utile**
normal **normal**
order **l'ordre** *(m)*
   in order **en ordre**
   out of order **en panne, en dérangement**
out of date **démodé**
ordinary **ordinaire**
pleasant **agréable**
poor **pauvre**
practical (im-) **(pas) pratique**
I prefer **je préfère** *(préférer)*
quality **la qualité**
   top quality **de haute qualité**
   poor quality **de mauvaise qualité**
right **juste**
strange **étrange, bizarre**
I succeed **je réussis**
success **le succès**
successful **qui réussit**
terrible, terrifying, terrible **terrifiant**
true **vrai**
I try **j'essaie** *(essayer)*
ugly **laid**
unpleasant **désagréable**
unsuccessful **qui est un échec**
I use **j'utilise**
use **l'emploi** *(m)*
useful **utile**
well **bien**
worse **plus mauvais, pire**
I would rather **je préférerais** *(préférer)*
wrong **mauvais, faux [-sse]**

How do you like our neighbor's garden? We do not like it at all.

Que pensez-vous du jardin de notre voisin? Nous ne l'aimons pas du tout.

I wish he would throw away that broken seat. It's only plastic anyway. We always buy the best!

Si seulement il jetait ce siège cassé. Ce n'est que du plastique de toute façon. Nous n'achetons que le meilleur!

And his lawn mower is out of order. He never puts it away, and now he'll have to get it fixed.

Et sa tondeuse à gazon est en panne. Il ne la range jamais et maintenant, il doit la faire réparer.

I fear he's not a very successful gardener. His vegetables are a complete failure.

Je crains qu'il ne soit pas un jardinier très accompli. Ses légumes sont un échec total.

I do like to keep the garden neat. I always put everything away.

J'aime garder le jardin en ordre. Je range toujours tout.

People always say our garden is the best on the street.

Les gens disent toujours que notre jardin est le plus beau de la rue.

WHAT SORT OF? DESCRIPTIONS AND JUDGMENTS

5e Comparisons

Regular comparatives and superlatives	
small	**petit**
smaller	**plus petit**
smallest	**le plus petit**

Irregular comparatives and superlatives	
bad	**mauvais**
worse	**pire, plus mauvais**

worst	**le pire, le plus mauvais**
good	**bon[ne]**
better	**meilleur**
best	**le meilleur**
well	**bien**
better	**mieux**
best	**le mieux**
much	**beaucoup**
more	**plus**
most	**le plus**

– Look at the children! Peter, our eldest son, is now the tallest. He's best at soccer, too. That's what he enjoys best.

– Regarde les enfants! Peter, notre fils aîné, est maintenant le plus grand. Il est aussi le meilleur au football. C'est ce qu'il aime le mieux.

John is now fairly large, almost as tall as Peter, and he really is too fat. He prefers to swim.

John est maintenant assez gros, presque aussi grand que Peter, mais il est vraiment trop gros. Il préfère la natation.

The smallish boy over there is Alan. He is quite small compared with the others, but on the other hand he's very confident. He doesn't behave as well as his brother.

Le garçon plutôt petit là-bas, c'est Alan. Il est assez petit comparé aux autres, mais d'un autre côté, il est très confiant. Il se comporte moins bien que son frère.

John has eaten the largest cake. He gets larger and larger.

John a mangé le plus gros gâteau. Il devient de plus en plus gros.

– Have you seen our latest products? They are just as cheap as the competition's. We cannot ask a higher price, as the greatest demand is for the cheaper product.

– Avez-vous vu nos derniers produits? Ils sont aussi bon marché que ceux de la concurrence. Nous ne pouvons pas demander un prix plus élevé, car la demande la plus forte est pour le produit le moins cher.

5f Materials

acrylic	l'acrylique (m)	manmade fibers	les fibres (f) artificielles
brick	la brique	metal	le métal
cambric	la batiste	mineral	le minéral
cardboard	le carton	nylon	le nylon
cashmere	le cachemire	oil	le pétrole
cement	le ciment	paper	le papier
chiffon	la mousseline	plastic	le plastique
china	la porcelaine	polyester	le polyester
concrete	le béton	pottery	la poterie
corduroy	le velours côtelé	satin	le satin
cotton	le coton	silk	la soie
crêpe	le crêpe	silver	l'argent (m)
denim	la toile de coton/jean	steel	l'acier (m)
felt	le feutre	stone	la pierre
flannel	la flanelle	suede	le daim
gas	le gaz	terylene®	le tergal
glass	le verre	towelling	le tissu éponge
gold	l'or (m)	velvet	le velours
iron	le fer	viscose	la viscose (f)
lace	la dentelle	wood	le bois
leather	le cuir	wool	la laine
linen	le lin		

– Which dress would you like? Silk is softer than wool, but it costs a lot.

The most beautiful dress is the one made of cotton. The colors are brighter and I think the cut is better, although it is not as warm as the wool dress.

It is not at all expensive. I prefer it to the others.

– All the same I would rather have the other.

– Did you succeed in finding something less expensive?
– Yes, this coat is a particularly good value. And it's better quality.

– **Quelle robe voudriez-vous? La soie est plus douce que la laine, mais elle coûte cher.**
La robe la plus belle est celle en coton. Les couleurs sont plus vives et je pense qu'elle est mieux coupée, bien qu'elle ne soit pas aussi chaude que la robe en laine. Elle n'est pas chère du tout. Je la préfère aux autres.
– **Mais je voudrais quand même prendre l'autre.**

– **Avez-vous réussi à trouver quelque chose de moins cher?**
– **Oui, ce manteau est d'un bon rapport qualité-prix et de meilleure qualité.**

⑥ The human mind and character

6a Human characteristics

active **actif [-ive]**
I adapt **je m'adapte**
amusing **amusant**
I annoy **j'agace, j'irrite**
bad **mauvais**
bad-tempered **qui a mauvais caractère**
I behave **je me conduis**
behavior **la conduite**
I boast **je me vante**
calm **calme**
care **le soin**
careful **soigneux [-se], prudent**
careless **peu soigneux [-se], inattentif [-ive]**
character **le caractère, le tempérament**
characteristic **la caractéristique**
characteristic *(adj)* **caractéristique**
charming **charmant**
cheerful **joyeux [-se], heureux [-se]**
clever **intelligent**
confident **confiant**

discipline **la discipline**
I disobey **je désobéis à**
dreadful **horrible**
evil **mauvais**
foolish **bête**
forgetful **étourdi**
friendly (un-) **(peu) aimable**
fussy **difficile, grincheux [-se]**
generous **généreux [-se]**
I get on with **je m'entends avec**
gifted **doué**
good **bon[ne]**
good-tempered **de bonne composition**
guilty **coupable**
habit **une habitude**
hard-working **travailleur [-se]**
I help **j'aide**
helpful **serviable**
honest (dis-) **(mal)honnête**
humor **l'humeur** *(f)*
humorous **qui a de l'humour**
immorality **l'immoralité** *(f)*
innocent **innocent**
intelligence **l'intelligence** *(f)*

Our neighbor is a lazy fellow, but very gifted.
He has a good sense of humor but is always boasting.

Notre voisin est un type paresseux mais très doué.
Il a le sens de l'humour, mais il est tout le temps en train de se vanter.

The pupils here are hard-working and well-behaved. We encourage self-confidence and self-discipline. Bad behavior and laziness are punished.

Les élèves ici sont travailleurs et bien élevés. Nous encourageons la confiance en soi et l'autodiscipline. Les mauvaises manières et la paresse sont punies.

intelligent **intelligent**
kind **gentil[le]**
kindness **la gentillesse, la bonté**
lazy **paresseux [-se]**
laziness **la paresse**
lively **vivant**
mad **fou [folle]**
manners **les manières** (f)
mean, stingy **mesquin**
memory **la mémoire**
mental(ly) **mental(ement)**
moral (im-) **(im)moral**
morality/morals **la moralité**
nervous **nerveux [-se]**
nice **bien, gentil[le], agréable, sympathique**
I obey **j'obéis à**
optimistic **optimiste**
patient (im-) **(im)patient**
personality **la personnalité**
pessimistic **pessimiste**
pleasant **plaisant**
polite (im-) **(im)poli**
popular **populaire**
quality **la qualité**
reasonable (un-) **(pas) raisonnable**
respect **le respect**
I respect **je respecte**
rude **grossier [-ère]**
sad **triste**
self-confidence **la confiance en soi**

self-esteem **l'amour-propre** (m)
sense **le sens**
  common sense **le bon sens**
  good sense **le bon sens**
sensible **raisonnable, avisé**
serious **sérieux [-se]**
shame **la honte**
shy **timide**
skill **l'habileté** (f)**, le talent, l'aptitude** (f)
skilful **habile, adroit, apte**
sociable (un-) **(peu) sociable**
strange **étrange**
stupid **stupide, idiot, bête**
stupidity **la bêtise, la stupidité**
suspicious **soupçonneux [-se], louche, suspect**
sympathetic **compatissant**
sympathy **la sympathie, la compassion**
talented **doué**
temperament **le tempérament**
temperamental **d'humeur instable**
I trust **je fais confiance à**
trusting **confiant**
unkind **peu aimable, pas gentil**
warm **chaleureux [-se]**
well-known **bien connu**
wise **sage, prudent**
wit **l'esprit** (m)
witty **spirituel[le], amusant**

Don't be so suspicious. Please trust me.

Ne soyez pas si soupçonneux. Faites-moi donc confiance.

The children have such different personalities. The eldest is very sensible and rather shy. Our daughter is more sociable and witty. The youngest is gifted but rather temperamental.

Les enfants ont des personnalités si différentes. L'aîné est très raisonnable et plutôt timide. Notre fille est plus sociable et amusante. La plus jeune est douée, mais elle a son caractère.

➤ THOUGHT PROCESSES 6c; EXPRESSING VIEWS 6d; HUMAN LIFE AND RELATIONSHIPS 7

THE HUMAN MIND AND CHARACTER

6b Feelings and emotions

I am afraid (of/that)   **j'ai peur (de/que)**

I am amazed (at)   **je suis très surpris/stupéfait/sidéré (par)**

amazement   **la surprise, la stupéfaction, l'étonnement** *(m)*

I amuse   **j'amuse**

I am amused by   **je trouve amusant**

amusement   **l'amusement** *(m)*

anger   **la colère**

angry   **en colère, furieux [-se]**

I am annoyed (at/about/with)   **je suis furieux [-se] (de/contre)**

anxiety   **l'anxiété** *(f)*

anxious   **anxieux [-se]**

I approve (of)   **j'approuve**

I am ashamed (of)   **j'ai honte (de)**

I am bored (by)   **je m'ennuie (par), j'en ai assez (de)**

boredom   **l'ennui** *(m)*

content (with)   **satisfait (de)**

cross (with)   **en colère (contre)**

delighted (about)   **ravi (de)**

I dislike   **je n'aime pas**

dissatisfaction   **le mécontentement**

dissatisfied (with)   **peu satisfait (de)**

embarrassed (about)   **gêné (par)**

embarrassment   **la gêne, l'embarras** *(m)*

emotion   **l'émotion** *(f)*

emotional   **émotionnel[le]**

I enjoy   **j'apprécie, j'aime**

envy   **l'envie** *(f)*

envious (of)   **envieux [-se] (de)**

fear   **la crainte**

I feel   **je ressens** *(ressentir)*, **je me sens** *(se sentir)*

I forgive   **je pardonne**

forgiveness   **le pardon**

I am frightened (of)   **j'ai peur (de)**

furious (about)   **furieux [-se] (de)**

fussy   **difficile, pinailleur [-se]**

grateful (for)   **reconnaissant (de)**

gratitude   **la reconnaissance, la gratitude**

grumpy   **grincheux [-se]**

happiness   **le bonheur**

happy (about)   **heureux [-se] (de)**

hate   **la haine**

I hate   **je hais** *(haïr)*, **je déteste**

We are very fond of our uncle. He has many good qualities.
However, he is often somewhat temperamental.
He hates it when we thank him, it makes him embarrassed.

**Nous aimons beaucoup notre oncle. Il a beaucoup de qualités. Toutefois, il a souvent des sautes d'humeur.
Il a horreur qu'on le remercie, ça le gêne.**

– I am really ashamed of my behavior yesterday. I was so upset and worried.

– J'ai vraiment honte de ma conduite d'hier. J'étais si bouleversée et inquiète.

– It really doesn't matter. I am thankful that you feel better.

– Cela n'a vraiment pas d'importance, je suis content que vous vous sentiez mieux.

– I am so glad you are not angry with me.

– Je suis si soulagé que vous ne soyez pas en colère contre moi.

I have a grudge against him **je lui en veux** *(vouloir)*
hope **l'espoir** *(m)*
I hope **j'espère** *(espérer)*
hopeful **plein d'espoir**
idealism **l'idéalisme** *(m)*
indifference **l'indifférence** *(f)*
indifferent (to) **indifférent (envers)**
I am indifferent **ça m'est indifférent/égal**
interest **l'intérêt** *(m)*
I am interested (in) **je m'intéresse (à)**
jealous **jaloux [-se]**
jealousy **la jalousie**
joy **la joie**
joyful **joyeux [-se]**
I like **j'aime bien**
I would like **je voudrais** *(vouloir)*
love **l'amour** *(m)*
I love **j'aime**
miserable (about) **malheureux [-se] (à cause de)**
misery **la tristesse, la déprime**
mood **l'humeur** *(f)*
in a good/bad mood **de bonne/ mauvaise humeur**
I'm pleased/glad that **je suis content/heureux [-se] que**
I prefer **je préfère** *(préférer)*
I regret **je regrette**
satisfaction **la satisfaction**
satisfied (with) **satisfait de**
surprise **la surprise**
I am surprised (at) **je m'étonne (de)**
thankful **reconnaissant**
unhappy **malheureux [-se]**
unhappiness **le malheur, la tristesse**
I am upset (about) **je suis vexé/ contrarié/peiné (à cause de)**
I want **je veux** *(vouloir)*
I wonder (at) **je m'étonne de, je suis étonné par**
I wonder if **je me demande si**
worried (about) **soucieux [-se] (au sujet de)**
worry **le souci**
I worry (about) **je me fais du souci (au sujet de)**
it worries me **cela m'inquiète** *(inquiéter)*

The boss is in a bad mood. He is cross with his secretary. She is bored with the work and doesn't care that he's annoyed.

I like our neighbor a lot but I'm worried about his wife. She takes care of her old mother, who has not adapted to life in town. She is often in a bad mood and very fussy.

Le patron est de mauvaise humeur. Il est en colère contre sa secrétaire. Elle trouve le travail ennuyeux et son humeur la laisse indifférente.

J'aime beaucoup notre voisin mais je me fais du souci pour sa femme. Elle s'occupe de sa mère, qui est âgée et ne s'est pas adaptée à la vie en ville. Elle est souvent de mauvaise humeur et très difficile.

THE HUMAN MIND AND CHARACTER

6c Thought processes

afterthought **la pensée après coup**
I analyze **j'analyse**
analysis **l'analyse** *(f)*
I assume **je suppose**
assuming that **à supposer que**
attention **l'attention** *(f)*
aware of (un-) **(in)conscient (de)**
I base . . . on **je base ... sur**
basic **de base**
basically **à la base**
basis **la base**
belief **la croyance, l'opinion** *(f)*
I believe (in) **je crois** *(croire)* **(à/en)**
certainty **la certitude**
certain, sure **certain, sûr**
coherent (in-) **(in)cohérent**
complex **le complexe**
inferiority **le complexe d'infériorité**
I comprehend **je comprends** *(comprendre)*
comprehensible **compréhensible**
I concentrate **je me concentre**
I concentrate (on) **je fixe mon attention (sur)**
I conclude (that) **je conclus** *(conclure)* **(que)**
conscious **conscient**
conscience **la conscience**
consciousness **la conscience**
I consider **je considère** *(considérer)* **que ...**
consideration **la considération**
I take into consideration **je tiens** *(tenir)* **compte (de)**
taking everything into consideration **tout compte fait**
I contemplate **je contemple**
context **le contexte**

on the contrary **au contraire**
controversial **controversé**
I decide **je décide**
decision **la décision**
I deduce **je déduis** *(déduire)*
I delude myself **je me fais des illusions**
delusion **l'illusion** *(f)*, **le fantasme**
I determine **je détermine**
I disbelieve **je me refuse à croire**
I distinguish **je distingue**
doubt **le doute**
I doubt **je doute**
doubtful **douteux [-se]**
doubtless/without a doubt **sans (aucun) doute**
exception **l'exception** *(f)*
evidence **la preuve**
evident **évident**
evidently **évidemment**
fact **le fait**
in fact **en fait**
false **faux [-sse]**
fantasy **la fantaisie**
fiction **la fiction**
for **pour**
I am for it **je suis pour**
I forbid **j'interdis** *(interdire)*
I forget **j'oublie**
genius (for) **le génie (de)**
I grasp **je saisis**
hypothesis **l'hypothèse** *(f)*
implication **l'implication** *(f)*
interesting **intéressant**
I imagine **je me réprésente, je m'imagine**
imagination **l'imagination**
I invent **j'invente**
invention **l'invention** *(f)*
issue **le problème** *(m)*
I judge **je juge**

judgment **le jugement**
justice **la justice**
I justify **je justifie**
I know *(place/person)* **je connais (connaître)**
I know that **je sais *(savoir)* que**
knowledge **la connaissance**
knowledgeable **bien informé**
logic **la logique**
logical **logique**
I go mad **je deviens** *(devenir)* **fou [folle]**
madness **la folie**
meaning **le sens**
it means **cela veut** *(vouloir)* **dire**
I meditate (on) **je médite (sur), je réfléchis (à)**
memory **la mémoire**
metaphysics **la métaphysique**
mind **l'esprit** *(m)*, **l'intelligence** *(f)*
a great mind **un grand esprit**
I misunderstand **je comprends *(comprendre)* mal**
misunderstanding **l'erreur** *(f)*, **la méprise, le malentendu**
motive **le motif, l'intention** *(f)*
it occurred to me that **il m'est venu à l'esprit que**
philosophy **la philosophie**
point of view **le point de vue**
I ponder **je considère *(considérer)*, je pèse** *(peser)*
premise **la prémisse**
I presume **je présume**
principle **le principe**
in/on principle **en/par principe**
problem **le problème**
proof **la preuve**
I prove **je prouve**
psychology **la psychologie**
psychoanalysis **la psychanalyse**
rational (ir-) *(thinking)* **rationnel[le] (déraisonnable)**

reality **la réalité**
I realize **je me rends compte de**
I reason *(conclude)* **j'en conclus *(conclure)***
I reason **je raisonne**
reason *(faculty of)* **la raison**
I recognize **je reconnais *(reconnaître)***
I reflect **je réfléchis**
relevant **significatif [-ve]**
I remember **je me rappelle *(se rappeler)*, je me souviens *(se souvenir)* de**
right **vrai, juste**
I am right **j'ai raison**
it is right **il est bon/juste**
I see **je vois** *(voir)*
I solve **je résous** *(résoudre)*
solution **la solution**
I speculate **je spécule**
subconscious **le subconscient**
I suppose **je suppose**
I summarize **je résume**
summary **le résumé**
theoretical **théoriquement**
theory **la théorie**
in theory **en théorie**
I think (of/about) **je pense (à)**
thought **la pensée**
true **vrai**
truth **la vérité**
I understand **je comprends**
understanding **la compréhension**
valid (in-) **(non) valable**
view **l'avis** *(m)*, **l'opinion** *(f)*
in my view **d'après moi, à mon avis**
wrong **faux [-sse]**
I am wrong **j'ai tort**
it is wrong **on a tort, c'est faux**

49

6d Expressing views

I accept **j'accepte**
I agree (with/about) **je suis d'accord (avec/au sujet de)**
I answer **je réponds**
answer **la réponse**
I argue **je (me) dispute**
argument **la discussion,**
I ask **je demande**
I ask (a question) **je pose (une question)**
brief **bref, bréve**
I contradict **je contredis (contredire)**
I criticize **je critique**
I define **je définis**
definition **la définition**
I deny **je nie**
I describe **je décris (décrire)**
description **la description**
I disagree (with/about) **je ne suis pas d'accord (avec/sur)**
I discuss **je discute (de)**

discussion **la discussion**
I maintain **je maintiens (maintenir)**
I mean **je veux (vouloir) dire**
opinion **l'opinion (f)**
in my opinion **à mon avis**
question **la question**
I question **je mets (mettre) en question**
a thorny question **une question épineuse**
I suggest **je suggère (suggérer)**
it is a question of **c'est une question de**
I say **je dis (dire)**
I state **je déclare**
statement **la déclaration**
suggestion **la suggestion**

Giving examples

as is known **tel que nous le connaissons**

– What do you think of the speaker?

– In my opinion he did not consider the basic problem.

In principle I agree with his views. On the one hand he proved the need for new housing. On the other hand he discussed the problems of finding a site.

– I suggest we try to analyze the problem carefully. Then we shall be able to judge the situation and come to a sound conclusion.

– **Que pensez-vous de la personne qui parle?**

– **A mon avis, il n'a pas abordé le problème essentiel.**

Je suis d'accord sur le principe. D'une part, il a démontré que l'on avait besoin de nouveaux logements, et de l'autre, il a discuté des problèmes pour trouver des sites.

– **Je propose que nous essayions d'analyser le problème avec soin. Nous serons alors en mesure de parvenir à une conclusion mesurée.**

etc./and so on **etc/ainsi de suite**
example/instance **un exemple**
for example **par exemple**
i.e. **c.a.d. (c'est à dire)**
namely **voire**
I quote **je cite**
such as **tel[le] que**

Comparing and contrasting

advantage **l'avantage** *(m)*
I compare **je compare**
comparison **la comparaison**
   in comparison with **comparé**
   avec/à, en comparaison avec
it contrasts with **il contraste avec**
contrast **le contraste**
   in contrast **par contraste**
I differ **je diffère**
difference **la différence**
different (from) **différent (de)**
disadvantage **l'inconvénient** *(m)*
dissimilar **dissemblable, différent**
   de
I distinguish **je distingue**
pros and cons **le pour et le contre**

relatively **relativement**
same **le/la même**
similar **qui ressemble, semblable**

Expressing reservations

even if **même si**
even so **malgré tout**
to some extent **jusqu'à un certain**
   point
at first sight **à première vue**
hardly **à peine**
in general **en général**
in the main **dans l'ensemble**
in part/partly **en partie**
perhaps/maybe **peut-être**
presumably **probablement, sans**
   doute
probably **probablement**
relatively **relativement**
reservation **la réserve**
unfortunately **malheureusement**
unusual(ly) **inaccoutumé**
virtually **pratiquement**
in a way **dans un sens**

---

conclusion **la conclusion**
   in conclusion **en conclusion**
finally **finalement**
first **premier**
firstly **premièrement**
   for one thing, for another
   d'abord, ensuite
furthermore **de plus, en outre**
on the one hand **d'une part**
   on the other hand **d'autre part**
initially **pour commencer**

last **dernier**
lastly **pour finir**
   at last **enfin, finalement**
next **suivant**
place **la place**
   in the first place **pour**
   commencer, d'abord
   in the second place **ensuite**
secondly **ensuite**
in short **en résumé**

– He is partly right about the
reasons for our difficulties, but
there is probably much more
behind it.

**– Il a raison en partie en ce qui
concerne la source de nos
problèmes, mais cette histoire
cache sans doute beaucoup de
choses.**

THE HUMAN MIND AND CHARACTER

Arguing a point

admittedly   **il faut le reconnaître**
all the same   **néanmoins,
   toutefois, quand même**
although   **bien que**
anyway   **de toute façon**
apart from   **à part**
as for   **quant à**
as I see it   **comme je le perçois**
as well   **également**
despite this   **en dépit de cela**
in effect   **en fait**
however   **cependant, toutefois**
incidentally   **à propos**
instead   **à la place**
instead of   **au lieu de**
just as important   **tout aussi
   important**
likewise   **de même**
no matter whether   **quoi qu'il en
   soit**
that may be so   **cela est peut-être
   vrai**
nevertheless   **néanmoins**
otherwise   **autrement**

in reality   **en réalité**
in many respects   **à plusieurs
   égards**
in my opinion   **à mon avis**
in return   **en revanche**
as a rule   **en règle générale**
so to speak   **pour ainsi dire**
in spite of   **en dépit de**
still,   **et pourtant,**
to tell the truth   **à vrai dire**
whereas   **tandis que, alors que**
on the whole   **dans l'ensemble**

Cause and effect

all the more (because)   **d'autant
   plus que**
as   **comme**
because   **parce que**
because of   **à cause de**
cause   **la cause**
consequence   **la conséquence**
consequently   **en conséquence**
effect   **un effet**
it follows that   **il en résulte que**
how?   **comment?**

In many respects things are not too bad. As a rule people try to obey the law. However, crime is still common, in spite of the efforts of the police. All the same, we are not discouraged.

À plusieurs égards les choses ne vont pas trop mal. En règle générale, les gens essaient d'obéir à la loi. Toutefois, les crimes sont encore fréquents en dépit des efforts de la police. Malgré tout, nous ne perdons pas l'espoir.

Honestly I'm extremely angry with him. Thanks to his carelessness we missed the plane. Fortunately there was another, but we got to Chicago completely exhausted.

Vraiment je suis très en colère contre lui. En raison de sa négligence, nous avons manqué l'avion. Heureusement, il y en avait un autre, mais nous sommes arrivés à Chicago complètement épuisés.

if **si**
reason **la raison**
for this reason **pour cette raison**
result **le résultat**
as a result **en conséquence**
provided that **à condition que**
since **puisque**
so long as **tant que**
therefore, so **ainsi, c'est pourquoi**
thus **ainsi**
whether **si**
why? **pourquoi?**

Emphasizing

above all **par-dessus tout**
in addition **en outre**
all the more **d'autant plus**
also **aussi**
both . . . and **à la fois/et ... et**
certainly **certainement**
clearly **clairement**
under no circumstances **en aucun cas**
completely **complètement**

especially **surtout, spécialement**
even (more) **encore (plus)**
without exception **sans exception**
I emphasize **je souligne**
extremely **extrêmement**
far and away **de loin**
fortunately **heureusement**
honestly **honnêtement**
just when **au moment précis où**
mainly **pour l'essentiel**
moreover **de plus**
naturally **naturellement**
not at all **pas du tout**
not in the least **pas le moins du monde**
obviously **de toute évidence**
in particular **en particulier**
particularly **particulièrement**
in every respect **à tous les niveaux**
I stress **je souligne**
thanks to **grâce à**
undeniably **sans aucun doute**
very **très**
and what is more **et qui plus est**

And what is more, he clearly didn't care at all. Obviously I shall tell his firm exactly what I think of him. Under no circumstances will I employ him again.

– How did he break his leg?

– When he got the ladder he did not notice it was broken. So he fell off it.

– Why did he want the ladder?

– Because he wanted to paint the house.

Et qui plus est, de toute évidence ça lui était complètement égal. Bien évidemment je dirai à son entreprise ce que je pense de lui. En aucun cas je ne le réemploierai.

– Comment s'est-il cassé la jambe?
– Lorsqu'il est allé chercher l'échelle, il n'a pas remarqué qu'elle était cassée et il en est tombé.
– Pourquoi avait-il besoin de l'échelle?
– Parce qu'il voulait peindre la maison.

7 Human life and relationships

7a Family and friends

Friendship

acquaintance **la connaissance**
boyfriend **le petit ami**
buddy **le/la pote**
classmate **le/la camarade de classe**
companion **le compagnon, la compagne**
friend (close) **un ami/une amie (proche)**
friendship **l'amitié** *(f)*
gang **la bande**
we get on well together **nous nous entendons bien**
I get on with **je m'entends avec**
we get together **nous nous retrouvons**
I get to know **j'apprends à connaître**
girlfriend **la petite amie**
I introduce **je présente**
pal **le copain, la copine**
pen pal **le/la correspondant[e]**
quarrel **la querelle**
I quarrel with **je me querelle avec**
family ties **les liens** *(m)* **de parenté**

school friend/pal **un ami/une amie d'école**

The family and relatives

adopted **adopté**
ancestor **un/une ancêtre**
ancestry **l'ascendance** *(f)*
aunt **la tante**
baby **le bébé**
brother **le frère**
brother-in-law **le beau-frère**
brothers and sisters **les frères et sœurs**
child **l'enfant** *(m)*
close relative **le parent proche**
closely related **proche parent**
commonlaw husband **l'époux de droit coutumier, le concubin**
commonlaw wife **l'épouse** *(f)* **de droit coutumier, la concubine**
cousin **le cousin, la cousine**
dad/pa **le papa**
daughter **la fille**
daughter-in-law **la bru, la belle-fille**
distant relative **le parent éloigné**
distantly related **parent éloigné**
elder **aîné**

We are good friends. I get on well with him. We have a good relationship.

Nous sommes de bons amis. Je m'entends bien avec lui. Nous avons une bonne relation.

No hard feelings!

Sans rancune!

We are more open with one another. We settle conflicts.

Nous sommes plus francs l'un envers l'autre. Nous réglons les différents.

---

elder/-est daughter **l'aînée** *(f)*
elder/-est son **l'aîné** *(m)*
family **la famille**
family tree **l'arbre** *(m)* **généalogique**
father **le père**
father-in-law **le beau-père**
fiancé(e) **le fiancé, la fiancée**
forebear **un aïeul, une aïeule**
foster **adoptif [-ve]**
genealogy **la généalogie**
goddaughter **la filleule**
godfather **le parrain**
godmother **la marraine**
godson **le filleul**
grandad/grandpa **le papy, le pépé**
grandchildren **les petits-enfants** *(m)*
granddaughter **la petite-fille**
grandfather **le grand-père**
grandmother **la grand-mère**
grandparents **les grands-parents** *(m)*
grandson **le petit-fils**
granny/grandma **la mamie, la mémé**
great-aunt **la grand-tante**
great-grandchild **l'arrière petit-fils** *(m)*, **l'arrière petite-fille** *(f)*
great-grandfather **l'arrière grand-père** *(m)*
great-grandmother **l'arrière grand-mère** *(f)*
great-nephew **le petit-neveu**

great-niece **la petite-nièce**
great-uncle **le grand-oncle**
guardian **le tuteur, la tutrice**
half-brother **le demi-frère**
half-sister **la demi-sœur**
husband **le mari, l'époux** *(m)*
maiden aunt **la tante vieille fille**
mother **la mère**
mother-in-law **la belle-mère**
mom, ma **la maman**
nephew **le neveu**
niece **la nièce**
only child **l'enfant** *(m)* **unique**
parents **les parents** *(m)*
partner **le conjoint, la conjointe**
related **apparenté**
relation, relative **le parent, la parente**
second cousin **le petit-cousin**
sister **la sœur**
son **le fils**
son-in-law **le gendre, le beau-fils**
spouse **l'épouse** *(f)*, **l'époux** *(m)*
stepbrother **le beau-frère**
stepdaughter **la belle-fille**
stepfather **le beau-père**
stepmother **la belle-mère**
stepsister **la belle-sœur**
stepson **le beau-fils**
twin brother **le frère jumeau**
twin sister **la sœur jumelle**
uncle **l'oncle** *(f)*
wife **la femme, l'épouse** *(f)*
younger/-est **cadet[te]**

– Have you any family?
– I come from a large family. I have four brothers and sisters. We have family problems.

– I have no close family. I am an only child.

We are distantly related.

– **As-tu de la famille?**
– **Je viens d'une famille nombreuse. J'ai quatre frères et sœurs. On a des problèmes familiaux.**

– **Je n'ai aucune famille proche. Je suis enfant unique.**

Nous sommes parents éloignés.

HUMAN LIFE AND RELATIONSHIPS

7b Love and children

Love and marriage

adultery **l'adultère**
affair **la liaison**
alimony **la pension alimentaire**
bachelor **le célibataire**
betrothal **les fiançailles** *(f)*
betrothed **fiancé**
breakdown *(marriage)* **la rupture**
bride **la mariée**
bridegroom **le marié**
bridesmaids **les demoiselles** *(f)* **d'honneur**
couple **le couple**
I court **je fais la cour à**
courtship **la cour**
divorce **le divorce**
divorced **divorcé**
I get divorced (from) **je divorce (de)**
divorcee **le/la divorcé[e]**
engaged **fiancé**
I get engaged (to) **je me fiance (avec)**
engagement **les fiançailles** *(f)*
I fall for/in love (with) **je tombe amoureux [-se] de**

I go out with **je sors** *(sortir)* **avec**
we are incompatible **nous ne sommes pas compatibles**
lover **l'amant** *(m)*
marriage **le mariage**
married **marié**
I get married (to) **je me marie (avec)**
married couple **le ménage**
I marry **j'épouse**
matrimony **le mariage**
mistress **la maîtresse**
newly married couple **les jeunes** *(m)* **mariés**
promiscuity **la promiscuité**
he is promiscuous **il est de mœurs faciles**
I separate from **je me sépare de**
separated **séparé**
separation **la séparation**
unmarried/single **célibataire**
unmarried/single mother **la mère célibataire**
wedding **les noces** *(f)*
widower/widow **le veuf/la veuve**

– We are madly in love. It was love at first sight.

– Nous sommes follement amoureux. Ça a été le coup de foudre.

– Are you married?
– We are getting engaged.

– Vous êtes mariés?
– Nous nous fiançons.

– She doesn't understand me. She is always nagging. She gets me worked up.
– He shouts at me. He drives me mad.
– All that's in the past now. Let's kiss and make up.

– Elle ne me comprend pas. Elle est toujours après moi. Elle m'énerve.
– Il crie après moi. Il me rend folle.
– Tout ça, c'est du passé maintenant. Faisons la paix.

Our relationship is breaking up.

Notre relation est en train de se briser.

LOVE AND CHILDREN **7b**

Birth and children

baby **le bébé**
baby carriage **la voiture d'enfant, la poussette**
babysitter **la gardienne d'enfants, le/la baby-sitter**
baptism **le baptême**
bib **le bavoir**
birth control **la régulation des naissances, la contraception**
birthrate **le taux de natalité**
birthday **l'anniversaire** *(m)*
I was born **je suis né[e]**
boy **le garçon**
I bring up/raise a child **j'élève *(élever)* un enfant**
I breast-feed **j'allaite, je donne le sein à**
child **l'enfant** *(m)*
childhood **l'enfance** *(f)*
christening **le baptême**
coil **le stérilet**
condom **le préservatif**
contraception **la contraception**
contractions **les contractions** *(f)*
crib **le lit d'enfant, le berceau**
diaper **la couche**
I deliver **j'accouche**
I am expecting a baby **j'attends un bébé**
family planning **le planning familial**
fertile (in-) **fécond (stérile)**
fertility **la fertilité**
fertiltity drug **le médicament contre la stérilité**
I give birth (to) **j'accouche (de)**
girl **la fille**

I go into labor **je commence à accoucher**
incubator **la couveuse**
infancy **la petite enfance**
infant **le nouveau-né**
infantile **infantile**
kid **le/la gosse, l'enfant**
lad **le gars**
lass **la jeune fille**
live birth **la naissance viable**
I look like **je ressemble à**
I have a miscarriage **je fais une fausse couche**
midwife **la sage-femme**
nanny **la nounou**
newborn child **le nouveau-né**
orphan **un orphelin, une orpheline**
pacifier **la tétine**
period **les règles** *(f)*
pill **la pilule**
pregnant **enceinte**
I remind . . . of . . . **je rappelle ... à ...** *(rappeler)*
saint's day **la fête**
sibling *(adj)* **fraternel[le]**
sibling rivalry **la rivalité fraternelle**
stillborn **mort-né**
teenaged **adolescent**
teenager **un adolescent, une adolescente**
teething **la pousse des dents**
toddler **le tout petit, la toute petite**
toy **le jouet**
triplets **les triplés** *(m)*
twin **le jumeau, la jumelle**

I'm on the pill.	**Je prends la pilule.**
I'm six months pregnant.	**Je suis enceinte de six mois.**
I spoil my child.	**Je gâte mon enfant.**
He looks like his mother.	**Il ressemble à sa mère.**

SOCIAL ISSUES 12   **57**

7c Life and death

Growing

adolescent **un adolescent, une adolescente**

adult **un/une adulte**

adult *(adj)* **adulte**

age **l'âge** *(m)*

I age (well) **je vieillis (bien)**

aged **âgé (de)**

centenarian **le/la centenaire**

child **l'enfant** *(m)*

he comes from **il vient de**

elder/-est **un aîné, une aînée**

elderly **les personnes** *(f)* **âgées**

elderly *(adj)* **vieux [vieille]**

female **la femme**

female *(adj)* **femelle**

foreigner **un étranger, une étrangère**

generation **la génération**

generation gap **le conflit des générations**

I grow old **je vieillis**

grown-up **l'adulte** *(m/f)*

I grow up **je deviens** *(devenir)* **adulte**

housewife **la femme au foyer**

life **la vie**

life insurance **l'assurance-vie** *(f)*

male **l'homme** *(m)*

male *(adj)* **mâle**

man **l'homme** *(m)*

mature **mûr**

maturity **la maturité**

menopause **la ménopause**

middle age **la cinquantaine**

new **nouveau [nouvelle]**

nickname **le surnom**

octogenarian **un/une octogénaire**

old **vieux [vieille]**

old age **la vieillesse**

old man, woman **le vieux, la vieille**

old people's home **maison de retraite**

pension **la pension**

When I grow up, I want to be an astronaut.

He respects his elders.

Next door, the couple are getting divorced. The children are suffering as the parents have separated.

– What about the elderly?
– Most try to stay on in their own homes rather than go into an old people's home.

Their pensions are barely adequate. However, the community looks after them well.

Quand je serai grand, je serai astronaute.

Il respecte ses aînés.

Le couple à côté de chez nous est en train de divorcer. Les enfants souffrent car les parents se sont séparés.

– Et les personnes âgées?
– La plupart des gens essaient de rester dans leur propre maison au lieu d'entrer dans une maison de retraite.
Leurs pensions sont à peine suffisantes. Cependant, la communauté s'occupe bien d'eux.

pensioner   **le retraité, la retraitée**
people   **les gens** *(m)*
permissive society   **la société permissive**
person   **la personne**
present   **présent**
in the prime of life   **dans la fleur de l'âge**
responsible   **responsable**
I retire   **je prends ma retraite**
retired   **en retraite**
retirement   **la retraite**
   early retirement   **la retraite anticipée**
septuagenarian   **le/la septuagénaire**
single   **célibataire**
spinster   **la vieille fille**
stranger   **un étranger, une étrangère**
surname   **le nom de famille**
I take after   **je tiens** *(tenir)* **de**
visit   **la visite**
I visit   **je rends visite**
woman   **la femme**
year   **l'année***(f)*
young *(adj)*   **jeune**
young person   **le/la jeune**
younger   **plus jeune**
youngest   **le/la plus jeune**
youth   **la jeunesse**
youth *(persons)*   **les jeunes** *(m/f)*

Death

afterlife   **la vie future/éternelle**
angel   **l'ange** *(m)*
ashes   **les cendres** *(f)*
autopsy   **l'autopsie** *(f)*
body   **le corps**
burial   **l'enterrement** *(m)*
I bury   **j'enterre**
corpse   **le cadavre, le corps**

he is cremated   **il est incinéré**
cremation   **la crémation**
crematorium   **le crématorium**
dead   **mort**
death   **la mort**
death rate   **le taux de mortalité**
death certificate   **l'acte** *(m)* **de décès**
he dies   **il meurt** *(mourir)*
epitaph   **l'épitaphe** *(f)*
eulogy   **le panégyrique**
funeral   **l'enterrement** *(m)*, **les obsèques** *(f)*
grave   **la tombe**
gravestone/tombstone   **la pierre tombale**
graveyard/cemetery   **la cimetière**
heaven   **le ciel, le paradis**
hell   **l'enfer** *(m)*
I inherit   **j'hérite**
inheritance   **la succession**
last rites   **les derniers sacrements** *(mpl)*
he lies in state   **il est exposé solennellement**
mortuary   **la morgue**
I mourn   **je pleure**
mourning   **le deuil**
I am in mourning for   **je porte le deuil de**
obituary   **la notice nécrologique**
he passes away   **il s'éteint** *(s'éteindre)*, **il disparaît** *(disparaître)*
remains   **les restes** *(m)*
he goes to heaven   **il va au ciel/paradis**
tomb   **le tombeau**
undertaker   **l'entrepreneur** *(m)* **de pompes funèbres**
will   **le testament**
   the last will and testament of   **les dernières volontés** *(f)* **de**

Daily life

8a The house

amenities **les aménagements** *(m)*
apartment **l'appartement** *(m)*
apartment house **l'immeuble** *(m)*
boarding house **la pension (de famille)**
(of) brick **en brique**
I build **je construis** *(construire)*
building **le bâtiment**
building plot **le terrain à bâtir**
building site **le chantier de construction**
bungalow **le pavillon**
caretaker **le gardien, la gardienne**
chalet **le chalet**
detached (single) house **la maison individuelle**
furnished apartment **l'appartement** *(m)* **meublé**
furnished house **la maison meublée**
freehold **la propriété foncière libre**

garbage collection **le ramassage d'ordures**
I have an addition built **je fais agrandir la maison**
house **la maison**
housing **le logement**
landlord/landlady **le/la propriétaire**
lease **le bail**
leased property **la propriété louée**
lodger/roomer **le/la locataire**
I modernize **je modernise**
mortgage **l'emprunt-logement** *(m)*
mortgage rate **le taux de l'emprunt-logement**
I move (house) **je déménage**
I move in **j'emménage**
I occupy **j'occupe**
I own **je possède**
owner-occupied **occupé par son/sa propriétaire**
penthouse **l'appartement** *(m)* **de grand standing**

– Are you hoping to buy your own home soon?
– Yes, we are trying to get a mortgage. We have found an older property, which we will modernize.

We are renting an apartment at the moment. The rent is very high, and the landlord is slow to make improvements

We are having a house built.

– **Espérez-vous acheter votre propre maison bientôt?**
– **Oui, nous essayons d'obtenir un emprunt-logement. Nous avons trouvé une propriété plus vieille que nous allons moderniser.**

Nous louons un appartement en ce moment. Le loyer est très élevé et le propriétaire est lent à faire des améliorations.

Nous faisons construire une maison.

partly furnished   **en partie meublé**
prefabricated house   **la maison en**
   préfabriqué
premises   **les locaux** *(m)*
public housing   **l'appartement** *(m)*
   loué à la municipalité, l'H.L.M. *(f)*
removal van   **le camion de**
   déménagement
rent   **le loyer**
I rent   **je loue**
sewage disposal   **l'évacuation** *(f)*
   des eaux usées
(of) stone   **de/en pierre**
street lighting   **l'éclairage** *(m)* **des**
   rues
subsidized housing   **l'H.L.M.** *(f)*
   (Habitation à Loyer Modéré)
I take out a mortgage   **je fais un**
   emprunt-logement
tenancy   **la location**
tenant   **le/la locataire**
terraced houses   **des maisons** *(f)*
   mitoyennes
unfurnished apartment
   l'appartement *(m)* **non-meublé**

Rooms

attic   **la mansarde**
basement   **le sous-sol**
bathroom   **la salle de bains, les**
   toilettes *(f)*
bedroom   **la chambre à coucher**
cellar   **la cave**
corridor   **le couloir**
dining room   **la salle à manger**
hall(way)   **l'entrée** *(f)*
kitchen   **la cuisine**
landing   **le palier**
living room   **le salon**
loft   **le grenier**
lounge   **le salon**
shower   **la douche**
sitting room, living room   **le salon,**
   la salle de séjour
study   **le bureau**
toilet   **le W.C.** *(m),* **le cabinet**
utility room   **la buanderie**
verandah   **la véranda**

Her penthouse is to let/for rent.   **Son appartement de grand**
standing est à louer.

My lease has two weeks to run.   **Mon bail se termine dans deux**
semaines.

We moved two years ago.   **Nous avons déménagé il y a**
deux ans.

The house has a fairly pleasant
view: it grows on you after a while!   **La vue depuis la maison est**
assez agréable. On s'y fait au
bout de quelque temps!

The whole house needs painting
before we sell it.   **Toute la maison a besoin d'être**
repeinte avant d'être vendue.

8b The household

aerial **l'antenne** *(f)*	functional **fonctionnel**
attached **attenant**	furnished **meublé**
back door **la porte de derrière**	furniture **les meubles** *(m)*
balcony **le balcon**	item of furniture **le meuble**
baseboard **la plinthe**	garage **le garage**
big **grand**	garbage can **la poubelle**
blind **le store**	gas **le gaz**
boiler **la chaudière**	glass *(material)* **le verre**
breakfast room **la petite salle à manger**	ground (first) floor **le rez-de-chaussée**
built-in **encastré**	gutter **la gouttière**
burglar alarm **la sonnerie d'alarme**	handle *(on drawer, door)* **la poignée**
button **le bouton**	handle *(on basket, jug)* **l'anse** *(f)*
carpet **la moquette**	hearth **le foyer**
ceiling **le plafond**	heating **le chauffage**
central **central**	central heating **le chauffage central**
chimney **la cheminée**	
clean **propre**	included **inclus**
closet **le placard mural, l'armoire**	key **la clé**
comfortable (un-) **(in)confortable**	keyhole **le trou de serrure**
cosy **douillet[te]**	lamp **la lampe**
cupboard **le placard**	lampshade **l'abat-jour** *(m)*
curtain **le rideau**	letterbox **la boîte aux lettres**
desk **le bureau**	lever **le levier**
dirty **sale**	lift **l'ascenseur** *(m)*
door **la porte**	lightbulb **l'ampoule** *(f)*
door handle **la poignée de la porte**	light **la lumière**
doorknob **le bouton de la porte**	lightswitch **l'interrupteur** *(m)*
doorbell **la sonnette**	lighting **l'éclairage**
doormat **le paillasson**	lock **la serrure**
downstairs **en bas**	it looks onto **il donne sur**
electric **électrique**	mantelpiece **le dessus de cheminée**
electric plug **la prise électrique**	mat **le tapis**
electric socket **la prise électrique**	mezzanine floor **la mezzanine**
electricity **l'électricité** *(f)*	modern **moderne**
extension cord **la rallonge**	new **nouveau, nouvelle, neuf [neuve]**
fireplace **la cheminée**	
floor **le sol**	nice **joli**
floor, story **l'étage** *(m)*	off *(switches, electrical apparatus)* **éteint**
floorboard **la planche**	
front door **la porte d'entrée**	off *(tap)* **fermé**

old   **vieux [vieille]**
on *(switches, electrical apparatus)*
    allumé
    on *(tap)*   **ouvert**
on the second floor   **au premier
    étage**
own   **propre**
passage   **le passage**
pipe   **le tuyau, le conduit**
plaster   **le plâtre**
plumbing   **la plomberie, la tuyauterie**
price   **le prix**
radiator   **le radiateur**
rent   **le loyer**
roof   **le toit**
roof tile   **la tuile**
room   **la pièce**
safety chain   **la chaîne de sûreté**
sale   **la vente**
shelf   **l'étagère** *(f)*
shutters   **les volets** *(m)*
situation   **la situation**
skylight   **la lucarne**
small   **petit**
spacious   **spacieux [-se]**
staircase   **l'escalier** *(m)*
stairs   **les escaliers** *(m)*
step   **la marche**
terrace   **la terrasse**
tidy   **bien rangé, en ordre**
tile   **le carreau**
toilet   **les toilettes** *(f)*
upper floor   **l'étage** *(m)* **supérieur**
upstairs   **en haut**
vase   **le vase**
view   **la vue**
wall   **le mur**
    interior wall   **la paroi**
    garden wall   **le mur (de clôture)**
wastepaper basket   **la corbeille (à
    papier)**
water   **l'eau** *(f)*
window   **la fenêtre**
windowsill   **le rebord de la fenêtre**
wire   **le fil**

wiring   **l'installation** *(f)* **électrique**
wood   **le bois**

Electrical goods

alarm clock   **réveille-matin**
answering machine   **le répondeur
    téléphonique**
cassette player   **le lecteur de
    cassettes**
cassette recorder   **le
    magnétophone**
clothes dryer   **le sèche-linge, le
    séchoir**
compact-disc player   **le lecteur de
    CD/disques lasers**
deepfreeze   **le congélateur**
dishwasher   **le lave-vaisselle**
electric appliance   **l'appareil** *(m)*
    ménager
electric stove   **la cuisinière
    électrique**
electric razor   **le rasoir électrique**
food mixer, beaters   **le batteur**
food processor   **robot de cuisine**
freezer   **le congélateur**
fridge/refrigerator   **le frigo, le
    réfrigérateur**
hi-fi   **la chaîne hi-fi**
iron   **le fer (à repasser)**
microwave oven   **le four à micro-
    ondes**
pants press   **le presse-pantalons**
personal stereo   **le baladeur**
radio   **la radio, le poste de radio**
record player   **le tourne-disque**
refrigerator   **le réfrigérateur**
spin dryer   **l'essoreuse** *(f)*
stereo system   **la chaîne stéréo**
tape player   **le lecteur de cassettes**
tape recorder   **le magnétophone**
TV set   **le poste de télévision**
vacuum cleaner   **l'aspirateur** *(m)*
video recorder   **le magnétoscope**
washing machine   **la machine à
    laver**

8c Furnishings

Lounge

armchair   **le fauteuil**
ashtray   **le cendrier**
bookshelf   **l'étagère** *(f)* **(à livres)**
bookcase   **la bibliothèque**
bureau   **le bureau**
coffee table   **la table basse**
cupboard, closet   **le placard**
cushion   **le coussin**
easy chair   **le fauteuil**
ornament   **l'ornement** *(m)*
picture   **le tableau**
   picture (portrait)   **le portrait**
photo   **la photo**
poster   **le poster**
pouffe   **le pouf**
rocking chair   **le fauteuil à bascule**
rug   **le tapis**
settee   **le canapé**
sofa   **la banquette**

Kitchen

bottle opener   **l'ouvre-bouteille(s)**
   (m)
bowl   **le bol**
can opener   **l'ouvre-boîte(s)** *(m)*
clothesline   **la corde à linge**
clothespeg   **la pince à linge**
coffee machine   **le percolateur**
coffee pot   **la cafetière**
colander   **la passoire**
cup   **la tasse**
cupboard   **le placard**
   wall-cupboard   **le placard mural**
cutlery   **les couverts** *(m)*
dish   **le plat**
dishcloth   **le torchon à vaisselle**
dishes   **la vaisselle**
dishwashing liquid   **le produit pour
   la vaisselle**
drain board   **l'égouttoir** *(m)*
fork   **la fourchette**
frying pan   **la poêle**

gas stove   **la cuisinière à gaz**
glass   **le verre**
   wine glass   **le verre à vin**
knife   **le couteau**
   carving knife   **le couteau à
   découper**
laundry detergent   **la lessive (en
   poudre)**
milk jug   **le pot à lait**
oven   **le four**
plate   **l'assiette** *(f)*
pepper shaker   **le poivrier, la
   poivrière, le moulin à poivre**
salt shaker   **la salière**
saucepan   **la casserole**
saucer   **la soucoupe**
scales   **la balance**
sink   **l'évier** *(m)*
sink unit   **l'évier** *(m)* **encastré**
spoon   **la cuillère**
stove   **la cuisinière**
tap/faucet   **le robinet**
teapot   **la théière**
tea towel/dish towel   **le torchon à
   vaisselle**
trash can   **la poubelle**
tray   **le plateau**

Dining room

chair   **la chaise**
candle   **la bougie, la chandelle**
candelabra   **le chandelier**
candlestick   **le bougeoir**
clock   **l'horloge** *(f)*, **la pendule**
dresser   **le vaisselier**
place setting   **le couvert**
plate warmer   **le chauffe-assiettes**
   (inv)
serviette   **la serviette**
sideboard   **le buffet**
table   **la table**
tablecloth   **la nappe**
table napkin   **la serviette de table**

Bedroom

alarm clock **le réveil**
bed **le lit**
  bunk bed **la couchette**
  double bed **le grand lit, le lit à deux personnes**
bedclothes **les couvertures** *(f)* et **les draps** *(m)*
bedding **la literie**
bedside table **la table de nuit**
bedspread **le couvre-lit**
blanket **la couverture**
chest of drawers **la commode**
dressing table **la coiffeuse**
duvet **la couette**
mattress **le matelas**
pillow **l'oreiller** *(m)*
quilt **l'édredon** *(m)*
sheet **le drap**
wardrobe **l'armoire** *(f)*
  hanging wardrobe **la penderie**

Bathroom

basin **le lavabo**
bath **la baignoire**
bathmat **le tapis de bain**
bidet **le bidet**
clothesbrush **la brosse à habits**
face washcloth **le gant de toilette**
laundry basket **le panier à linge sale**
mirror **le miroir**
nailbrush **la brosse à ongles**
plug **la prise**
scales **le pèse-personne**
shower **la douche**
sink **le lavabo**
soap **le savon**
tap **le robinet**
toilet **les toilettes** *(f)*
toilet paper **le papier hygiénique**
toothbrush **la brosse à dents**
towel **la serviette**
towel rail **le porte-serviettes** *(invar)*
washbasin **la cuvette de lavabo**

The washing machine doesn't work. Can you repair it?

La machine à laver ne marche pas. Pouvez-vous la réparer?

Come into the dining room.

Entrez dans la salle à manger.

The bed has not been changed.
The hot water faucet doesn't work!

Le lit n'a pas été changé.
Le robinet d'eau chaude ne fonctionne pas!

The toilet will not flush!

La chasse d'eau ne fonctionne pas!

The bathroom mirror is cracked.

Le miroir de la salle de bains est fendu.

Can I take a bath? Have you any shampoo? Could we have some clean towels?

Est-ce que je peux prendre un bain? As-tu du shampooing? Pourrions-nous avoir des serviettes propres?

I can't find the socket for the razor.

Je ne trouve pas la prise du rasoir.

➤ HOUSEHOLD GOODS AND TOILETRIES 9b; FARMING AND GARDENING 24c; TOOLS App.8b

8d Daily routine

bath **le bain**	time *(of day)* **l'heure** *(f)* **de la journée**
bed **le lit**	work **le travail**
breakfast **le petit déjeuner**	
daily **journalier [-ère]**	
dinner **le dîner, le repas du soir**	
dishes (to be washed) **la vaisselle**	
evening meal **le dîner**	
garbage **les ordures** *(f)*	
home **la maison**	
at home **à la maison**	
housekeeper **la gouvernante**	
housework **le ménage**	
laundry **le linge, la lessive**	
lunch **le déjeuner**	
maid **femme de ménage**	
routine **la routine**	
school **l'école** *(f)*	
shopping **les achats** *(m)*	
sleep **le sommeil**	
spare time **le temps libre**	
supper **le souper**	
tea **le thé**	
time *(commodity)* **le temps**	

Actions

I break **je casse**
I bring **j'apporte**
I buy **j'achète** *(acheter)*
I carry **je porte**
I change (clothes) **je me change**
I chat **je bavarde**
I clean **je nettoie** *(nettoyer)*
I clear (away) **je débarrasse**
I cook **je fais la cuisine**
I close **je ferme**
I dampen **j'humecte**
I darn **je raccommode**
I decorate **je décore**
I defrost **je décongèle**
I dirty **je salis**
I do **je fais**
I drink **je bois** *(boire)*
I dry **je sèche**

We usually get up at seven o'clock. We have breakfast at eight.	**Nous nous levons normalement à sept heures. Nous prenons le petit déjeuner à huit heures.**
Lunch is in the dining room. Dinner will be at nine p.m.	**Le déjeuner est servi dans la salle à manger. Le dîner sera servi à neuf heures du soir.**
The table has not been cleared!	**La table n'a pas été débarrassée!**
My husband cooks on Saturdays.	**Mon mari fait la cuisine le samedi.**
Don't forget to put out the garbage and turn off the lights.	**N'oublie pas de sortir les ordures et d'éteindre les lumières.**
She does the dusting and cleaning for us on Fridays.	**Elle fait la poussière et le ménage pour nous tous les vendredis.**

I dry up **j'essuie** *(essuyer)*
I dust **je fais la poussière**
I eat **je mange**
I empty **je vide**
I fasten **j'attache**
I fill **je remplis**
I garden/work in the yard **je fais du jardinage**
I get dressed **je m'habille**
I get undressed **je me déshabille**
I get up **je me lève**
I go to bed **je vais au lit**
I go to sleep **je m'endors** *(s'endormir)*
I go to the toilet **je vais aux toilettes**
I grow *(vegetables)* **je cultive**
I have breakfast **je prends le petit déjeuner**
I have lunch **je déjeune**
I have tea **je prends le thé**
I heat **je chauffe**
I iron **je repasse**
I knit **je tricote**
I knock **je frappe**
I lay the table **je mets** *(mettre)* **la table**
I leave **je pars** *(partir)*
I let *(allow)* **je laisse**
I live **j'habite**
I lock **je ferme à clé**
I make **je fais**
I mend/fix **je répare**
I microwave **je passe au four à micro-ondes**
I move **je bouge**
I open **j'ouvre**
I paint **je peins** *(peindre)*
I polish **je cire**
I prepare **je prépare**
I press (the button) **j'appuie** *(appuyer)* **(sur le bouton)**
I put right **je remets** *(remettre)* **en place**
I put on *(clothes)* **je mets** *(mettre)*
  I put on *(radio, TV)* **j'allume**

I rent **je loue**
I repair **je fais des réparations, je répare**
I rest **je me repose**
I ring *(telephone)* **j'appelle** *(appeler)*
  I ring *(doorbell)* **je sonne**
I rinse **je rince**
I scrub **je frotte**
I sew **je couds**
I share **je partage**
I shine **je fais briller**
I shop **je fais les courses**
I shower **je prends une douche**
I shut/close **je ferme**
I sit (down) **je m'assieds** *(s'asseoir)*
I sleep **je dors** *(dormir)*
I speak **je parle**
I stand **je me tiens** *(se tenir)* **debout, je suis debout**
I stand up **je me mets** *(se mettre)* **debout**
I start **je commence**
I stop **j'arrête**
I sweep **je balaie**
I switch/turn off **j'éteins** *(éteindre)*, **je ferme**
I switch/turn on **j'allume, j'ouvre**
I take off **j'enlève** *(enlever)*
I throw away **je jette** *(jeter)*
I tie **je noue**
I tidy/straighten up **je range**
I unblock **je débouche**
I undo **je défais** *(défaire)*
I use **j'utilise**
I wake up **je me réveille**
I wallpaper **je pose du papier peint**
I wash (car, clothes) **je lave**
I wash dishes **je fais la vaisselle**
I wash (myself) **je me lave**
I watch TV **je regarde la télévision**
I wear **je porte**

➤ FARMING AND GARDENING 24c; CLOTHING 9c

Shopping

9a General terms

article **l'article** *(m)*
automatic door **la porte automatique**
automatic teller, ATM **le distributeur de billets**
bank card **la carte bancaire**
bank note **le billet**
bargain **l'affaire** *(f)*
basement **le sous-sol**
business **les affaires** *(f)*
cash register **la caisse**
cash register receipt **le ticket de caisse**
catalog **le catalogue**
change *(money)* **la monnaie**
cheap **bon marché**
checkout **la caisse**
choice **le choix**
closed **fermé**
coin **la pièce**
costly **coûteux [-se]**
credit **le crédit**
credit card **la carte de crédit**
currency **la devise**
customer information **les renseignements** *(m)*
customer service **le service**

relation clientèle
day off/closed **le jour de congé/ de fermeture**
department **le rayon**
discount **la réduction**
elevator **l'ascenseur** *(m)*
entrance **l'entrée** *(f)*
escalator **l'escalier** *(m)* **roulant**
exit **la sortie**
expensive **cher [-ère]**
fashion **la mode**
fire door **la porte de secours**
fire exit **la sortie de secours**
fitting room **le salon d'essayage**
free **gratuit**
free gift **le cadeau gratuit**
it is good value **c'est bon marché**
handbag **le sac à main**
instructions for use **le mode d'emploi**
item **l'article** *(m)*
label **l'étiquette** *(f)*
mail order **la vente par correspondance**
manager **le gérant, la gérante**
market **le marché**
money **l'argent** *(m)*

Anything else?/Is that all?
Are you being served?

Can I help you?
Do you want anything in particular?
What would you like?
Who's next?
Whose turn is it?

Et avec ça? Ce sera tout?
On vous sert? On s'occupe de vous?
Je peux vous aider?
Vous cherchez quelque chose de précis?
Vous désirez?
Qui est le suivant/la suivante?
C'est à qui le tour?

note **le billet**
open **ouvert**
opening hours **les heures** *(f)* **d'ouverture**
packet **le paquet**
pocket **la poche**
pound *(weight/money)* **la livre**
PULL **tirer**
purse **le porte-monnaie, le sac à main**
PUSH **pousser**
quality **la qualité**
real/genuine **véritable**
receipt **le reçu**
reduction **la réduction**
refund **le remboursement**
refundable **remboursable**
sale **les soldes** *(f)*
security guard **le garde**
self-service **le libre-service**
sales person **le vendeur, la vendeuse**
shopkeeper **le commerçant**
shoplifting **le vol à la tire**
shopping **les courses** *(f)*
shopping basket **le panier**
shop/store **le magasin, la boutique**
shopping list **la liste de courses**
shopping trip **la tournée des magasins**
shopping cart **le chariot**
shut **fermé**
slice **la tranche**
special offer **l'offre** *(f)* **spéciale, la**

promotion
stairs **les escaliers** *(m)*
summer sale **les soldes** *(f)* **d'été**
trader **le négociant, le marchand**
traveler's check **le chèque de voyage**
wallet **le portefeuille**

Actions

I change **je change**
I choose **je choisis**
I decide **je décide**
I dress **je m'habille**
I exchange **j'échange**
I gift-wrap **je fais un paquet cadeau**
I have on/wear **je porte**
I order **je commande**
I pay **je paie** *(payer)*
I put on **je mets** *(mettre)*
I line up **je fais la queue**
I select **je sélectionne, je choisis**
I sell **je vends**
I serve **je sers** *(servir)*
I shop **je fais les courses**
I shoplift **je vole**
I show **je montre**
I spend (money) **je dépense**
I steal **je vole**
I take off **j'enlève** *(enlever)*
I try on **j'essaie** *(essayer)*
I wait **j'attends**
I wear **je porte**
I weigh **je pèse** *(peser)*

How much is it? **C'est combien?**
I've no change. **Je n'ai pas de monnaie.**
Can I pay by check? **Est-ce que je peux payer par chèque?**

Can you change this bill? **Est-ce que vous pouvez me faire de la monnaie?**

Do you take credit cards? **Est-ce que vous acceptez les cartes de crédit?**

9b Household goods and toiletries

Toiletries

aftershave	l'après-rasage *(m)*
antiperspirant	le déodorant
brush	la brosse
comb	le peigne
condom	le préservatif
cosmetics	les produits *(m)* de beauté
cotton wool	le coton hydrophile
deodorant	le déodorant
face cream	la crème de soins pour le visage
glasses	les lunettes *(f)*
hairbrush	la brosse à cheveux
lipstick	le rouge à lèvres
makeup	le maquillage
nail file	la lime à ongles
perfume	le parfum
razor	le rasoir
razor blades	les lames *(f)* de rasoir
sanitary napkin	la serviette périodique/hygiénique
shampoo	le shampooing
soap	le savon
spray	le vaporisateur, l'atomiseur *(m)*
sunglasses	les lunettes *(f)* de soleil
suntan lotion	le lait solaire
talcum powder	le talc
tampon	le tampon
tissues	le mouchoir en papier, les Kleenex®
toilet water	l'eau *(f)* de toilette
toilet paper	le papier hygiénique
toiletry	les produits *(m)* de toilette
toothpaste	le dentifrice
toothbrush	la brosse à dents
watch	la montre

Expressions of quantity

a bar of	une barre de ...
a bottle of ...	une bouteille de ...
a can of ...	une boîte de ...
a hundred gram(me)s of ...	cent grammes de ...
a kilo of ...	un kilo de ...
a liter of	un litre de ...
a packet of ...	un paquet de ...
a pound of	une livre de ...
a slice of ...	une tranche de ...

Household items

aluminum foil	le papier d'aluminium
bottle	la bouteille
bowl	l'assiette *(f)* creuse, le bol
cling-wrap	le Scellofrais®
clothespeg	la pince à linge
cup	la tasse
dish	le plat
dishwashing liquid	le liquide-vaisselle
fork	la fourchette
glass	le verre
jar	le pot
jug	le pichet, la cruche
knife	le couteau
laundry detergent	la lessive, la poudre à laver
matches	les allumettes *(f)*
paper napkin	la serviette en papier
paper towel	le Sopalin®, l'essuie-tout *(m)* *(invar)*
plate	l'assiette *(f)*
pot	la marmite, la casserole
saucer	le soucoupe
scouring pad	l'éponge *(f)* à gratter, le tampon à récurer
string	la ficelle

Basic foodstuffs

bacon   **le bacon, le lard**
baguette   **la baguette**
baked beans   **les haricots** *(m)*
  blancs à la sauce tomate
beer   **la bière**
bread   **le pain**
  rye bread   **le pain de seigle**
  sliced bread   **le pain coupé en**
  tranches
  white bread   **le pain blanc/bis**
  whole-grain bread   **le pain**
  complet
butter   **le beurre**
cakes   **les gâteaux** *(m)*
candy   **les bonbons** *(m)*
cereals   **les céréales** *(f)*
chocolate spread   **la pâte à tartiner**
  au chocolat
condiments   **les condiments** *(m)*
cola   **le coca®**
coffee   **le café**
cookies   **les biscuits (sucrés)**
crackers   **les biscuits (salés)** *(m)*
cream   **la crème**
custard   **la crème anglaise**
dessert   **le dessert**
egg   **l'œuf** *(m)*
fish   **le poisson**
french fries   **les frites** *(f)*
fruit   **le fruit**
garlic   **l'ail** *(m)*
ham   **le jambon**
jam   **la confiture**
juice   **le jus**
lemonade   **la limonade**
loaf   **le pain**
  round loaf   **la miche**
macaroni   **les macaronis** *(m)*

margarine   **la margarine**
marmalade   **la confiture/**
  marmelade d'oranges
mayonnaise   **la mayonnaise**
meat   **la viande**
milk   **le lait**
mustard   **la moutarde**
oil   **l'huile** *(f)*
olive oil   **l'huile** *(f)* **d'olive**
pasta   **les pâtes** *(f)*
pâté   **le pâté**
peanut butter   **le beurre de**
  cacahuète
pepper   **le poivre**
pizza   **la pizza**
pork   **le porc**
pototo chips   **les chips** *(f)*
pudding   **le pouding**
roll *(bread)*   **le petit pain**
salt   **le sel**
sandwich   **le sandwich**
sardines   **les sardines** *(f)*
sauce   **la sauce**
sausage *(cold, sliced)*   **le**
  saucisson
  sausage *(hot)*   **la saucisse**
soup   **la soupe, le potage**
spaghetti   **les spaghettis** *(m)*
spice   **l'épice** *(m)*
sugar   **le sucre**
sunflower oil   **l'huile** *(f)* **de tournesol**
tea bag   **le sachet de thé**
toasted sandwich   **le croque-**
  monsieur
vegetables   **les légumes** *(m)*
vinegar   **le vinaigre**
wine   **le vin**
yogurt   **le yaourt**

I'd like something for a cough.   **Je voudrais quelque chose**
  contre la toux.

Whole or sliced?   **Entier ou en tranches?**
Have you anything cheaper?   **Est-ce que vous avez quelque**
  chose de moins cher?

9c Clothing

anorak/parka l'anorak *(m)*
bathing suit/swimming trunks le maillot de bain
beautiful beau [belle]
big grand
bikini le bikini
blouse le chemisier
boot la botte, la chaussure
bra le soutien-gorge
brand new tout neuf [toute neuve]
cap la casquette
cardigan le cardigan, le gilet
checked à carreaux
clothes les habits *(m)*, les vêtements *(m)*
clothing les vêtements *(m)*
coat le manteau, la veste
color-fast qui ne déteint pas, grand teint
colorful coloré, aux couleurs vives
cravate la cravate
denim la toile de jean, le jean
dress la robe
drip-dry infroissable
elegant élégant
embroidered brodé
fashionable à la mode
glove le gant
handkerchief le mouchoir
hat le chapeau
heel le talon
high-heeled les talons *(m)* hauts
hood la cagoule
in the latest fashion à la dernière mode
jacket la veste
jewelry les bijoux *(m)*
jumper le pull
knitted tricoté
knitwear le tricot
ladies' wear les vêtements *(m)* pour dames
lingerie la lingerie

long long[ue]
long-sleeved à manches longues
loose ample
loud, flashy tape-à-l'œil, voyant
low-heeled à talons plats
matching coordonné
men's wear les vêtements *(m)* pour hommes
pair la paire
panties le slip
pants le pantalon
plain uni
printed imprimé
pajamas le pyjama
raincoat l'imperméable *(m)*
sandal la sandale
scarf le foulard, l'écharpe *(f)*
shirt la chemise
shoe la chaussure
shoelace le lacet
short-sleeved à manches courtes
silky soyeux [-se]
size la taille
  size *(shoes)* la pointure
skirt la jupe
slip la combinaison
small petit
smart élégant, chic
sneakers les baskets *(f)*
sock la chaussette
soft doux [-ce]
stocking le bas
striped rayé
suit le costume
sweater le pull
sweatshirt le sweat-shirt
tie la cravate
tight serré, étroit
tights le collant
too big/small trop grand/petit
trousers le pantalon
T-shirt le T-shirt, le tee-shirt
ugly affreux [-se], moche
umbrella le parapluie
underpants le slip, la culotte

underwear **les sous-vêtements** *(m)*
unfashionable **démodé**
vest **le tricot de peau**

Alterations and repairs

alteration **la retouche**
I alter **je retouche**
belt **la ceinture**
buckle **la boucle**
button **le bouton**
I (dry)clean **je nettoie** *(nettoyer)* **(à sec)**
collar **le col**
cuff *(shirt/blouse)* **le poignet, le revers**
dressmaker **la couturière**
dressmaking **la couture**
dry cleaning **la teinturerie**
hat pin **l'épingle** *(f)* **à chapeau**
hem **l'ourlet** *(m)*
I hem **je fais l'ourlet**
hole **le trou**
I iron **je repasse**
knitting machine **la machine à tricoter**

knitting needle **l'aiguille** *(f)* **à tricoter**
material **le tissu**
needle **l'aiguille** *(f)*
patch **la pièce**
I patch **je rapièce**
pin **l'épingle** *(f)*
pocket **la poche**
I press **je repasse**
I repair **je raccommode**
safety pin **l'épingle** *(f)* **de sûreté**
I sew **je couds**
sewing machine **la machine à coudre**
I shorten **je raccourcis**
sleeve **la manche**
snap fastener **le bouton-pression**
I stitch **je recouds**
I take in/let out **je reprends** *(reprendre)*, **j'élargis**
tailor **le tailleur**
tailored **bien taillé, bien coupé**
thread **le fil**
zip(per) **la fermeture-éclair, le zip**

Can I try it on?
Do you have the same in red?

I bought it on sale.
I like it.
I prefer . . .
I take/wear size . . .
I would like it in brown.
I would like to change . . .
I would rather have . . .
I'll take the big one.
I'd like it two sizes bigger.

It suits me.
That's is not quite right.
They don't go together.
What color?
Would you like me to wrap it up?

Je peux l'essayer?
Est-ce que vous avez le/la même en rouge?

Je l'ai acheté en solde.
Il/elle me plaît.
Je préfère …
Je fais du …
Je le/la voudrais en marron.
Je voudrais changer …
Je préférerais prendre …
Je prends le/la grand[e].
Je voudrais le/la même deux tailles au-dessus.

Il/elle me va bien.
Ça ne va pas tout à fait.
Ils/elles ne vont pas ensemble.
Quelle couleur?
Voulez-vous que je l'emballe?

➤ THE SENSES 5b; LEISURE AND SPORTS 16

10 Food and drink

10a Drinks and meals

Drinks

alcoholic	**alcoolisé**
aperitif	**l'apéritif** *(m)*
beer	**la bière**
black coffee	**le café noir**
brandy	**le cognac**
champagne	**le champagne**
chocolate (drinking)	**le chocolat (chaud)**
cider	**le cidre**
cocktail	**le cocktail**
coffee	**le café**
coffee with milk	**le café au lait**
cola	**le coca**
draught beer	**la bière pression**
drink	**la boisson**
dry	**sec [sèche]**
fizzy	**gazeux [-se], mousseux [-se]**
fruit juice	**le jus de fruit**
juice	**le jus**
lemonade	**la limonade**

low-alcohol	**l'alcool** *(m)* **léger**
orange/lemonade	**l'orangeade** *(f)***/la citronnade**
milk	**le lait**
milkshake	**le milk-shake**
mineral water	**l'eau** *(f)* **minérale**
nonalcoholic	**non alcoolisé**
red wine	**le vin rouge**
sherry	**le vin de Xérès**
sparkling	**mousseux [-se]**
spirits	**les alcools** *(m)* **forts**
straight	**sec [sèche], sans eau**
sweet	**sucré**
tea	**le thé**
water	**l'eau** *(f)*
bottled water	**l'eau non gazeuse, l'eau plate**
with ice	**avec de la glace**
whiskey	**le whisky**
white wine	**le vin blanc**
wine	**le vin**

---

cafeteria	**la cafétéria**
canteen	**la cantine**
hot dog stall	**le stand de hot dogs**
pizza parlor	**la pizzéria**
restaurant	**le restaurant**
self-service	**le libre-service**
snack bar	**le snack-bar**
take-away	**à emporter**

Where can we get a drink around here?	**Où peut-on boire un verre par ici?**
Can you tell me where the nearest cafe is, please?	**Pouvez-vous m'indiquer le café le plus proche, s'il vous plaît?**
Can I have a mineral water and two coffees with milk, please.	**Puis-je avoir une eau minérale et deux cafés au lait, s'il vous plaît?**

Drinking out

bar   **le bar**
barman/barmaid   **le serveur, la serveuse**
beer hall   **la brasserie**
bottle   **la bouteille**
cafe   **le café**
coffee bar   **le café**
cellar   **la cave**
coffee shop   **le salon de thé**
counter/bar   **le comptoir, le bar**
cup   **la tasse**
I drink   **je bois**
glass   **le verre**
pub(lic-house)   **le bar, le pub**
refreshments   **les rafraîchissements** *(m)*
saucer   **la soucoupe**
sip   **la petite gorgée**
straw   **la paille**
teaspoon   **la petite cuillère**
wine cellar   **la cave à vin**
wine glass   **le verre de vin**
wine-tasting   **la dégustation de vin**

Meals

appetizer   **le hors-d'œuvre**
breakfast   **le petit déjeuner**
course   **le plat**
   first course   **l'entrée** *(f)*
dessert   **le dessert**
I dine   **je dîne**
dinner   **le dîner**
I eat   **je mange**
I have a snack   **je prends un casse-croûte**
I have breakfast   **je prends le petit déjeuner**
I have dinner   **je dîne**
I have lunch   **je déjeune**
lunch   **le déjeuner**
main   **principal**
meal   **le repas**
snack   **le casse-croûte, l'en-cas**
supper   **le souper**

Eating out

I add up the bill   **je calcule l'addition** *(f)*
bill/check   **l'addition** *(f)*, **la note**
bowl   **le bol**
charge   **le prix**
cheap   **pas cher, bon marché**
children's menu   **le menu d'enfant**
I choose   **je choisis**
it costs   **il coûte**
cover charge   **le couvert**
I decide   **je décide**
expensive   **cher**
first course   **l'entrée** *(f)*
fixed price   **le prix fixe**
fork   **la fourchette**
inclusive   **inclus**
inclusive price   **prix net**
knife   **le couteau**
main course   **le plat principal**
menu   **le menu**
menu of day   **le menu du jour**
napkin   **la serviette**
I order   **je commande**
order   **la commande**
place setting   **le couvert**
plate   **l'assiette** *(f)*
portion   **la portion**
reservation   **la réservation**
I serve   **je sers**
service   **le service**
set menu   **la carte, le menu**
side dish   **le plat d'accompagnement**
spoon   **la cuillère**
table   **la table**
tablecloth   **la nappe**
tip/gratuity   **le pourboire**
I tip   **je donne un pourboire**
toothpick   **le cure-dent**
tourist menu   **le menu touriste**
tray   **le plateau**
waiter   **le serveur**
waitress   **la serveuse**
wine list   **la liste des vins**

10b Fish and meat

Fish & seafood

anchovy	**l'anchois** *(m)*
clam	**la palourde**
cockles	**les coques** *(f)*
cod	**la morue**
crab	**le crabe**
crayfish	**l'écrevisse** *(f)*, **la langouste**
eel	**l'anguille** *(f)*
fish	**le poisson**
flounder	**le flet**
frog's legs	**les cuisses** *(f)* **de grenouilles** *(f)*
hake	**le colin**
herring	**le hareng**
lobster	**le homard**
mullet	**le rouget**
mussels	**les moules** *(f)*
octopus	**la pieuvre**
oyster	**l'huître** *(f)*
pike	**le brochet**

plaice	**le carrelet, la plie**
prawn	**la crevette**
salmon	**le saumon**
sardine	**la sardine**
scampi	**la langoustine**
sea bass	**le loup**
seafood	**les fruits** *(m)* **de mer**
shell	**le coquillage**
shellfish	**le crustacé**
shrimp	**la crevette**
snails	**les escargots** *(m)*
sole	**la sole**
sprat	**le sprat**
squid	**le calmar**
swordfish	**l'espadon** *(m)*
trout	**la truite**
tuna	**le thon**
turbot	**le turbot**
whitebait	**la blanchaille**
whiting	**le merlan**

What is there for starters?	**Qu'y a-t-il en hors-d'œuvres?**
Would you prefer cod or sole?	**Vous préféreriez de la morue ou de la sole?**
– Shall we try the chicken?	**– On essaie le poulet?**
– I'd like a pork chop.	**– J'aimerais une côtelette de porc.**
Can we both have steak, one rare and one well cooked?	**Est-ce qu'on peut prendre tous les deux un bifteck, l'un saignant et l'autre bien cuit?**
May I have a clean teaspoon?	**Puis-je avoir une petite cuillère propre, s'il vous plaît?**

Meat

bacon **le lard, le bacon**
beef **le bœuf**
beefburger **le hamburger**
bolognese **(à la) bolognaise**
brains **la cervelle**
casserole **le ragoût en cocotte**
chop **la côtelette**
cold table **le buffet froid**
cutlet **la côtelette**
escalope **l'escalope** *(f)*
ham **le jambon**
hamburger **le hamburger**
hot dog **le hot-dog**
kidney **le rognon**
lamb **l'agneau** *(m)*
liver **le foie**
marrow **la moelle**
meat **la viande**
meatballs **les boulettes** *(f)* **de viande**
minced beef **le bifteck haché**
mixed grill **le mélange de grillades**
mutton **le mouton**
offal **les abats** *(m)*
oxtail **la queue de bœuf**
paté **le pâté**

pork **le porc**
rabbit **le lapin**
rib **la côte**
salami **le salami**
sausage **la saucisse**
  sausage *(cold, sliced)* **le saucisson**
sirloin **le faux-filet**
steak **le steak**
stew **le ragoût**
tenderloin steak **le médaillon**
veal **le veau**

Poultry

capon **le chapon**
chicken **le poulet**
  chicken breast **le blanc de poulet**
duck **le canard**
duckling **le caneton**
goose **l'oie** *(f)*
pheasant **le faisan**
pigeon **le pigeon**
poultry **la volaille**
quail **la caille**
turkey **la dinde**
woodcock **la bécasse**

Traditional dishes

bœuf bourguignon rich beef stew with vegetables, braised in red wine

bouillabaisse fish and seafood stew

bourride fish stew (chowder) from Marseilles

canard à l'orange braised duck with oranges and orange liqueur

chateaubriand double fillet steak

coq au vin chicken stewed in red wine

coquilles St-Jacques scallops in a creamy sauce, served on half the shell

entrecôte rib or rib-eye steak

matelote fish stew (generally eel) with wine

quenelles light dumplings made of fish, fowl, or meat

quiche a flan with a rich filling of cheese, vegetables, meat, or seafood

FOOD AND DRINK

10c Vegetables, fruit, and desserts

Vegetables

artichoke **l'artichaut** *(m)*
asparagus **l'asperge** *(f)*
avocado **l'avocat** *(m)*
beans **les haricots** *(m)*
beets **la betterave rouge**
broccoli **les brocolis** *(m)*
brussels sprout **les choux** *(m)* **de Bruxelles**
cabbage **le chou**
carrot **la carotte**
cauliflower **le chou-fleur**
celeriac **le céleri-rave**
celery **le céleri**
chick pea **le pois chiche**
corn **le maïs**
corn on the cob **l'épi** *(m)* **de maïs**
cucumber **le concombre**
eggplant **l'aubergine** *(f)*
endive/chicory **l'endive** *(f)*
garlic **l'ail** *(m)*
gherkin **le cornichon**
green bean **le haricot vert**
herb **l'herbe** *(f)* **aromatique**
leek **le poireau**
lentil **les lentilles** *(f)*
lettuce **la laitue**
marrow **la courge**
mushroom **le champignon**
onion **l'oignon** *(m)*
parsley **le persil**
parsnip **le panais**
pea **le petit pois**
pepper (red/green) **le poivron (rouge/vert)**

potato **la pomme de terre**
pumpkin **la citrouille, la courge**
radish **le radis**
rice **le riz**
salad **la salade**
spinach **les épinards** *(m)*
sugar pea, pea pods **le pois mange-tout**
tomato **la tomate**
turnip **le navet**
vegetable **le légume**
vegetable *(adj)* **végétal**
watercress **le cresson**
zucchini **la courgette**

Fruit and nuts

apple **la pomme**
apricot **l'abricot** *(m)*
banana **la banane**
berry **la baie**
bilberry **la myrtille**
blackberry **la mûre**
black currant **le cassis**
Brazil nut **la noix du Brésil**
bunch of grapes **la grappe de raisins**
cherry **la cerise**
chestnut **le marron, la châtaigne**
coconut **la noix de coco**
currant **la groseille**
date **la date**
fig **la figue**
fruit **le fruit**
gooseberry **la groseille à maquereau**

I want a tomato salad.	**Je veux une salade de tomates.**
Does it have garlic in it?	**Il y a de l'ail dedans?**
Two strawberry ice creams.	**Deux glaces à la fraise**
Have you got any apple pie?	**Avez-vous de la tarte aux pommes?**

grape **le raisin**
grapefruit **le pamplemousse**
hazelnut **la noisette**
kiwi fruit **le kiwi**
lemon **le citron**
lime **le citron vert**
melon **le melon**
nectarine **la nectarine, le brugnon**
nut **la noisette**
olive **l'olive** *(f)*
orange **l'orange** *(f)*
passion fruit **le fruit de la passion**
peach **la pêche**
peanut **la cacahuète**
pear **la poire**
piece of fruit **le morceau de fruit**
pineapple **l'ananas** *(m)*
pip **le pépin**
plum **la prune**
pomegranate **la grenade**
prune **le pruneau**
raisin **le raisin**
raspberry **la framboise**
red currant **la groseille**
rhubarb **la rhubarbe**
stone **le noyau, le pépin**
strawberry **la fraise**
sultana **les raisins** *(m)* **de Smyrne**
tangerine **la mandarine**
walnut **la noix**

Dessert

bun **la brioche**
cake **le gâteau**
caramel **le caramel**
chocolate **le chocolat**
chocolates **les chocolats** *(m)*
cake **le gâteau**
cookie **le biscuit**
cream **la crème**
creme caramel **la crème caramel**
custard **la crème anglaise**
custard tart **le flan**
dessert **le dessert**
doughnut **le beignet**
flan **la tarte**
fresh fruit **le fruit frais**
fruit of the day/season **le fruit du jour/de saison**
fruit salad **la salade/macédoine de fruits**
ice cream **la glace**
mousse **la mousse**
pancake **la crêpe**
pastry **la pâtisserie**
pie **la tarte**
pudding **le pudding, le pouding**
tart **la tourte**
trifle **la charlotte russe**
vanilla **la vanille**
whipped cream **la crème Chantilly**
yogurt **le yaourt**

Traditional dishes

julienne de légumes shredded vegetable soup
soupe à l'oignon French onion soup

crêpe suzette large pancakes simmered in orange juice and flambéd with orange liqueur
mille-feuille cream slice

omelette norvégienne baked Alaska
poire belle Hélène pear with vanilla ice cream and chocolate sauce
profiterole puff pastry filled with whipped cream or custard
sorbet water ice/sherbet
velouté de tomates cream of tomato soup

10d Cooking and eating

Food preparation

I bake **je fais cuire**
baked **cuit au four**
barbeque **le barbecue**
I beat **je bats (battre)**
beaten **battu**
I boil **je fais bouillir**
boiled **bouilli**
bone **l'os (m)**
boned **désossé**
   boned (fish) **sans arêtes**
I bone **je désosse, j'ôte les arêtes de**
I braise **je braise**
braised **braisé**
(in) breadcrumbs **(en) miettes**
breast **le blanc**
I carve **je découpe**
I chop **je hache**
I clear the table **je débarrasse la table**
I cook **je fais la cuisine**
cooking/cuisine **la cuisine**
I cut **je coupe**

I dice **je coupe en cubes**
dough **la pâte**
I dry up **j'essuie (essuyer)**
flour **la farine**
food preparation **la préparation culinaire**
fried **frit**
I fry **je fais frire**
I garnish with **je garnis de**
I grate **je rape**
grated **rapé**
gravy **le jus, la sauce**
I grill **je fais griller**
grilled **grillé**
ingredient **l'ingrédient (m)**
large **grand**
I set the table **je mets (mettre) la table**
leg (of lamb) **la patte, le gigot d'agneau**
I marinate **je fais mariner**
marinated **mariné**
medium (rare) **à point**
medium-sized **moyen[ne]**

Fruit salad

Ingredients:
2 apples, 2 pears, 2 oranges, 1 banana, 100g cherries, 100g grapes

Peel and slice apples, pears, oranges and the banana. Wash grapes and cherries, add to bowl. Add 100ml of orange juice. Chill before serving.

Salade de fruits

Ingrédients:
2 pommes, 2 poires, 2 oranges, 1 banane, 100g de cerises, 100g de raisin

Pelez et coupez les pommes, les poires, les oranges, et la banane. Lavez le raisin et les cerises et ajoutez-les aux fruits; mettez-les dans un saladier. Ajoutez 100ml de jus d'orange. Tenez au frais avant de servir.

milk   **le lait**
I mix   **je mélange**
mixed   **mélangé**
olive oil   **l'huile** *(f)* **d'olive**
pastry   **la pâte**
   puff pastry   **la pâte feuilletée**
   short(crust) pastry   **la pâte brisée**
peel   **la pelure**
I peel   **je pèle** *(peler),* **j'épluche**
peeled   **pelé, épluché**
I pour   **je verse**
rare   **saignant**
recipe (for)   **la recette (de)**
roast   **le rôti**
I roast   **je fais rôtir**
in sauce   **en sauce**
I sift   **je tamise, je passe au tamis**
I slice   **je coupe (en tranches)**
sliced   **(coupé) en tranches**
I spread   **j'étends**
stewed   **à l'étouffée**
sunflower oil   **l'huile** *(f)* **de tournesol**
I toast   **je fais griller**
toasted   **grillé**
I wash up   **je fais la vaisselle**
I weigh   **je pèse** *(peser)*
well-done   **bien cuit**
I whip   **je fouette**
whipped   **fouetté**
I whisk   **je bats** *(battre),* **je remue, je fouette**
whisked   **battu, fouetté**

Eating

additive   **l'additif** *(m)*
I am hungry   **j'ai faim**
I am thirsty   **j'ai soif**
appetite   **l'appétit** *(m)*
appetizing   **appétissant**
bad   **mauvais**
I bite   **je mords**
bitter   **amer [-ère]**
calorie   **la calorie**

low calorie   **à basses calories**
I chew   **je mâche**
cold   **froid**
delicious   **délicieux [-se]**
diet   **le régime**
   I'm on a diet   **je suis/me mets** *(se mettre)* **au régime**
fatty/oily   **gras[se]**
fresh   **frais [fraîche]**
fresh(ly)   **fraîche(ment)**
healthy *(appetite)*   **bon[ne], robuste**
   healthy *(food)*   **sain**
I help myself   **je me sers** *(servir)*
hot   **chaud**
hunger   **la faim**
hungry   **affamé, qui a faim**
I like   **j'aime**
mild   **doux [-ce], léger [-ère]**
I offer   **j'offre** *(offrir)*
I pass (salt)   **je passe (le sel)**
piece   **le morceau**
I pour   **je verse**
I provide   **je fournis**
salty   **salé**
I serve   **je sers** *(servir)*
   dinner is served   **le dîner est servi**
sharp   **coupant**
slice   **la tranche**
I smell   **je sens** *(sentir)*
soft   **doux [-ce]**
spicy   **épicé**
stale *(bread)*   **rassis**
   (cheese)   **dur**
still, not fizzy   **non gazeux [-se]**
strong   **fort**
I swallow   **j'avale**
tasty   **qui a du goût**
thirst   **la soif**
thirsty   **assoiffé**
I try   **j'essaie** *(essayer)*
vegan   **végétalien[ne]**
vegetarian   **végétarien[ne]**

Sickness and health

11a Accidents and emergencies

accident **l'accident** *(m)*
ambulance **l'ambulance** *(f)*
I attack **j'attaque**
black eye **l'œil** *(m)* **poché**
I bleed **je saigne**
blood **le sang**
bomb **la bombe**
break **la fracture**
I break **je casse**
  I broke a leg **je me suis cassé la jambe**
breakage **la fracture, la rupture**
broken **cassé**
bruise **la contusion, l'hématome** *(m)*, **le bleu**
I bruise easily **je me fais facilement des bleus**
  I bruise *(someone)* **je fais un bleu à**
burn **la brûlure**
I burn **je (me) brûle**

casualty **l'urgence** *(f)*
casualty department **le service des urgences**
I collide **j'entre en collision**
collision **la collision**
I crash (into) **j'entre en collision (avec)**
crash **la collision, un accident**
I crush **j'écrase**
dead **mort**
death **la mort**
I die **je meurs** *(mourir)*
emergency **l'urgence** *(f)*
emergency exit **la sortie de secours**
emergency services **les services** *(m)* **de secours**
it explodes **il explose**
explosion **l'explosion** *(f)*
I extinguish **j'éteins** *(éteindre)*
I fall **je tombe**

There has been an accident! We need an ambulance quickly.

Il vient d'y avoir un accident. Il nous faut une ambulance, vite!

– My friend is injured. Are you a doctor? Do you know first aid?

– Mon ami est blessé. Vous êtes médecin? Savez-vous donner les premiers secours?

– I'm sorry, I have never done any first aid training.
– Then where's the nearest hospital?

– Je suis désolé. Je n'ai jamais pris de cours de secourisme.
– Où est l'hôpital le plus proche alors?

fatal **fatal**
fine **bien**
fire **le feu**
fire brigade **les pompiers** *(m)*
fire engine **le camion des pompiers**
fire extinguisher **l'extincteur** *(m)*
firefighter **le pompier**
first aid **les premiers secours** *(m)*
fracture **la fracture**
graze, scratch **l'écorchure** *(f)*
   I grazed my knee **je me suis écorché le genou**
Help! **Au secours!**
hospital **l'hôpital** *(m)*
I've had an accident **j'ai eu un accident**
I've hurt myself **je me suis fait mal (à)**
impact **l'impact** *(m)*
incident **l'incident** *(m)*
I injure **je blesse**
injury **la blessure**
injured **blessé**
   I've injured myself **je me suis blessé[e]**
insurance **l'assurance** *(f)*
I insure **j'assure**
I kill **je tue**

killed **tué**
life belt **la ceinture de sécurité**
life jacket **le gilet de sauvetage**
oxygen **l'oxygène** *(f)*
paramedic **l'auxiliare** *(m/f)* **médical(e)**
I recover **je recupère, je me remets** *(-mettre)*
recovery **la récupération**
I rescue **je sauve**
rescue **le sauvetage**
rescue services **les services** *(m)* **de sauvetage**
I run over **j'écrase**
I rush **je me dépêche**
safe **sauf [-ve], sauvé**
safe and sound **sain et sauf [saine et sauve]**
safety belt **la ceinture de sécurité**
I save **je sauve**
seatbelt **la ceinture de sécurité**
terrorist attack **l'attaque** *(f)* **de terroristes**
third-party insurance **l'assurance** *(f)* **au tiers**
witness **le témoin**
I wound **je (me) blesse**
wounded **blessé**

Call the fire department! Someone is trapped in the wreckage of the car.

Appelez les pompiers! Quelqu'un est coincé dans les débris de la voiture.

She has cut her hand badly.

Elle s'est coupé profondément la main.

I think I have broken my arm. It hurts a lot.

Je crois que je me suis cassé le bras. Ça fait très mal.

It was your fault, not mine.

Vous êtes en tort, pas moi.

Statistics show that the most likely place for accidents is in the home.

Les statistiques montrent que la plupart des accidents se produisent à domicile.

➤ MEDICAL TREATMENT 11c; HEALTH AND HYGIENE 11d

SICKNESS AND HEALTH

11b Illness and disability

alive **vivant**
all right **bien**
arthritis **l'arthrite** *(f)*
asthma **l'asthme**
I bleed **je saigne**
blind **aveugle**
blood **le sang**
breath **le souffle**
I breathe **je respire**
breathless **à bout de souffle**
broken **cassé**
cancer **le cancer**
chest cold **le catarrhe**
I catch cold **je prends** *(prendre)*
  froid, je suis enrhumé
cold **le rhume**
constipated **constipé**
constipation **la constipation**
convalescence **la convalescence**
I am convalescing **je suis en**
  convalescence
cough **la toux**
I cough **je tousse**
I cry **je pleure**
I cut **je (me) coupe**

dead **mort**
deaf **sourd**
  deaf-mute **le sourd-muet, la**
  sourde-muette
deafness **la surdité**
death **la mort**
depressed **déprimé**
depression **la dépression**
  (nerveuse)
diarrhea **la diarrhée**
I die **je meurs** *(mourir)*
diet **le régime, la diète**
disabled **handicapé**
disease **la maladie**
dizziness **le vertige,**
  l'étourdissement *(m)*
dizzy **pris de vertige**
drug **le médicament, la drogue**
drugged **drogué**
drunk **ivre, saoul**
dumb **muet[te], abasourdi**
earache **la douleur à l'oreille**
  I have an earache **j'ai mal à**
  l'oreille
I feel dizzy **j'ai la tête qui tourne,**

– What's wrong?
– My foot hurts.

I can't breath very well.

I have been sick/thrown up several
times. I had the flu last week.

She said she felt very dizzy.

I feel dizzy if I stand up.

I don't usually faint!
But the dizziness is wearing off.

– Qu'est-ce qui ne va pas?
– J'ai mal au pied.

Je n'arrive pas à respirer
correctement.

J'ai vomi plusieurs fois. J'ai eu
la grippe la semaine dernière.

Elle a dit qu'elle était prise d'un
violent vertige.

J'ai la tête qui tourne si je me
lève.

Je m'évanouis très rarement.
Mais mon vertige a l'air de
s'atténuer.

---

je suis pris *(prendre)* de vertige

I feel ill/unwell   **je me sens *(se sentir)* mal, je ne me sens pas bien**

fever   **la fièvre**

feverish   **fièvreux [-se]**

flu   **la grippe**

I get drunk   **je me saoule**

I got better   **je me suis remis *(remettre)***

handicapped   **le handicapé, la handicapée**

handicapped *(adj)*   **handicapé**

I had an operation   **j'ai été opéré**

I have a headache   **j'ai mal à la tête**

heart attack   **la crise cardiaque**

high blood pressure   **l'hypertension** *(f)*

HIV positive   **séro-positif [-ve]**

hurt   **blessé**

I hurt   **j'ai mal à**

it hurts   **ça fait mal**

where does it hurt?   **où avez-vous mal?**

illness   **la maladie**

I am ill/sick   **je suis malade**

I live   **je vis *(vivre)*, je suis en vie**

I look (ill)   **j'ai l'air (malade)**

mental illness   **la maladie mentale**

mentally sick   **malade mental**

migraine   **la migraine**

mute   **le muet, la muette**

mute *(adj)*   **muet[te]**

pain   **la douleur**

painful   **douloureux [-se]**

pale   **pale**

paralyzed   **paralysé**

paraplegic   **paraplégique**

pregnant   **enceinte**

pregnancy   **la grossesse**

rheumatism   **le rhumatisme**

sick   **malade**

I am sick/vomit   **je vomis**

I sneeze   **j'éternue**

sore throat   **le mal à la gorge**

sting   **la piqûre**

it stings   **ça pique**

stomachache   **le mal à l'estomac**

stomach upset   **l'indigestion** *(f)*

symptom   **le symptôme**

I take drugs   **je me drogue**

temperature   **la température**

I have a temperature   **j'ai de la température/fièvre**

travel sickness   **le mal des transports**

My children have diarrhea; I seem to be constipated.

Mes enfants ont la diarrhée; je pense que je suis constipé.

I don't know what is wrong with you. It's only a stomachache.

Je ne sais pas ce qui ne va pas chez toi. Ce n'est qu'une indigestion.

I am pregnant!

Je suis enceinte!

He seems to have a temperature.
He had an operation recently.
He seems to be recovering.

Il a l'air d'avoir de la température
Il a été opéré récemment.
Il a l'air de se remettre.

I suffer from high blood pressure.
I have a sore throat.
I have a migraine coming on.

Je fais de l'hypertension.
J'ai mal à la gorge.
Je sens que je vais avoir une migraine.

➤ ILLNESSES AND DISEASES App.11c; HEALTH AND HYGIENE 11d

11c Medical treatment

antiseptic   l'antiseptique *(m)*
appointment   le rendez-vous
bandage   la bande, le bandage
blood   le sang
blood test   l'analyse *(f)* de sang
blood pressure   la tension artérielle
capsule   la capsule
chemotherapy   la chimiothérapie
critical   critique
cure   le traitement, la guérison
danger to life   le danger mortel
dangerous   dangereux [-se]
death   la mort
doctor (Dr.)   le médecin (Dr)
doctor's office   le cabinet médical
dressing   le pansement, le bandage
drop   la goutte

drug   le médicament
I examine   j'examine
examination   l'examen *(m)*
I fill   je remplis
four times a day   quatre fois par jour
I have   j'ai
heating   le chauffage
hospital   un hôpital
I improve   je me rétablis, je me remets *(remettre)*
injection   la piqûre
insurance certificate   le certificat médical
I look after   je m'occupe de
lozenge   la pastille
medical   médical, l'examen *(m)* médical

Call a doctor!
Is he a good doctor?

Appelez un docteur!
C'est un bon médecin?

Will I need an operation? I have my medical insurance.

Est-ce que j'ai besoin d'une opération? J'ai mon assurance médicale.

He does not like injections.
He has never had an x-ray.

Il n'aime pas les piqûres.
On ne lui a jamais fait de radio.

Can I have a prescription? I have lost my tablets.

Est-ce que vous pouvez me faire une ordonnance? J'ai perdu mes comprimés.

An increasing number of people use alternative medicine and techniques, like homeopathy and reflexology.

De plus en plus, les gens utilisent les médecines parallèles ainsi que des techniques comme l'homéopathie et la réflexologie.

Stress-related illness is on the increase.

Les maladies provoquées par le stress augmentent.

medicine **le médicament**
medicine *(science)* **la médecine**
midwife **la sage-femme**
nurse **un infirmier, une infirmière**
I nurse **je soigne**
office hours **les heures** *(f)* **de consultation**
I operate **j'opère**
operation **l'opération** *(f)*
patient **le malade, le patient**
pharmacist **le pharmacien, la pharmacienne**
physiotherapy **la kinésithérapie**
physiotherapist **le/la kinésithérapeute**
pill **la pillule**
plaster (of paris) **le plâtre de Paris**
I prescribe **je prescris**
prescription **l'ordonnance** *(f)*
radiation therapy **la radiothérapie**
receptionist **le/la réceptionniste**
service **le service**
I set **je fixe**
spa, hot baths **la station thermale**
specialist **le spécialiste**
stitch **le point**
surgery **la chirurgie**
syringe **la seringue**
tablet **le comprimé**
therapeutic **thérapeutique**
therapy **les soins** *(m)*
therapist **le thérapeute**
thermometer **le thermomètre**
I treat **je soigne**
treatment **le traitement**
ward **la salle d'hôpital**
wound **la blessure**
x-ray **la radiographie**

Dentist and optician

abscess **l'abcès** *(m)*
anesthetic **l'anesthésique** *(m)*
bifocals **à double foyer, bifocal**
contact lens **le verre de contact**
hard/soft lenses **les verres durs/souples**
contact lens fluid **le liquide pour verres de contact**
crown **la couronne**
dental treatment **le traitement dentaire**
dentist **le dentiste**
dentures **le dentier**
drill **la fraise**
drilling **le fraisage**
I extract **j'arrache**
eye **l'œil** *(m)* (pl **les yeux**)
eyesight **la vue**
eyestrain **la vue fatiguée**
eye test **l'examen** *(m)* **de la vue**
false **faux [fausse]**
filling **le plombage**
frame **la monture**
glasses **les lunettes** *(f)*
gum **la gencive**
lens **le verre**
I'm far-sighted/near-sighted **je suis presbyte/myope**
optician **un opticien, une opticienne**
pupil **la pupille**
spectacle case **l'étui** *(m)* **à lunettes**
sty **l'orgelet** *(m)*
sunglasses **une paire de lunettes de soleil**
tinted **teinté**
tooth **la dent**
I have toothache **j'ai mal aux dents**

11d Health and hygiene

Physical state

ache **la douleur**
aching **endolori, douloureux [-se]**
asleep **endormi**
awake **éveillé**
blister **l'ampoule** *(f)*
boil **le furoncle**
comfort **le confort**
comfortable **confortable, à l'aise**
discomfort **le malaise**
dizziness **le vertige**
dizzy **pris de vertige**
drowsiness **la somnolence**
drowsy **somnolent**
faint **pris de vertige**
I exercise **je fais de l'exercice**
exercise bike **le vélo de santé/d'apportement**
I faint **je m'évanouis**
I feel (well) **je me sens** *(se sentir)* **(bien)**
fit **en forme**
fitness **la forme**
I'm hot/cold **j'ai chaud/froid**
health **la santé**
healthy **en bonne santé, sain**
hunger **la faim**
hungry **affamé**
ill/sick **malade**
I lie down **je m'allonge**
I look **j'ai l'air**
nausea **la nausée**
queasy **nauséeux**

recovery **la convalescence**
I recuperate/recover **je me rétablis, je guéris**
I relax **je me détends**
I rest/have a rest **je me repose**
sick **malade**
I sleep **je dors** *(dormir)*
sleepy **ensommeillé**
stamina **la vigueur**
strange **drôle, bizarre**
thirst **la soif**
I am thirsty **j'ai soif**
tired **fatigué**
I am tired **je suis fatigué**
tiredness **la fatigue**
uncomfortable **mal à l'aise**
under the weather **mal en point**
unfit **pas en forme**
unwell **malade, indisposé**
virile **viril**
I wake up **je me réveille**
well **bien**
well-being **le bien-être**

Beauty and hygiene

acne **l'acné** *(f)*
bath **le bain**
beauty **la beauté**
beauty contest **le concours de beauté**
beauty salon/parlor **l'institut** *(m)*/ **le salon de beauté**
beauty treatment **les soins** *(m)* **de**

– I don't feel at all well!
– You should rest!

I need a shower.

– **Je ne me sens pas bien du tout.**
– **Vous devriez vous reposer!**

J'ai besoin de prendre une douche.

beauté
I burp/belch **j'ai un renvoi**
I brush **je (me) brosse**
brush **la brosse**
I clean **je nettoie** *(nettoyer)* , **je (me) lave**
clean **propre**
I clean my teeth **je me lave les dents**
comb **je peigne**
I comb my hair **je me peigne les cheveux**
condom **le préservatif**
contraceptive **le moyen de contraception**
contraception **la contraception**
I cut **je coupe**
dandruff **les pellicules** *(f)*
I defecate **je défèque**
diet **le régime**
I am on a diet **je me mets** *(se mettre)* **au régime**
dirty **sale**
electric razor **le rasoir électrique**
fleas **les puces**
fresh air **l'air** *(m)*, **le frais**
hairbrush **la brosse à cheveux**
haircut **la coupe de cheveux**
I have my hair cut **je me fais couper les cheveux**
hairdo **la coiffure**
healthy *(person)* **en bonne santé**
healthy *(diet)* **sain**
hungry **affamé**
I am hungry **j'ai faim**

hygienic **hygiénique**
hygiene **l'hygiène** *(f)*
laundry *(establishment)* **le pressing, la blanchisserie**
laundry *(linen)* **le linge**
lice/nits **les poux** *(m)*
I'm losing my hair **je perds mes cheveux**
I menstruate **j'ai mes règles**
menstruation **les règles** *(f)*, **la menstruation**
nailbrush **la brosse à ongles**
nutritious **nutritif [-ve]**
period **les règles** *(f)*
period pains **les douleurs** *(f)* **menstruelles**
razor **le rasoir**
sanitary **sanitaire**
sanitary napkin **la serviette hygiénique/périodique**
scissors **les ciseaux** *(m)*
shampoo **le shampooing**
I shave **je (me) rase**
shower **la douche**
soap **le savon**
I take a bath/shower **je prends** *(prendre)* **un bain/une douche**
tampon **le tampon**
toothbrush **la brosse à dents**
toothpaste **le dentifrice**
towel **la serviette**
I wash **je (me) lave**
wash cloth **le gant de toilette**

I'd like a haircut, please. Don't cut it too short.

Je voudrais me faire couper les cheveux, s'il vous plaît; pas trop court.

A little more off the back and sides, please.

Dégagez un peu plus derrière et sur les côtés.

Please trim my mustache.

Pourriez-vous me rafraîchir la moustache.

➤ HOUSEHOLD GOODS AND TOILETRIES 9b; HAIRDRESSER App.11d

12 Social issues

12a Society

abnormal **anormal**	difficulty **la difficulté**
alternative **le choix**	effect **l'effet** (m)
amenity **l'équipement** (m)	effective **efficace**
anonymous **anonyme**	fact **le fait**
attitude **l'attitude** (f)	finance **la finance**
available **disponible**	financial **financier**
basic **de base**	frustrated **frustré**
basis **la base**	frustration **la frustration**
burden **le fardeau**	guidance **les conseils** (m)
campaign **la campagne**	increase **l'augmentation** (f)
care **le soin**	inner city **les quartiers** (m)
cause **la cause**	**pauvres, les vieux quartiers**
change **le changement**	**déshérités**
circumstance **la circonstance**	insecurity **l'insécurité** (f)
community **la communauté**	institution **l'institution** (f)
compulsory **obligatoire**	loneliness **la solitude**
contribution **la contribution**	lonely **seul**
cost **le coût**	long-term **à long terme**
I counsel **je conseille**	measure **la mesure**
counselling **les conseils** (m)	negative **négatif**
criterion **le critère**	normal **normal**
debt **la dette**	policy/policies **la politique**
I am in debt **je suis endetté**	positive **positif [-ve]**
dependence **la dépendance**	power **le pouvoir**
dependent **dépendant**	prestige **le prestige**
depressed (region)	problem **le problème**
économiquement faible	protest movement **le mouvement**
depression **la dépression**	**de protestation**
deprived **privé de**	I provide (for/with) **je fournis**

– There are immense social problems in the inner city.

– Il y a d'importants problèmes sociaux dans les quartiers défavorisés.

– What are the causes?

– Quelles en sont les causes?

– People are frustrated and lonely, often as a result of unemployment.

– Les gens sont frustrés et seuls, souvent à cause du chômage.

provision   la provision
psychological   **psychologique**
quality of life   la qualité de la vie
question/issue   le problème,
   la question
rate   le taux
responsibility   la responsabilité
responsible (ir-)   (ir)responsable
result   le résultat
right *(human)*   le droit
role   le rôle
rural   rural
scarcity   la pénurie
scheme   le projet
I am on the scrap heap   je suis
   mis *(mettre)* au rebus
secure (in-)   (pas) en sécurité
security   la sécurité
self-esteem   l'amour-propre *(m)*
short-term   à court terme
situation   la situation
social   social
society   la société
stable (un-)   (in)stable
stability (in-)   l'(in)stabilité *(f)*
statistics   les statistiques *(f)*
status   le statut
stigma   le stigmate
stress   le stress
stressful   stressant
structure   la structure
superfluous   superflu
support   le soutien
urban   urbain
value   la valeur

Some useful verbs

it affects   il a des conséquences
I can afford to   je peux *(pouvoir)*
   me permettre (de)
I am alienated   je suis exclu
I break down   je craque
I campaign   je fais campagne
I care for   je m'occupe de
I cause   j'occasionne
it changes   il change
I contribute   je contribue
I cope, manage   je me débrouille
I depend on   je dépends de
I deprive   je prive
I discourage   je décourage
I dominate   je domine
I encourage   j'encourage
I help   j'aide
I increase   j'augmente
I lack   je manque de
I look after   je m'occupe de
I need   j'ai besoin de
I neglect   je néglige
I owe   je dois *(devoir)*
I protest   je proteste
I put up with   je supporte
I rely on   je compte sur
I respect   je respecte
I share   je partage
I solve   je résous *(résoudre)*
I suffer from   je souffre *(souffrir)*
   de
I support   je soutiens *(soutenir)*
I tackle   j'aborde
I value   j'estime

Financial difficulties lead to loss of status and family problems. The quality of life suffers because of it.

Les difficultés financières entraînent la perte de statut et les problèmes familiaux. La qualité de la vie en souffre.

We attempt to offer guidance and counseling.

Nous essayons de donner des conseils.

SOCIAL ISSUES

12b Social services and poverty

Social services

aid	l'aide *(f)*
agency	l'agence *(f)*
authority	l'autorité *(f)*
benefit	l'allocation *(f)*
I benefit	je bénéficie
charity	l'organisation *(f)* caritative
claim	la réclamation
I claim	je réclame
claimant	le demandeur
disability	l'invalidité *(f)*
disabled	invalide
I am eligible for	j'ai droit à
frail	fragile
frailty	la fragilité
grant	la bourse
handicap	le handicap
handicapped	handicapé
ill health	la mauvaise santé
loan	le prêt
maintenance	la pension alimentaire
official	officiel[le]
reception center	le centre d'accueil
Red Cross	la Croix Rouge

refuge	le refuge
refugee	le réfugié, la réfugiée
I register	je m'inscris *(s'inscrire)*
registration	l'inscription *(f)*
Salvation Army	l'Armée *(f)* du Salut
service	le service
social security	la sécurité sociale
social services	les services *(m)* sociaux
social worker	un assistant social, une assistante sociale
support	le soutien
I support	je soutiens *(soutenir)*
unemployment benefit, welfare, income support	l'allocation *(f)* chômage
well-being	le bien-être

Wealth and poverty

affluence	la richesse
I beg	je mendie
beggar	le mendiant, la mendiante
I am broke	je suis fauché
debt	la dette
in debt	endetté
deprivation	la privation
deprived	privé de

There is a reception center for the homeless that provides food and clothing.	Il y a un centre d'accueil pour les sans-abris qui fournit de la nourriture et des vêtements.
Many charities are active in this way. The physically handicapped can apply for help too.	De nombreuses organizations de bienfaisance sont actives dans ce sens. Les handicapés physiques peuvent aussi demander de l'aide.
They are particularly vulnerable to unemployment.	Ils sont particulièrement vulnérables au chômage.
Not everyone gets the dole, as many have not worked for a long time.	Tout le monde n'a pas droit à l'allocation chômage, car beaucoup n'ont pas travaillé depuis longtemps.

destitute **sans ressources**
living standards **le niveau de vie**
millionaire **le millionnaire**
need **le besoin**
nutrition **l'alimentation** *(f)*
poor **pauvre**
poverty **la pauvreté**
I live in poverty **je vis** *(vivre)* **dans le besoin**
rich **riche**
subsistence **la subsistance**
tramp/vagrant **le clochard**
vulnerability **la vulnérabilité**
vulnerable **vulnérable**
wealth **la richesse, les richesses**
I am well-off **je vis** *(vivre)* **dans l'aisance** *(f)*

Unemployment

I cut back *(on jobs)* **je réduis**
I dismiss **je licencie, je congédie**
dismissal **le licenciement**
dole **l'indemnité** *(f)*, **le chômage**
I give notice **je donne mon préavis**
job **l'emploi** *(m)*
job center **l'agence** *(f)* **nationale pour l'emploi, l'ANPE**
job creation scheme **le plan de création d'emplois**
layoff **le licenciement**
laid off, terminated **licencié**
I've been laid off **j'ai été licencié**
long-term unemployed **les chômeurs** *(m)* **de longue durée**
I have lost my job **j'ai été privé de mon emploi**
part-time **à temps partiel**
part-time work **le chômage partiel**
retraining **le recyclage**
I am retrained **je me recycle**
I refuse a job **je rejette** *(rejeter)* **une offre d'emploi**
I resign **je démissionne**
skill **la compétence**
termination pay **l'indemnité** *(f)* **de licenciement**
training program **le programme de formation**
unemployable **incapable de travail**
unemployed **au chômage**
unemployment **le chômage**
unemployment benefit/insurance **l'allocation** *(f)* **de chômage**
unemployment rate **le taux de chômage**
vacancy **le poste vacant**

– How high is the level of unemployment? – In some areas it is about 15%.
– Can people retrain or work part-time?

– Yes, sometimes, and many take early retirement.

My brother was laid off some months ago. He has to report every two weeks to the employment office.

– Quel est le niveau du chômage?
– Dans certaines régions, il est d'environ quinze pour cent.
– Est-ce que les gens peuvent se recycler ou travailler à temps partiel?
– Oui, parfois, et beaucoup prennent une retraite anticipée.

Mon frère a été licencié il y a quelques mois. Il doit venir signer tous les quinze jours à l'ANPE.

SOCIAL ISSUES

12c Housing and homelessness

accommodation **le logement**
apartment **l'appartement** *(m)*
   apartment house **l'immeuble** *(m)*
I build **je construis**
building **le bâtiment**
   building land **le terrain à bâtir**
   building site **le chantier de construction**
camp **le camp**
comfortable/homey **confortable, accueillant**
commune **la commune**
I commute **je fais la navette**
commuter **le navetteur [-se]**
delapidated **délabré**
I demolish **je démolis**
demolition **la démolition**
it deteriorates **il s'abîme**
digs/pad **les piaules** *(f)*
drab **morne, gris**

I evict **j'expulse**
it falls down **il tombe en ruine**
furnished **meublé**
homeless **sans-abri**
homelessness **la vie sans domicile fixe**
hostel **l'auberge** *(f)*
house **la maison**
housing **le logement**
   housing association **l'association** *(f)* **de logement**
   housing policy **la politique de logement**
   housing shortage **la crise du logement**
inner city **les vieux quartiers** *(m)* **déshérités, les quartiers** *(m)* **défavorisés**
landlord **le/la propriétaire**

– Are they hoping to renovate the city center?
– Yes, many houses will be pulled down. Others will be modernized.

– Espèrent-ils rénover le centre-ville?
– Oui, de nombreuses maisons seront démolies. D'autres seront modernisées.

We live in a house near the shopping center. The advantage is that we do not have to commute to work.

Nous habitons une maison près du centre commercial. L'avantage est que nous ne faisons pas la navette pour aller au travail.

My sister lives on a new estate in the suburbs. She has a long journey every day to work.

Ma sœur habite dans un nouveau lotissement en banlieue. Elle a un long trajet pour aller au travail chaque jour.

It is impossible to find a furnished apartment to rent.

C'est impossible de trouver un appartement meublé à louer.

living conditions **les conditions** *(f)* **de vie**
I maintain **j'entretiens** *(entretenir)*
I modernize **je modernise**
mortgage **l'emprunt-logement** *(m)*
I move *(house)* **je déménage**
I occupy **j'occupe**
overcrowded **surpeuplé**
overcrowding **le surpeuplement**
own *(adj)* **propre**
I own **je suis propriétaire de**
public housing **les logements** *(m)* **sociaux**
I pull down **je démolis**
real estate agent **l'agent** *(m)* **immobilier**
I redevelop **je redéveloppe**
I renovate **je rénove**
I rent **je loue**
rent **le loyer**
I repair **je répare**

repairs **les réparations** *(f)*
shantytown **le bidonville**
shelter **l'abri** *(m)*
slum **le taudis**
I sleep in the street **je couche dehors**
slum clearance **l'aménagement** *(m)* **des quartiers insalubres**
speculator **le spéculateur, la spéculatrice**
squalid **misérable, sordide**
I squat **je squatte**
squatter **le squatter**
suburb **la banlieue**
tenant **le/la locataire**
town planning **l'urbanisme** *(m)*
urban **urbain**
urban development **le développement urbain**
unfurnished **non meublé**
wasteland **le terrain vague**

– Why do so many houses in France stand empty?
–The houses deteriorate fast and squatters move in.

–Aren't the town planners intending to demolish the houses?

– Yes, but at the same time so many are homeless. They sleep rough or squat.
– Is the municipality still building public housing?

– Not enough. Living conditions in the blocks of apartment houses are extremely poor. They are overcrowded and the landlords no longer repair them.

– **Pourquoi est-ce que tant de maisons en France sont vides?**
–**Les maisons se détériorent rapidement et les squatters y emménagent.**

–**Est-ce que les urbanistes n'envisagent pas de démolir les maisons?**

– **Si, mais en même temps, il y a tant de sans-abri. Ils couchent dehors ou squattent.**
– **Est-ce que le conseil municipal construit toujours des immeubles?**

– **Pas assez. Les conditions de vie dans les immeubles sont extrêmement mauvaises. Ils sont surpeuplés et les propriétaires ne le réparent plus.**

12d Addiction and violence

abuse **le mauvais traitement**
I abuse *(person)* **je maltraite**
act of violence **l'acte** *(m)* **de violence**
addict **le/la toxicomane**
addiction **la dépendance**
addictive **qui crée une dépendance**
aggression **l'agression** *(f)*
aggressive **agressif [-ve]**
alcohol **l'alcool** *(m)*
alcoholic **un/une alcoolique**
alcoholism **l'alcoolisme** *(m)*
anger **la colère**
angry **en colère**
I attack **j'attaque**
attack **l'attaque** *(f)*
I beat up **je bats** *(battre)*
I bully **je brutalise**
bully **la brute**
consumption **la consommation**
dangerous **dangereux [-se]**
I drink **je bois** *(boire)*
I get drunk **je m'enivre**
drunk **ivre, saoul**
drunk driving **la conduite en état**

d'ivresse
I dry out **je suis** *(suivre)* **une cure de désintoxication**
effect **l'effet** *(m)*
fatal **fatal**
fear **la peur**
I fear **j'ai peur**
force **la force**
gang **le gang, la bande**
harassment **le harcèlement**
hoodlum, thug **le voyou**
hostile **hostile**
hostility **l'hostilité** *(f)*
insult **l'insulte** *(f)*
I insult **j'insulte**
intoxication **l'ivresse** *(f)*
legal (il-) **(il)légal**
I legalize **je légalise**
I mug **j'agresse**
mugger **l'agresseur** *(m)*
nervous **nerveux [-se]**
nervousness **la nervosité**
pimp **le souteneur, le proxénète**
pimping **le proxénétisme**
porno **porno**
pornography **la pornographie**

Violence and vandalism are common in the inner city. Sometimes gangs mug tourists on the streets or terrorize citizens.

La violence et le vandalisme sont choses communes en ville. Les bandes agressent parfois les touristes dans la rue ou terrorisent les citoyens.

They beat up rivals and threaten the safety of the community.

Ils battent leurs rivaux et menacent la sécurité de la communauté.

Older people and women are sometimes afraid to go out alone.

Les personnes âgées et les femmes ont parfois peur de sortir seules.

prostitution **la prostitution**
rehabilitation **la réhabilitation**
I revert **je retourne**
I seduce **je séduis** *(séduire)*
sexual harassment **le harcèlement sexuel**
skinhead **le skinhead**
I smoke **je fume**
stimulant **stimulant**
stimulation **la stimulation**
I terrorize **je terrorise**
theft **le vol**
I threaten **je menace**
vandal **le/la vandale**
vandalism **le vandalisme**
victim **la victime**
violent **violent**

Drugs

addicted to drugs **intoxiqué**
AIDS **le SIDA**
angel dust **la poudre d'ange**
cannabis **le cannabis**
cocaine **la cocaïne**
crack **le crack**
I deal **je traite**
drug **la drogue**

drug scene **le monde de la drogue**
drug traffic **le trafic de la drogue**
ecstasy **l'ecstasy** *(m)*
I get infected **je suis contaminé**
glue **la colle**
hard drugs **les drogues** *(f)* **dures**
hashish **le hasch**
I have a fix **je me drogue**
heroin **l'héroïne** *(f)*
I inject **je m'injecte, je me pique**
junkie **le drogué, la droguée**
I kick (the habit) **je renonce (à la drogue)**
LSD **le LSD**
marijuana **la marijuana**
narcotic **le narcotique**
pusher **le revendeur**
I sniff **j'inhale, je sniffe**
soft drugs **les drogues** *(f)* **douces**
solvent **le solvant**
stimulant **stimulant**
syringe **la seringue**
I take drugs/a fix **je me drogue**
tranquilizer **le tranquillisant**
withdrawal **l'état** *(m)* **de manque**

Many young people have a drug problem. They start by sniffing solvents, or by taking soft drugs. Marijuana is the most common.

Beaucoup de jeunes ont des problèmes de drogue. Ils commencent par inhaler des solvants, ou par prendre des drogues douces. La marijuana est la drogue la plus commune.

They quickly become addicted. Then they go on to hard drugs.

Ils deviennent rapidement intoxiqués. Puis ils passent aux drogues dures.

The drug scene is troubling because many people become dealers or turn to crime.

Le monde de la drogue est inquiétant car tant de gens deviennent fournisseurs ou criminels.

12e Prejudice

asylum seeker **la personne qui cherche asile**
I call names **j'injurie**
citizenship **la citoyenneté**
civil liberties **les libertés** (f) **civiques**
country of origin **le pays natal**
cultural **culturel[le]**
culture **la culture**
I discriminate **je fais une discrimination**
discrimination **la discrimination**
dual nationality **la double nationalité**
emigrant **un émigrant, une émigrante**
emigration **l'émigration** (f)
equal (un-) **(in)égal**
equal opportunities **l'égalité** (f) **des chances**
equal pay **le salaire égal**
equal rights **l'égalité** (f) **des droits**
equality (in-) **l'(in)égalité** (f)
ethnic **ethnique**
far right **l'extrême droite** (f)
fascism **le fascisme**

fascist **le/la fasciste**
foreign (adj) **étranger [-ère]**
foreign worker **un ouvrier étranger, une ouvrière étrangère**
freedom **la liberté**
    freedom of movement **la liberté de mouvement**
    freedom of speech **la liberté d'expression**
ghetto **le ghetto**
human rights **les droits** (m) **de l'homme**
I immigrate **j'immigre**
immigrant **un immigrant, une immigrante**
immigrant (settled) **un immigré, une immigrée**
immigration **l'immigration** (f)
I integrate **j'intègre** (intégrer)
integration **l'intégration** (f)
intolerance **l'intolérance** (f)
intolerant **intolérant**
majority **la majorité**
minority **la minorité**
mother tongue **la langue maternelle**
I persecute **je persécute**

– Is racism a serious problem?

– **Est-ce que le racisme est un problème grave?**

– What about the ethnic minority population resident here?

– **Et à propos de la population de minorité ethnique qui réside ici?**

persecution **la persécution**
politically correct **politiquement correct**
prejudice **le préjugé**
prejudiced **plein de préjugés**
rabid **farouche**
race riot **l'émeute** *(f)* **raciale**
racism **le racisme**
racist **le/la raciste**
  racist *(adj)* **raciste**
refugee **le réfugié, la réfugiée**
I repatriate **je rapatrie**
residence permit **le permis de séjour**
right **le droit**
  right to asylum **le droit d'asile**
  right to residence **le droit de séjour**
stereotypical **stéréotypique**
I stand up for **je défends**
tolerance **la tolérance**
tolerant (in-) **(in)tolérant**
I tolerate **je tolère** *(tolérer)*
work permit **le permis de travail**

feminism **le féminisme**
feminist **la féministe**
heterosexual **l'hétérosexuel** *(m)*
  heterosexual **hétérosexuel[le]**
homosexual/gay **l'homosexuel** *(m)*
  homosexual **homosexuel[le]**
homosexuality **l'homosexualité** *(f)*
lesbian **la lesbienne**
  lesbian *(adj)* **lesbienne**
male **mâle**
sexual **sexuel[le]**
sexuality **la sexualité**
women's liberation **la libération de la femme**
women's rights **les droits** *(m)* **de la femme**

Sexuality
_____

female **la femme**
feminine **féminin**

– Unfortunately they tend to get the worst jobs and to be paid less.

– **Malheureusement, ils ont tendance à être offert les pires emplois et à être moins payés.**

The law still discriminates against homosexuals, although society is getting more tolerant. Gay people have become more open about their sexuality.

La loi fait toujours une discrimination contre les homosexuels bien que la société devienne plus tolérante. Les homosexuels parlent plus ouvertement de leur sexualité.

The feminist movement is still demanding equal rights for women.

Le mouvement féministe demande toujours l'égalité des droits pour les femmes.

13 Religion

13a Ideas and doctrines

agnostic **agnostique**
Anglican **anglican**
apostle **l'apôtre** *(m)*
atheism **l'athéisme** *(m)*
atheist **l'athée** *(m/f)*
atheistic **athée**
authority **l'autorité** *(f)*
belief **la croyance**
I believe (in) **je crois** *(croire)* **(en)**
believer **le croyant**
blessed **béni**
Buddha **le Bouddha**
Buddhism **le bouddhisme**
Buddhist **le/la Bouddhiste**
calvinist **le/la calviniste**
he canonizes **il canonise**
cantor **le chantre**
Catholic **catholique**
charismatic **charismatique**
charity **la charité**
Christ **le Christ**
Christian **chrétien[ne]**
Christianity **le christianisme**
church **l'église** *(f)*
commentary **le commentaire**
conscience **la conscience**
conversion **la conversion**

covenant **l'alliance** *(f)*
disciple **le disciple**
divine **divin**
duty **le devoir**
ecumenism **l'œcuménisme** *(m)*
ethical **éthique, moral**
evil **le mal**
faith **la foi**
faithful **fidèle**
the faithful **les fidèles** *(m)*
fast **le jeûne**
I forgive **je pardonne (à)**
forgiveness **le pardon**
free will **le libre-arbitre**
fundamentalism **l'intégrisme** *(m)*
fundamentalist **intégriste**
god **le dieu**
goddess **la déesse**
Gospel **l'évangile** *(m)*
grace **la grâce**
heaven **le ciel**
Hebrew **hébreu, hébraïque**
hell **l'enfer** *(m)*
heretical **hérétique**
Hindu **hindou**
Hinduism **l'Hindouisme** *(m)*
holiness **la sainteté**

The five pillars of Islam are belief in the One True God and that Mohammed is his Prophet, prayer, fasting, giving alms, and pilgrimage to Mecca.

Les cinq piliers de l'Islam sont l'attestation de la foi qu'il il n'est de divinité que Dieu et que Mahomet est son prophète, la prière rituelle, le jeûne du ramadan, l'aumône légale, et le pèlerinage à la Mecque.

holy **saint**
Holy Spirit **le Saint-Esprit**
hope **l'espoir** *(m)*
human **humain**
human being **l'être** *(m)* **humain**
humanism **l'humanisme** *(m)*
humanity **l'humanité** *(f)*
infallibility **l'infaillibilité** *(f)*
infallible **infaillible**
Islam **l'Islam** *(m)*
Islamic **islamique**
Jesus **Jésus**
Jew **juif, juive**
Jewish **juif [-ve]**
Judaic **judaïque**
Judaism **le judaïsme**
Lord **le Seigneur**
merciful **clément**
mercy **la miséricorde**
Messiah **le Messie**
Mohammed **Mohammed, Mahomet**
moral **moral**
morality **la moralité**
Muslim **le musulman, la musulmane**
Muslim *(adj)* **musulman**
myth **le mythe**
New Testament **le Nouveau Testament**
nirvana **le nirvana**
Old Testament **l'Ancien Testament** *(m)*
orthodox **orthodoxe**
pagan **païen[ne]**

parish **la paroisse**
Pentateuch **le Pentateuque**
prophet **le prophète**
Q'uran/Koran **le Coran**
redemption **la rédemption**
religion **la religion**
sacred **sacré**
saint **le saint, la sainte**
Saint Peter **Saint Pierre**
he sanctifies **il sanctifie**
Satan **Satan** *(m)*
he saves **il sauve**
Scripture **l'Ecriture** *(f)*
service **le service**
Sikh **le sikh**
Sikhism **le Sikhisme**
Shintoism **le Shintoïsme**
sin **le péché**
sinful **pécheur**
soul **l'âme** *(f)*
spirit **l'esprit** *(m)*
spiritual **spirituel**
spirituality **la spiritualité**
Talmud **le Talmud**
Taoism **le Taoïsme**
theological **théologique**
theology **la théologie**
Torah **la Torah**
traditional **traditionnel**
Trinity **la Trinité**
true **vrai**
truth **la vérité**
vision **la vision**
vocation **la vocation**

Religious fundamentalism can lead to fanaticism and intolerance in any religion.

L'intégrisme religieux peut mener au fanatisme et à l'intolérance dans n'importe quelle religion.

There is considerable disagreement about the ordination of women to the priesthood.

Il existe énormément de désaccords sur la question des femmes prêtres et de leur ordination.

➤ RELIGIOUS GROUPS App.13b

RELIGION

13b Faith and practice

archbishop   l'archevêque *(m)*
baptism   le baptême
bar mitzvah   la bar-mitzva
I bear witness to   je témoigne de
Bible   la Bible
biblical   biblique
bishop   l'évêque *(m)*
bishopric/see   l'évêché *(m)*
cathedral   la cathédrale
chapel   la chapelle
christening   le baptême
clergy   le clergé
clergyman   l'ecclésiastique *(m)*
communion   la communion
   Holy Communion   la Sainte
   Communion
community   la communauté
I confess *(sins)*   je me confesse
   I confess *(faith)*   je confesse
confession   la confession

confirmation   la confirmation
congregation   l'assemblée *(f)*
   congregation *(of cardinals)*   la
   congrégation
convent   le couvent
I convert *(others)*   je convertis
   I convert *(self)*   je me convertis
diocese   le diocèse
Eucharist   l'Eucharistie *(f)*
evangelical   évangélique
evangelist   évangéliste
I give alms   je fais l'aumône *(f)*
I give thanks (to God)   je rends
   grâces (à Dieu)
Imam   l'Imam, l'Iman *(m)*
intercession   l'intercession *(f)*
laity   les laïcs *(m)*
lay   laïque
layperson   le laïc
the Lord's Supper   la Sainte Cène

Bishops in the Church of England are not afraid to speak about social problems.

Les évêques de l'Eglise Anglicane n'ont pas peur de se prononcer sur les problèmes sociaux.

The sacrament of Holy Communion will be celebrated on Sunday at 9 o'clock.

L'Eucharistie sera célébrée dimanche à neuf heures.

The parish council meets regularly.

Le conseil de la paroisse se réunit régulièrement.

Those who are called to ministry must demonstrate their vocation before being accepted in theological colleges.

Ceux qui ont la vocation du saint ministère doivent le démontrer avant qu'on les accepte pour faire des études en théologie.

The Baptist tradition is very strong in the American South.

La tradition baptiste est très forte dans le sud des Etats-Unis.

mass   **la messe**
I meditate   **je médite**
meditation   **la méditation, le recueillement**
minister   **le pasteur (protestant)**
I minister to the parish   **je dessers (desservir) la paroisse**
ministry   **le saint ministère**
mission   **la mission**
missionary   **le missionnaire**
monastery   **le monastère**
monk   **le moine**
mosque   **la mosquée**
mullah   **le mollah**
nun   **la religieuse**
parish   **la paroisse**
parishioner   **le paroissien, la paroissienne**
pastor   **le pasteur**
pastoral   **pastoral**
Pope   **le Pape**
I praise   **je loue**
I pray (for)   **je prie (pour)**

prayer   **la prière**
prayerful   **recueilli, méditatif [-ve]**
priest   **le prêtre**
rabbi   **le rabbin**
I repent   **je me repens** *(se repentir)*
repentance   **le repentir**
repentant   **repenti**
I revere   **je vénère** *(vénérer)*
reverence   **la révérence**
reverent   **respectueux [-se]**
rite   **le rite**
ritual   **le rituel**
sacrament   **le sacrement**
synagogue   **la synagogue**
synod   **le synode**
temple   **le temple**
witness   **le témoin**
I witness   **je témoigne**
worship   **le culte, l'adoration** *(f)*
I worship   **j'adore**

A few Muslim schoolgirls in France have come into conflict with the authorities because they choose to wear the veil at school.

Quelques collégiennes musulmanes en France sont entrées en conflit avec les autorités pour avoir choisi de porter le foulard islamique à l'école.

Every Muslim is called to prayer five times a day.

Tout musulman est appelé à la prière cinq fois par jour.

During the holy month of Ramadan, Muslims fast from dawn to dusk. The month ends with the celebrations of the festival of Eid.

Pendant le mois sacré du Ramadan, les musulmans jeûnent dès l'aube jusqu'au coucher du soleil. Le mois se termine par les fêtes de l'Id.

Passover is a very important Jewish holiday.

La Pâque est une fête judaique trés importante.

Business and economics

14a Economics of work

I administer	**j'administre**
I agree (to do)	**je me mets** *(se mettre)* **d'accord (pour faire)**
agreement	**l'accord** *(m)*
bureaucracy	**la bureaucratie**
business	**les affaires** *(f)*
a business	**une entreprise**
capacity *(industrial)*	**les moyens** *(m)* **de production**
commerce	**le commerce**
commercial	**commercial**
company	**la compagnie**
deal	**l'affaire** *(f)*
I deliver	**je livre**
demand	**la demande**
the product is in demand	**le produit est très demandé**
development	**le développement**
I earn (a living)	**je gagne (ma vie)**
I employ	**j'emploie** *(employer)*
employment	**l'emploi** *(m)*
executive	**le cadre**
I export	**j'exporte**
exports	**les exportations** *(f)*
fall	**la chute, la baisse**
goods	**les marchandises** *(f)*
it grows	**il se développe**
I import	**j'importe**
I increase	**j'augmente**
increase	**l'augmentation** *(f)*

industrial output	**le rendement, la production**
industry	**l'industrie** *(f)*
I invest	**j'investis**
investment	**l'investissement** *(m)*
layoffs	**des licenciements** *(m)*
living standards	**le niveau de vie**
I manage	**je gère** *(gérer)*
management	**la gestion**
multinational	**multinational**
I negotiate	**je négocie**
one-to-one	**face à face, seul à seul**
priority	**la priorité**
I produce	**je produis**
producer	**le producteur**
production line	**la chaîne de fabrication**
productivity	**la productivité**
quality	**la qualité**
I raise (prices)	**je hausse (les prix)**
reliability	**la fiabilité, la qualité**
raise	**la hausse**
wage increase	**la hausse des salaires**
semiskilled	**spécialisé**
services	**les services** *(m)*
I set (priorities)	**je décide (des priorités)**
sick leave	**le congé de maladie**

Unemployment is rising to 12%.	**Le chômage monte à douze pour cent.**
The unions called for a reduction in the average weekly hours of work.	**Les syndicats ont demandé une réduction des heures de travail hebdomadaires moyennes.**

I sign *(contracts)* **je signe**

skilled labor **la main- d'œuvre qualifiée**

social unrest **l'agitation** *(f)* **sociale, les troubles** *(m)* **sociaux**

social welfare **la sécurité sociale**

I strengthen **je renforce, je consolide**

supply **la provision**

trade unionism **le syndicalisme**

unemployment **le chômage**

unemployment benefit **allocation de chômage** *(f)*

unskilled labor **la main- d'œuvre non-spécialisée**

work ethic **l'attitude** *(f)* **moraliste envers le travail**

workforce **la main-d'œuvre**

working week **la semaine de travail**

Industrial/labor dispute

I am on strike **je fais grève**

I strikebreak **je brise la grève**

I boycott **je boycotte**

I cross the picket line **je traverse le piquet de grève**

demonstration **la manifestation**

dispute **le conflit**

I slow down **je fais la grève perlée**

industrial/labor dispute **le conflit social**

I join the union **je me syndique**

I lock out **je ferme l'usine aux ouvriers**

lockout **le lock-out**

minimum wage **le SMIC**

I picket **je fais partie d'un piquet de grève**

picket **le piquet de grève**

productivity bonus **la prime à la productivité**

I resume work **je reprends le travail**

settlement **l'accord** *(m)*

strike **la grève**

general strike **la grève générale**

wildcat strike **la grève sauvage**

I strike/go on strike **je fais grève**

strike ballot **le scrutin**

strikebreaker **le briseur de grève**

striker **le gréviste**

trade union **le syndicat**

unfair dismissal **le licenciement injuste**

the profession is forming a union **la profession se syndique**

unionized labor **la main-d'œuvre syndiquée**

unrest **l'agitation** *(f)*

I am a union member **je suis syndiqué**

wage demand **la revendication salariale**

work-to-rule **la grève du zèle**

work stoppage **l'arrêt** *(m)* **de travail**

The Department of Commerce hope these measures will enhance the country's competitiveness. The unions fear they will facilitate job losses.

Le Département du Commerce espère que ces mesures encourageront la compétitivité. Les syndicats craignent qu'elles rendent plus faciles les licenciements.

➤ AT WORK 14b; SOCIAL SERVICES AND POVERTY 12b; PROFESSIONS AND JOBS App.14b

BUSINESS AND ECONOMICS

14b At work

I am away on business **je suis en déplacement**
boring **ennuyeux [-se]**
business trip **le voyage d'affaires**
I buy **j'achète** *(acheter)*
canteen **la cantine**
career **la carrière**
disciplinary proceedings **des mesures** *(f)* **disciplinaires**
I follow a training course **je suis/fais un stage**
free **libre**
grant **la subvention**
I grant *(someone)* **j'accorde à**
holiday/vacation **les vacances** *(f)*, **le congé**
job **le poste, l'emploi** *(m)*
job satisfaction **la satisfaction au travail**
misconduct **l'inconduite** *(f)*
occupation **l'occupation** *(f)*
I'm off work **je ne travaille pas, je ne suis pas de service**
post **le poste**
profession **la profession**
professional **professionnel[le]**
I qualify **j'obtiens** *(obtenir)* **mon diplôme/brevet**
research **la recherche, les recherches**
I sell **je vends**
tax **la taxe, l'impôt** *(m)*
I tax **j'impose**
taxes **les impôts** *(m)*
I toil **je travaille dur**
training **la formation**
training course **le stage**
vocation **la vocation**
wage-earner **le salarié, la salariée**
warning *(verbal)* **l'avertissement** *(m)*
    written warning **l'avis** *(m)*
I work **je travaille**
work **le travail, le boulot** *(fam)*
worker **l'ouvrier** *(m)*

Company personnel and structure

accounting department **le service de la comptabilité**
apprentice **l'apprenti** *(m)*
assistant **un/une assistant[e]**
associate **l'associé** *(m)*
board of directors **le conseil d'administration**
boss **le patron, la patronne**
colleague **le/la collègue**
I delegate **je délègue** *(déléguer)*
department **le département**
director **le directeur**
division **la division**
employee **un/une employé[e]**
employer **l'employeur** *(m)*
labor **le travail**
management **la direction, la gestion**
manager **le directeur**
manageress **la directrice**
managing director/CEO **le PDG**
marketing department **les responsables** *(m/f)* **du marketing**
personal assistant **le/la secrétaire particulier [-ère]**
president **le/la président[e]**
production department **les responsables** *(m/f)* **de la production**
I report to **je suis sous les ordres directs de**
I am responsible for **je suis responsable de**
sales department **les responsables** *(m/f)* **des ventes**
secretary **le/la secrétaire**
specialist **le/la spécialiste**
staff/personnel **le personnel**
supervisor **le supérieur, le chef de service, le directeur**
team **l'équipe** *(f)*
trainee **le/la stagiaire**
I transfer **je suis muté**
vice president **le vice-président**

In the office

business lunch **le déjeuner d'affaires**
business meeting **la réunion**
computer **l'ordinateur** *(m)*
conference call **l'audioconférence** *(f)*
conference room **la salle de conférence**
desk **le bureau**
I dictate **je dicte**
dictating machine **le dictaphone**
electronic mail **le courrier électronique**
extension **le poste**
fax **le fax, la télécopie**
fax machine **le télécopieur**
I fax **j'envoie** *(envoyer)* **par télécopie**
file **le dossier**
I file **je classe**
filing cabinet **le classeur (vertical)**
intercom **l'interphone** *(m)*
open plan **non cloisonné**
photocopier **la photocopieuse**
photocopy **la photocopie**
I photocopy **je photocopie**
pigeonhole **le casier**
reception **la réception**
receptionist **le/la réceptionniste**
swivel chair **le fauteuil pivotant**
typing pool **la dactylo** *(fam)*
wastebasket **la poubelle**
word processor **la machine à traitement de texte**
workstation **le poste de travail**

In the factory and on site

automation **l'automatisation** *(f)*
blue-collar worker **le col bleu**
bulldozer **le bulldozer**
car/automobile industry **l'industrie** *(f)* **automobile**
component **la pièce**
concrete **le béton**
construction industry **la construction**
crane **la grue**
foreman **le contremaître, le chef d'équipe**
forklift truck **le chariot de levage**
I forge **je forge**
industry **l'industrie** *(f)*
heavy/light **lourde/légère**
I manufacture **je fabrique**
manufacturing **la fabrication**
mass production **la production de masse**
mining **l'exploitation** *(f)* **minière**
power industry **l'énergie** *(f)*
precision tool **l'outil** *(m)* **de précision**
prefabricated **préfabriqué**
process **le processus**
I process **je traite**
product **le produit**
raw materials **les matières** *(f)* **premières, le matériau**
robot **le robot**
scaffolding **l'échafaudage** *(m)*
I smelt **je fonds**
steel smelting **la sidérurgie**
textile industry **le textile**

While my wife works for a bank, my son works in a factory on the production line and my daughter works in an office all day, I enjoy the peace and quiet of working at home as a writer.

Pendant que ma femme travaille dans une banque, mon fils travaille à la chaîne dans une usine, et ma fille travaille toute la journée dans un bureau, moi je profite de la tranquillité chez moi pour exercer le métier d'écrivair écrivain.

▶ COMPUTERS 15d; STATIONERY App.22b

BUSINESS AND ECONOMICS

14c Working Conditons

Conditions and remuneration

I am employed **je suis employé**

apprenticeship **l'apprentissage** *(m)*

benefit **l'allocation** *(f)*

I clock in **je pointe (à l'arrivée)**

I clock out **je pointe (à la sortie)**

company car **la voiture de fonction**

contract **le contrat**

expenses **les frais** *(m)*

expense account **les frais** *(m)* **de représentation**

flextime **l'horaire** *(m)* **mobile**

freelance **indépendant**

I work freelance **je travaille en free-lance**

full-time **à temps plein**

income **le revenu**

overtime **des heures** *(f)* **supplémentaires**

overworked **surchargé de travail**

part-time **à temps partiel**

payday **le jour de paie/paye**

pay slip **la feuille de paie/paye**

pay raise **l'augmentation** *(f)* **de salaire**

payroll **le registre du personnel**

pension **la retraite, la pension**

permanent **permanent**

I retire **je prends** *(prendre)* **ma retraite**

retirement **la retraite**

salary **le salaire**

self-employed **qui travaille à son compte**

sexual harassment **le harcèlement sexuel**

shift **la période de travail, le poste d'équipe**

day/night shift **le poste de jour/nuit**

temporary **temporaire**

– The conditions in this office are not good enough for your secretary, Mr. Martin.

– What do you mean?

– The place is cold, badly lit, and poorly ventilated. And you have far too many electrical appliances plugged into one socket.
Unless you make considerable changes within three months, I shall be forced to close the office down. I shall come back next week to discuss your plans. Good-bye!

– Les conditions de travail de ce bureau ne sont pas assez bonnes pour votre secrétaire, Monsieur Martin.

– Que voulez-vous dire?

–Les locaux sont froids, mal éclairés, et mal ventilés. Et vous avez trop d'appareils électriques branchés à la même prise.
Si vous n'effectuez pas de changements importants dans les trois mois à venir, je serai obligé de fermer ce bureau. Je reviens la semaine prochaine pour discuter de vos plans. Au revoir, Monsieur!

Job application

I advertise for a secretary   **je fais paraître une annonce pour trouver une sécretaire**

advertisement   **l'annonce** *(f)*

I have been laid off   **j'ai été licencié**

I apply for a job   **je fais une demande d'emploi, le postule**

classified ad   **la petite annonce**

curriculum vitae/resumé   **le curriculum vitae, le c.v.**

discrimination   **la discrimination**
   racial   **raciale**
   sexual   **sexuelle**

employment agency   **l'agence** *(f)* **de placement**

help wanted   **offres** *(f)* **d'emploi**

job center *(government)*   **l'Agence** *(f)* **Nationale pour l'Emploi (l'ANPE)**

I find a job   **je trouve un emploi**

interesting   **intéressant**

interview   **l'entretien** *(m)*

I interview   **je convoque pour un entretien**

job application   **la demande d'emploi**

I look for   **je cherche**

opening *(vacancy)*   **le débouché**

I promote *(someone)*   **je nomme ... à un poste**

I am promoted   **je suis promu**

promotion   **la promotion, l'avancement** *(m)*

qualification   **le diplôme, le brevet**

qualified   **qualifié, compétent**

I start work (for)   **je commence à travailler (pour)**

I take on *(employee)*   **j'embauche**

trial period   **la période d'essai**

vacancy   **le poste libre**

work experience   **le stage (non rémunéré)**

– Hello. Could I speak to the personnel manager, please.

– Speaking. What can I do for you?

– I saw your advertisement in the local paper for a sales executive: to start work next month.

– That's right.
– Could you send me the job description and application forms?
– Certainly.

– How many references are you asking for?
– Two, including your present or last employer.

– **Allô. Je voudrais parler au directeur du personnel, s'il vous plaît.**

– **C'est moi-même. Que puis-je faire pour vous?**

– **J'ai vu l'annonce que vous avez fait paraître au journal régional pour chercher un cadre commercial pouvant commencer le travail le mois prochain.**

– **C'est ça.**
– **Voulez-vous m'envoyer les détails du poste et le dossier à remplir pour faire ma demande, s'il vous plaît? – Bien sûr.**

– **Combien de noms faut-il donner en référence?**
– **Deux, dont votre employeur actuel, ou le plus récent.**

BUSINESS AND ECONOMICS

14d Finance and industry

account   **le compte bancaire**
advance   **l'avance** *(f)*
advertising   **la publicité**
audit   **la vérification des comptes,
l'audit** *(m)*
bill   **la facture**
board   **le conseil**
bonds   **le bon, le titre**
branch *(of company)*   **la
succursale, la branche**
budget   **le budget**
capital   **les capitaux** *(m)*
capital expenditure   **la dépense
d'investissement**
chamber of commerce   **la chambre
de commerce**
collateral   **le nantissement**
company   **la société, la compagnie**
I consume *(resources)*   **je
consomme**
consumer goods   **les biens** *(m)* **de
consommation**
consumer spending   **les dépenses**
(f) **des ménages**
cost of living   **le coût de la vie**
costing   **l'estimation** *(f)* **du prix de
revient**
costs   **les coûts** *(m)*
credit   **le crédit**
debit   **le débit**
deflation   **la déflation**

economic   **économique**
economy   **l'économie** *(f)*
funds   **les fonds** *(m)*
government spending   **les
dépenses** *(f)* **publiques**
income   **le revenu**
income tax   **l'impôt** *(m)* **sur le
revenu**
installment   **l'acompte** *(m)*, **le
versement partiel**
interest rate   **le taux d'intérêt**
I invest in   **j'investis en/dans**
investment   **l'investissement** *(m)*
invoice   **la facture**
labor costs   **les coûts** *(m)* **de la
main-d'œuvre**
liability   **la responsabilité**
manufacturing industry   **la
fabrication industrielle**
market   **le marché**
market economy   **l'économie** *(f)* **de
marché**
marketing   **la commercialisation,
le marketing**
merchandise   **la marchandise**
national debt   **l'endettement** *(m)*
national
I nationalize   **je nationalise**
notice   **l'avis** *(m)*
output   **la production, le
rendement**

A spiraling budget deficit caused
panic on the stock exchange
today.

**Aujourd'hui, la spirale du déficit
budgétaire a causé la panique à
la bourse.**

The company informed
shareholders that this year's
operating profits will not match the
level seen last year.

**L'entreprise a annoncé à ses
actionnaires que les profits
d'exploitation de cette année
seront moins avantageux que
ceux de l'année dernière.**

pay   **le salaire, la paie**
price   **le prix**
price war   **la guerre des prix**
private sector   **le secteur privé**
I privatize   **je privatise**
product   **le produit**
production   **la production, la fabrication**
public sector   **le secteur public**
quota   **le quota**
real estate/realty   **l'immobilier** *(m)*
retail sales   **les ventes** *(f)* **au détail**
retail trade   **la vente au détail**
salaries   **les salaires** *(m)*, **les traitements** *(m)*
sales tax   **la taxe à l'achat**
service sector   **le secteur tertiaire**
share   **l'action** *(f)*
shares going up/down   **des actions** *(f)* **en hausse/en baisse**
statistics   **les statistiques** *(f)*
stock exchange/market   **la bourse**
stock market index   **l'indice** *(m)* **de la Bourse**
I subsidize   **je subventionne**
subsidy   **la subvention**
supply and demand   **l'offre** *(f)* **et la demande**
supply costs   **les coûts** *(m)* **de l'approvisionnement**
I tax   **je taxe, j'impose**
tax   **la taxe, l'impôt** *(m)*
tax increase   **la hausse des impôts**
taxation   **la taxation, l'imposition** *(f)*
taxation level   **le taux d'imposition**
turnover   **le chiffre d'affaires**
valued-added sales tax/VAT   **la T.V.A.**
viable   **viable, qui a des chances de réussir**
wages   **les salaires** *(m)*

Personnel

accountant   **le/la comptable**
actuary   **un/une actuaire**
auditor   **le vérificateur de comptes**
banker   **le banquier**
  investment banker   **le banquier d'acceptation**
  merchant banker   **le banquier de commerce**
bank manager   **le directeur d'agence bancaire**
broker   **le courtier**
  insurance broker   **le courtier d'assurances**
consumer   **le consommateur, la consommatrice**
investor   **l'investisseur** *(m)*
speculator   **le spéculateur, la spéculatrice**
stockbroker   **l'agent** *(m)* **de change**
trader *(Wall St.)*   **le contrepartiste**

There is no area of electrical retailing where there isn't strong competition.

The commercial store owners are embarking on a program of cuts in an effort to restore profitability.

La concurrence est très forte dans tous les domaines de l'électroménager.

Les propriétaires des commerces s'engagent dans un programme de réductions des coûts afin d'essayer de rétablir la rentabilité.

BUSINESS AND ECONOMICS

14e Banking and the economy

Banking and personal finance

account **le compte**
automatic teller **la caisse automatique**
bank **la banque, l'agence** *(f)* **bancaire**
bank loan **le crédit bancaire**
I bank (money) **je dépose en banque**
bankrupt **failli, en faillite**
cash **les espèces** *(f)*
I cash a check **je touche/j'encaisse un chèque**
cash card **la carte de retrait, la carte bleue**
cashier **la caisse, le guichet**
cashpoint **le distributeur automatique, la billetterie**
I change **je change**
check **le chèque**
credit card **la carte de crédit**
credit union **la société de crédit immobilier**
currency **la monnaie, la devise**
deposit *(in a bank)* **le dépôt**
deposit *(returnable)* **la caution**

down payment/deposit **des arrhes** *(f)*
Eurocheque **l'eurochèque** *(m)*
exchange rate **le taux de change**
installment plan **la vente à crédit**
I have a credit of **(j'ai) un crédit de**
in deficit **en déficit**
in the red **à découvert**
I lend **je prête**
loan **le prêt** *(m)*, **l'avance** *(f)*
mortgage **l'emprunt-logement** *(m)*, **l'hypothèque** *(f)*
I mortgage **j'obtiens** *(-tenir)* **un emprunt-logement, j'hypothèque**
I open (an account) **j'ouvre** *(ouvrir)* **un compte**
overdraft **le découvert**
repayment **le remboursement**
I save **je mets** *(mettre)* **de côté, je fais des économies**
savings **l'épargne** *(f)*, **les économies** *(f)*
traveler's check **le chèque de voyage**
I withdraw **je retire (de)**

– Good morning. I'd like to open an account here, if possible.

– **Bonjour, madame. Je voudrais ouvrir un compte dans cette banque, si c'est possible.**

– Certainly, sir. What sort of account do you need?

– **Certainement, monsieur. Quel genre de compte vous faut-il?**

– Just a normal checking account. Are overdraft facilities available for students?

– **Un compte courant, avec un carnet de chèques. Est-ce qu'il existe des possibilités de découvert pour les étudiants?**

– I need to check that for you, sir, but I don't think so.

– **Je dois vérifier cela pour vous, monsieur, mais je ne pense pas.**

Growth

amalgamation   l'amalgamation *(f)*, la fusion

appreciation   la hausse, l'augmentation *(f)*

assets   les biens *(m)*, le capital

assurance   la garantie

auction   la vente aux enchères

boom   la montée en flèche, la forte hausse, le boom

competition   la concurrence

economic miracle   le miracle de l'économie

efficiency   la capacité, l'éfficacité *(f)*

growth   la croissance

merger   la fusion, le fusionnement

profit   le profit, le bénéfice

profitable   rentable, lucratif [-ve]

progress   le progrès

prosperity   la prospérité

prosperous   prospère, florissant

quality control   le contrôle/la gestion de la qualité

recovery   la reprise

research and development   la recherche et le développement

takeover   le rachat

takeover bid   l'OPA *(m)* (offre publique d'achat)

Decline

bankrupt   failli, en faillite

credit squeeze   les restrictions *(f)* de crédit

debt   la dette

it is declining   il est en baisse

deficit   le déficit

depreciation   la dépréciation

I dump   je dépose

inflation   l'inflation *(f)*

inflation rate   le taux d'inflation

loss   la perte

no-growth economy   l'économie *(f)* sans croissance

slowdown   le ralentissement

slump   la récession, la crise

spending cuts   les compressions *(f)* budgétaires

stagnant   stagnant

stagnation   la stagnation

– Did you hear about Woodland Toys? Unfortunately, they went bankrupt.

– Why was that?

– They borrowed too heavily in order to introduce a new line, which just didn't sell!

– And what was it?

– A range of battery-powered toys; just couldn't compete with the video and computer games!

– Tu as entendu la nouvelle des Jouets Woodland? Malheureusement, ils ont fait faillite.

– Pourquoi?

– Ils ont trop emprunté afin de lancer un nouveau produit qui n'a pas pris.

– Et qu'est-ce que c'était?

– Une gamme de jouets fonctionnant sur piles. Ça ne pouvait pas réussir contre la concurrence des jeux vidéo et des jeux électroniques!

➤ ECONOMICS OF WORK 14a; FINANCE AND INDUSTRY 14d; TRADE 27c

15 Communicating with others

15a Social discourse

Meetings

I accept **j'accepte**
appointment **le rendez-vous**
I become **je deviens** *(devenir)*
ball **le bal**
banquet **le banquet**
I'm busy **je suis pris**
I celebrate **je célèbre, je fête**
celebration **la fête, les festivités** *(f)*
club **le club**
I come and see **je viens** *(venir)*
   voir
I dance **je danse**
date **la date**
diary/datebook **l'agenda** *(m)*
I drop in on **je passe voir**
I expect **je m'attends à**
I fetch **je vais chercher**
I have fun **je m'amuse**
I greet **je salue**
guest **un invité, une invitée**
handshake **la poignée de main**
I invite **j'invite**
invitation **l'invitation** *(f)*
I join **je rejoins** *(rejoindre)*
I keep **je garde**
I meet **je rencontre**
meeting **la rencontre**
party **la réunion**
reception **la réception**
I see **je vois** *(voir)*
I shake hands with **je serre la**
   main à/de
I spend *(time)* **je passe**
social life **la vie mondaine**
I take part **je participe**
I talk **je parle**
I visit *(someone)* **je rends visite à**
visit **la visite**

Greetings and congratulations

bow/curtsey **la révérence**
I bow/curtsey (to) **je fais une**
   révérence (à)
Cheers! **Santé!**
Come in! **Entrez!**
I congratulate **je félicite**
Congratulations! **Félicitations!** *(f)*
Excuse me **Excusez-moi**
Good evening **Bonsoir**
Good morning/afternoon **Bonjour**
Hallo/hello **Salut!**
Happy Christmas **Joyeux Noël**
Happy Easter **Joyeuses Pâques**
Happy New Year **Bonne Année**
Here's to . . . **A la santé de ...**
Hi! **Salut!**
I toast **je porte un toast**
toast **le toast**
Well done! **Félicitations!**

Introduction

Bill, meet Jane **Bill, voici Jane**
How do you do?/How are you?
   Comment allez-vous?
I introduce myself **je me présente**
I introduce **je présente**
introduction **la présentation**
Ladies and Gentlemen
   Mesdames, Messieurs
Madam **Madame**
May I introduce . . .? **Puis-je vous**
   présenter ...?
Miss **Mademoiselle**
Mr. **M. (Monsieur)**
Mrs. **Mme (Madame)**
Ms. **Madame**
I'd like you to meet **j'aimerais**
   vous faire rencontrer

Pleased to meet you   **Enchanté de faire votre connaissance**
I say!   **dites donc!**
Sir   **Monsieur**
This is . . .   **Voici ...**
I welcome   **je souhaite la bienvenue (à)**
Welcome to   **Bienvenue à**

Pleasantries

I address (someone)   **je m'adresse à**
I address as tu   **je tutoie (tutoyer)**
I address as vous   **je vouvoie (vouvoyer)**
Best regards from ...   **Meilleures salutations (f) de ...**
Bless you!/Gesundheit!   **A vos souhaits!**
Much better, thank you   **Beaucoup mieux, merci**
I'm fine, thank you   **Je vais bien, merci**
I hope you get well soon   **J'espère que vous irez bientôt mieux**
How are you keeping?   **Comment vous portez-vous?**
My regards to ...   **Mes amitiés à ...**
so-so   **comme ci, comme ça**
Very well, thank you   **Très bien, merci**
Your (very good) health!   **A votre santé!**

Thanking

I thank   **je remercie**
No, thank you!   **Non, merci!**
thanks!   **merci!**
thanking   **le remerciement**
I'm grateful to you for   **je vous suis reconnaissant de**
Nice/good of you to . . .   **C'est gentil à vous de ...**
It's a pleasure   **C'est un plaisir**
Many thanks   **Mille remerciements**
Not at all!   **Pas de quoi!**

Thank you so much   **Merci beaucoup**
With pleasure   **Avec plaisir**

Apologizing

I apologize   **je m'excuse**
I do apologize   **je tiens (tenir) à m'excuser**
apology/excuse   **l'excuse (f)**
Excuse me, please   **Excusez-moi, s'il vous plaît**
I excuse   **j'excuse**
Forget it!   **N'en parlons plus!**
I forgive   **je pardonne**
it doesn't matter (at all/a bit)   **cela ne fait rien (du tout)**
it matters   **c'est important**
not at all   **pas du tout**
I beg your pardon   **je vous demande pardon**
I'm (so very) sorry (that ...)   **je suis (vraiment) désolé (que** +subj)
Unfortunately, I can't!   **Malheureusement, je ne peux pas!**

Farewells

All the best!   **Beaucoup de bonheur!**
Best wishes!   **Mes/Nos meilleurs vœux!**
Bye!   **Au revoir!**
Cheerio!   **Salut!**
Good luck!   **Bonne chance!**
Good-bye   **Au revoir**
I say good-bye   **je dis au revoir**
Good night!   **Bonne nuit!**
Have a good time!   **Amusez-vous bien!**
Have a safe journey home!   **Rentrez bien!**
See you later!   **A tout à l'heure!**
I will see you later/ tomorrow   **Je vous verrai plus tard/demain**
Sweet dreams!   **Faites de beaux rêves!**

15b Comments and interjections

Approval and disapproval

I approve   **j'approuve**
Is this all right?   **Est-ce que ça va?**
That's all right!   **Ça va!**
Excellent!   **Excellent!**
You should(n't) have . . .   **vous (n')auriez (pas) dû** +inf
Tut-tut, Tsk-tsk   **Allons! Allons!**
What a shameful business!   **Quelle honte!**

Permission and obligation

That's (quite) all right   **C'est bon**
allowed   **autorisé**
I allow   **j'autorise**
I am allowed to . . .   **je suis autorisé à ...**
it is not allowed/permitted   **ce n'est pas autorisé/permis**
Can I . . . ?   **Puis-je ...?**
I can (not)   **je (ne) peux (pas)**
you cannot/can't   **vous ne pouvez pas**
I have to   **je dois**
May I . . . ?   **Pourrais-je ...?**
I may (not)   **je (ne) pourrais (pas)**
I must (not)   **je (ne) dois (pas)**
No   **Non**
Not now/here/tonight   **Pas maintenant/ici/ce soir**
obligation   **l'obligation** *(f)*
I ought to . . .   **je devrais ...**
you ought to . . .   **vous devriez ...**
permitted   **permis**
permission   **la permission**
I'm (not) supposed to   **je (ne) suis (pas) censé**
Have you got time to . . . ?   **Avez-vous le temps de ...?**
You're welcome!   **Je vous en prie!**

Surprise

oh dear!   **oh mon Dieu!, oh là là!**
Fancy (that)!   **Tiens!**

Good God!   **Mon Dieu!**
Goodness!   **Seigneur!**
Is that so?   **Est-ce vrai?**
Really!   **Vraiment!**
I surprise   **je surprends**
surprising   **surprenant**
Does that surprise you?   **Est-ce que cela vous surprend?**
Ugh!   **Pouah!**
Well?   **Et bien?**
So what?   **Et alors?**
Wow!   **Super! Formidable!**

Hesitating

Just a minute/moment!   **Une minute/Un moment!**
I hesitate   **j'hésite**
What's his/her name?   **Quel est son nom?**
How shall I put it?   **Comment dire?**
Now let me think   **Laissez-moi réfléchir maintenant**
or rather . . .   **ou plutôt ...**
that is to say . . .   **c'est-à-dire ...**
That's not what I meant to say   **Ce n'est pas ce que je voulais dire**
thingamajig   **le machin, le truc**
Well . . .   **Et bien ...**

Listening & agreeing

I believe so/not   **je crois/je ne crois pas**
Certainly (not)!   **Certainement (pas)!**
definite(ly)   **certain, sûr, certainement, sûrement, bien sûr**
Don't you think (that) . . . ?   **Ne crois-tu pas (que) ...?**
Exactly!/Just so!   **Exactement!**
Indeed   **En effet**
never   **jamais**
no!   **non!**
of course (not)!   **bien sûr (que non)!**

Oh! **Oh!**

Quiet! **Silence!**

I quite agree **je suis entièrement d'accord**

Really? **Vraiment?, Ah bon?**

Rubbish! **Quelle blague!**

Shh! **Chut!**

That's correct **C'est exact**

That's not fair **Ce n'est pas juste**

That's not right **Ce n'est pas exact**

That's not so **Ce n'est pas ainsi**

That's wrong **C'est faux**

I think/don't think so **je pense que oui/non**

true **vrai**

Uh-huh! **Oui, oui!, Oh oui!**

wrong **faux**

Yes! **Oui!**

Yes, please **Oui, s'il vous plaît**

you're wrong **tu as tort**

Clarification and meaning

a kind/sort of . . . **un genre/une sorte de ...**

Can you speak more slowly, please? **Pouvez-vous parler plus lentement, s'il vous plaît?**

Could you repeat that, please? **Pourriez-vous répéter cela, s'il vous plaît?**

Did you say . . . ? **Avez-vous dit ...?**

Do you mean . . . ? **Est-ce que vous voulez dire ...?**

er . . . **euh ...**

Is that clear? **C'est clair?**

I mean **je veux dire**

I said that . . . **j'ai dit que ...**

slowly **lentement**

The same to you *(polite)* **Vous de même**

That's just what I meant **C'est exactement ce que je voulais dire**

That's just what I had in mind **C'est exactement ce à quoi je pensais**

That's not what I had in mind/meant **Ce n'est pas ce à quoi je pensais**

That's just what I need **C'est précisément ce dont j'ai besoin**

What did you say? **Qu'est-ce que vous avez dit?**

What do you mean by . . . ? **Que voulez-vous dire par ...?**

What I said was . . . **J'ai dit que ...**

What is the matter? **Qu'est-ce qui se passe?**

you know **vous savez**

– What make of computer did you want, sir?

– **Quel marque d'ordinateur désirez-vous, monsieur?**

– Wait a moment. I'll have to think about it . . .

– **Attendez un instant. Il faut que je réfléchisse ...**

– Was it this one?

– **C'était celui-ci?**

– No, I don't think so. I need one that is easy to use and has a lot of memory.

– **Non, je ne pense pas. Il me faut un ordinateur qui soit facile à utiliser, et qui ait beaucoup de mémoire.**

COMMUNICATING WITH OTHERS

15c Mail and telephone

Mail

abroad   **à l'étranger**
addressee   **le/la destinataire**
airmail letter   **la lettre par avion**
airmail   **par avion**
answer   **la réponse**
collection   **la levée**
I correspond   **je corresponds**
correspondence   **la correspondance**
correspondent   **le correspondant, la correspondante**
counter   **le guichet**
customs declaration   **la déclaration de douane**
envelope   **l'enveloppe** *(f)*
express delivery   **la distribution express**
I finish *(letter)*   **je termine**
first-class   **normal**
greetings   **les salutations** *(f)*
I hand in   **je remets** *(remettre)*
letter   **la lettre**
letter carrier   **le facteur, la factrice**
letter rate   **le tarif d'une lettre**
mail   **le courrier**

mailbox   **la boîte aux lettres**
news   **les nouvelles** *(f)*
package   **l'emballage** *(m)*
parcel   **le colis**
parcel-post   **le tarif d'un colis**
penpal   **le correspondant, la correspondante**
I post/mail   **je poste**
post office   **la poste**
post restante   **la poste restante**
post/mail   **le courrier**
postage   **les tarifs** *(m)* **postaux**
postage paid   **port payé**
postal order   **le mandat postal**
postcard   **la carte postale**
I receive   **je reçois** *(recevoir)*
recorded/registered mail   **le courrier recommandé**
reply   **la réponse**
sealed   **cacheté**
I send   **j'envoie** *(envoyer)*
sender   **un expéditeur, une expéditrice**
stamp   **le timbre**
I write   **j'écris** *(écrire)*
ZIP code   **le code postal**

When does the mail arrive?

Quand est-ce que le courrier arrive?

I haven't heard from her for ages.

Je n'ai pas eu de ses nouvelles depuis bien longtemps.

Dear Sir,
I am writing on behalf of my father, concerning...
I look forward to hearing from you.

Monsieur,
Je vous écris de la part de mon père, en ce qui concerne …
Dans l'attente de votre réponse …

Yours sincerely

Je vous prie d'agréer, monsieur/madame, l'expression de mes sentiments les meilleurs

Telephone and
telecommunications

answering machine **le répondeur téléphonique**
button **le bouton**
call box **la cabine téléphonique**
cell/mobile phone **un (téléphone) portable**
collect call **l'appel** *(m)* **en P.C.V.**
conversation **la conversation**
dial **le cadran**
electronic mail (E-mail) **le courrier électronique**
engaged *(phone)* **occupé**
extension **le poste**
fax **la télécopie, le fax**
fax modem **le modem de fax**
local call **la communication urbaine**
long-distance call **la communication interurbaine**
operator **le/la standardiste**
out of order **en panne**
party line **le téléphone rose**
receiver **le combiné**
slot **la fente**
subscriber **un abonné, une abonnée**
telecommunications links **les liai-**
sons *(f)* **de télécommunications**
telegraph **le télégraphe**
telephone **le téléphone**
telephone booth **la cabine**
telephone directory **l'annuaire** *(m)* **téléphonique**
unlisted **sur la liste rouge**
wrong number **le mauvais numéro**
zero **le zéro**

Telephoning

I call **j'appelle** *(appeler)*
I call again **je rappelle** *(rappeler)*
I connect **je mets** *(mettre)* **en communication**
I dial **je compose**
I fax **j'envoie** *(envoyer)* **une télécopie/un fax**
I hang up **je raccroche**
I hold **je patiente**
I pick up *(the phone)* **je décroche**
I press **j'appuie** *(appuyer)*
I put . . . through (to) **je passe ... (à)**
I speak to **je parle à**
I telephone/phone/call **je téléphone**
I transmit **je transmets** *(transmettre)*

Do you have change for the telephone? Can I dial direct?

Avez-vous de la monnaie pour le téléphone? Puis-je appeler par l'automatique?

– This is Jean-Luc (speaking). Could you put me through to François?

– C'est Jean-Luc à l'appareil. Pourriez-vous me passer François?

– Please wait/hold! ... Are you still there? I'm afraid he's not in.

– Veuillez patienter!/Ne quittez pas! ... Vous êtes toujours en ligne? Je regrette, il n'est pas ici.

– I will call back later.

– Je rappellerai plus tard.

This is Cambridge 503244.

Ici Cambridge 503244. (cinquante, trente-deux, quarante-quatre).

119

COMMUNICATING WITH OTHERS

15d Computers

Computer applications

adventure game **le jeu d'aventure**
application **l'application** *(f)*
artificial intelligence **l'intelligence**
(f) **artificielle**
bar code **le code à barres**
bar code reader **le lecteur de**
code à barres
browser **un navigateur**
calculator **la calculatrice**
computer **l'ordinateur** *(m)*
computer science/studies
l'informatique *(f)*
computerized **informatisé**
desktop publishing/DTP **la**
publication assistée par
ordinateur (PAO)
email **le courrier électronique,**
l'email
grammar-check **le correcteur de**
grammaire
information technology **la**
technologie de l'information
information **une information**
internet **l'internet**

optical reader **le lecteur optique**
simulation **la simulation**
simulator **le simulateur**
spell-check **le correcteur**
d'orthographe
thesaurus **le thésaurus, le**
dictionnaire de synonymes
website **un site**
word processor **la machine de**
traitement de texte
word processing **le traitement de**
texte

Word processing and operating

I access **j'accède (accéder) à**
I append **j'ajoute**
I back up **je sauvegarde**
I browse **je feuillette**
I cancel **j'annule**
I click **je clique**
I communicate **je communique**
I copy **je copie**
I count **je compte**
I create **je crée**
I cut and paste **je coupe et colle**

Which disk drive are you using?	**Quel lecteur de disques utilisez-vous?**
What size disks does it use?	**De quelle taille de disque avez-vous besoin?**
Can you repair this keyboard?	**Pouvez-vous réparer le clavier?**
How do you turn down the brightness?	**Comment est-ce qu'on baisse l'intensité?**
What do the function keys do?	**A quoi servent les touches de fonction?**
I'm surfing the internet to find a hotel.	**Je surfe sur internet por trouver un hôtel.**
These computers are on a local area network.	**Ces ordinateurs sont sur un réseau local.**

I debug **je débogue**
I delete **j'efface**
I download **je transfère**
  (transférer)
I emulate **j'imite**
I enter **j'entre**
I erase **j'efface**
I exit **je sors**
I export **j'exporte**
I file **je classe**
I format **je formate**
I forward **je fais suivre**
I handle (text) **je traite (texte)**
I import **j'importe**
I install **j'installe**
keyboard **le clavier**
keyboard operator **un opérateur/**
  une opératrice de saisie
I list **je liste**
I log on/off **j'entre/je sors** *(sortir)*
I log **j'enregistre**
I make bold **je mets** *(mettre)* **en**
  caractères gras
I merge **je fusionne**
I move **je déplace**
I open (a file) **j'ouvre** *(ouvrir)* **(un**
  fichier)
I print (out) **j'imprime**

I (word) process **je traite**
I program **je programme**
I quit **j'abandonne**
I read **je lis** *(lire)*
I reboot **je réinitialise, je**
  réamorce
I receive **je reçois** *(recevoir)*
I record **j'enregistre**
I remove **j'efface**
I replace **je remplace**
I reply **je réponds**
I retrieve **j'extrais**
I run **je parcours**
I save **je sauvegarde**
I search **je cherche**
I send **j'envoie**
I shift **je décale**
I sort **je classe**
I store **je mets** *(mettre)* **en**
  mémoire
I switch on/off **j'allume/j'éteins**
  (éteindre)
I tabulate **je mets** *(mettre)* **en**
  colonnes
I update **je mets** *(mettre)* **à jour**
I underline **je souligne**

– How easy is this spreadsheet to use?
– You can always consult the pull-down menu.

– **Ce tableur est-il facile à utiliser?**
– **Vous pouvez toujours regarder le menu qui défile vers le bas.**

This disk is corrupted. It has wiped my file!
Have you checked for a virus?

Ce disque est corrompu. Il a effacé mon fichier!
Avez-vous vérifié qu'il n'y a pas de virus?

Which operating system do you use?

Quel système d'exploitation utilises-tu?

Don't show me your password!

Ne me montrez pas votre mot de passe!

I don't like this software package.

Je n'aime pas ce progiciel.

16 Leisure and sport

16a Leisure

activity **l'activité** (f)
amateur **amateur**
archeology **l'archéologie** (f)
archery **le tir à l'arc**
I begin **je commence**
I belong to **je fais partie de**
book **le livre**
boring **ennuyeux [-se]**
camera **l'appareil** (m) **photo**
card **la carte**
card game **le jeu de cartes**
card table **la table de jeu**
casino **le casino**
cinema/movie theater **le cinéma**
closed **fermé**
club **le club**
I collect **je collectionne**
coin **la pièce**
connoisseur (of) **le connaisseur/la connaisseuse (de)**
crossword puzzles **les mots** (m) **croisés**
collection **la collection**

collectors fair **la foire des collectionneurs**
I decide **je décide**
discotheque **la discothèque**
I dislike **je n'aime pas**
DIY/do-it-yourself **le bricolage**
energy **l'énergie** (f)
energetic **énergique**
enthusiasm **l'enthousiasme** (m)
entrance **l'entrée** (f)
entry fee **le prix d'entrée**
excitement **l'exaltation** (f)
exciting **passionnant**
excursion **l'excursion** (f)
exit **la sortie**
fair **la fête foraine**
fascinating **fascinant**
I fish **je pêche, je vais à la pêche**
finished **fini**
free time **le temps libre**
fun **amusant**
I gamble **je joue de l'argent**
I get in line/queue **je fais la queue**

– What is your favourite hobby?

– Well, I used to go for a drive in the country every Sunday, but I have no time for hobbies nowadays. Sometimes I go fishing, which is recommended for stressed executives.

I can meet you at the swimming pool or, if you prefer, at the gym.

– **Quel est ton passe-temps préféré?**

– **Eh bien, tous les dimanches, je partais en voiture à la campagne, mais maintenant, je n'ai plus de temps pour les passe-temps. Parfois, je vais à la pêche, ce qui est recommandé pour les cadres stressés.**

On peut se rencontrer à la piscine, ou si tu préfères, à la salle de gym/au gymnase.

I go out **je sors** *(sortir)*
guide **le/la guide**
guided tour **la visite guidée**
hobby/pastime **le passe-temps**
holiday/vacation **les vacances** *(f)*
interest **l'intérêt** *(m)*
interesting **intéressant**
I join **je m'inscris** *(s'inscrire)* **à**
leisure **le loisir**
I like **j'aime**
line/queue **la queue**
I listen to **j'écoute**
I look **je regarde**
market **le marché**
  antiques market **le marché d'antiquités**
  flea market **le marché aux puces**
I meet **je rencontre**
meeting place **le lieu de rencontre**
member **le membre**
membership **l'adhésion** *(f)*
nightclub **la boîte de nuit**
open **ouvert**
organization **une organisation**
I organize **j'organise**
picnic **le pique-nique**
place **le lieu**
I play **je joue**

pleasure **le plaisir**
politics **la politique**
I prefer **je préfère**
private **privé**
public **publique**
I read **je lis** *(lire)*
ready **prêt**
season **la saison**
season ticket **l'abonnement** *(m)*
secluded **isolé**
slide **la diapositive**
spectator **le spectateur, la spectatrice**
I start (doing) **je commence (à faire)**
I stop (doing) **j'arrête (de faire)**
I stroll **je me promène**
subscription **l'abonnement** *(m)*
television **la télévision**
ticket **le billet**
time **l'heure** *(f)*
theater **le théâtre**
tour/visit **la visite**
vacation **les vacances** *(f)*
I visit **je visite, je rends visite à**
visit **la visite**
I walk **je marche**
I watch **je regarde**
youth club **le centre de jeunes**
zoo **le zoo**

– What do you like doing on a rainy day?
– Perhaps playing cards but not with my brother: he cheats!

– Shall we take the children to the zoo?
– Good idea. If we take Eve's children and their school friends as well we can have a group rate.

– **Qu'est-ce que tu aimes faire les jours de pluie?**
– **Peut-être jouer aux cartes mais pas avec mon frère, il triche!**

– **Et si nous emmenions les enfants au zoo?**
– **Bonne idée. Si nous emmenons les enfants d'Eve et leurs copains d'école, nous pourrons bénéficier d'un prix de groupe.**

➤ SPORTS AND EQUIPMENT 16c; PHOTOGRAPHY App.16c

LEISURE AND SPORT

16b Sporting activity

against **contre**	game **le jeu**
I aim **je vise**	I get fit **je me mets** *(se mettre)* **en forme**
archer **l'archer** *(m)*	goal **le but**
athlete **un/une athlète**	ground/stadium **le terrain**
athletic **athlétique**	gym(nasium) **la salle de gym, le gymnase**
ball **la balle**	
ball *(large)* **le ballon**	I hit **je frappe, je touche**
bath towel **la serviette de bain**	hit **la frappe**
bet **le pari**	ice rink **la patinoire**
boat **le bateau**	I ice skate **je fais du patin à glace**
boxer **le boxeur**	injury **la blessure**
I bowl **je joue aux boules**	instructor **le moniteur, la monitrice**
captain **le capitaine**	
I catch **j'attrape**	I jog **je fais du jogging**
champion **le champion, la championne**	jogger **le jogger**
	I jump **je saute**
championship **le championnat**	jump **le saut**
I climb **je grimpe**	I kick (ball) **je shoote (dans le ballon)**
climber **le grimpeur, la grimpeuse**	
coach **un entraîneur, une entraîneuse**	lawn **la pelouse**
	lawn *(tennis)* **le gazon**
cup *(sport)* **la coupe**	league **la ligue**
cycle **le vélo**	locker room **le vestiaire**
I cycle **je fais du vélo**	I lose **je perds** *(perdre)*
defeat **la défaite**	I lift weights **je fais des haltères**
I dive **je plonge**	marathon **le marathon**
I do (sport) **je fais (du sport)**	match **le match**
effort **l'effort** *(m)*	medal **la médaille**
endurance **l'endurance** *(f)*	gold/silver/bronze **d'or/ d'argent/de bronze**
equipment **le matériel**	
I exercise **je fais des exercices**	muscle **le muscle**
I fall **je tombe**	I'm not in shape **je ne suis pas en forme**
fall **la chute**	
finals **la finale**	Olympic Games (winter, summer) **les Jeux** *(m)* **Olympiques**
fit **en pleine forme**	
fitness **la forme**	

It is a remarkable achievement for the national team, which has performed extremely well.

C'est un exploit remarquable pour l'équipe nationale qui a extrêmement bien joué.

(d'hiver, d'été)

opponent **un/une adversaire**

pedal **la pédale**

pentathlon **le pentathlon**

physical **physique**

I pitch **je lance**

pitcher **le lanceur**

I play **je joue**

player **le joueur, la joueuse**

point **le point**

professional **le professionnel, la professionnelle**

I race **je fais une course**

race **la course**

referee **l'arbitre** *(m)*

rest **le repos**

result **le résultat**

I ride **je fais du cheval**

riding school **l'école** *(f)* **d'équitation**

roller skating **le patinage à roulettes**

I row **je fais de l'aviron**

I run **je cours** *(courir)*

run **la course**

runner **le coureur**

sailing school **l'école** *(f)* **de voile**

I sail **je fais de la voile**

sail **la voile**

I score (a goal) **je marque (un but)**

score **le score**

I shoot *(ball, puck)* **je shoote**

I shoot (at a target) **je tire (sur la cible)**

I shoot pool **je joue au billard américain**

I ski **je fais du ski**

ski slope **la piste**

show **le spectacle**

skier **le skieur, la skieuse**

ski lift **le remonte-pente**

sponsor **le sponsor**

sponsorship **le sponsoring**

sport **le sport**

sports field **le terrain de sport**

sprint **le sprint**

stadium **le stade**

stamina **l'endurance** *(f)*

strength **la force**

supporter **le/la supporter**

I swim **je nage**

table tennis **le tennis de table**

team **l'équipe** *(f)*

team sport **le sport d'équipe**

I throw **je lance**

I tie (draw) **je fais match nul**

tie (draw) **le match nul**

timing/timekeeping **le chronométrage**

touchdown **le but**

tournament **le tournoi**

track **la piste**

I train **je m'entraîne**

trainer **un entraîneur, une entraîneuse**

training **l'entraînement** *(m)*

triumph **le triomphe**

trophy **le trophée**

victory **la victoire**

I win **je gagne**

workout **la séance d'entraînement**

world championship **le championnat du monde**

world cup **la coupe du monde**

The team has been training in very trying weather conditions and each athlete was ready to give his best.

L'équipe s'est entraînée dans des conditions climatiques très pénibles et chaque athlète était prêt à donner le meilleur de lui-même.

LEISURE AND SPORT

16c Sports and equipment

Sports

aerobics **l'aérobic** *(m)*
archery **le tir à l'arc**
athletics **l'athlétisme** *(m)*
badminton **le badminton**
baseball **le baseball**
basketball **le basketball**
bowling **le jeu de boules**
 tenpins **le bowling (à dix quilles)**
boxing **la boxe**
climbing (rock) **l'escalade** *(f)*
 free climbing **la libre escalade** *(f)*
crew **l'équipage** *(m)*
cricket **le cricket**
cycling **le cyclisme**
decathlon **le décathlon**
diving **la plongée**
 deep-sea diving **la plongée sous-marine**
football **le football American**
hang gliding **le delta-plane**
handball **le handball**
hockey **le hockey**
horse racing **les courses** *(f)* **de chevaux**
horseback riding **l'équitation** *(f)*
ice hockey **le hockey sur glace**
ice skating **le patinage (sur glace)**
jogging **le jogging**
motor racing **les courses** *(f)* **automobiles**
parapenting **le parapente**
polo **le polo**
pool **le billard américain**
racing **les courses** *(f)*
riding **l'équitation** *(f)*
rugby **le rugby**
sailing **la navigation à voile**
skiing **le ski**
 alpine skiing **le ski alpin**

cross-country skiing **le ski de fond**
downhill skiing **le ski de descente**
snooker **le billard**
soccer **le football**
swimming **la natation**
table tennis **le tennis de table**
tennis **le tennis**
volleyball **le volleyball**
water polo **le water-polo**
weightlifting **l'haltérophilie** *(f)*
weight training **la musculation (en salle)**
wind surfing **la planche à voile**

Leisure wear and sports clothes

anorak **l'anorak** *(m)*
bathing suit **le maillot de bain**
boots **les bottes** *(f)*
cycling shorts **le short de cycliste**
dancing shoes **les chaussures** *(f)* **de danse**
gardening gloves **les gants** *(m)* **de jardinage**
hiking boots **les chaussures** *(f)* **de marche**
leotard **le collant**
parka **le parka**
rugby shirt **la chemise de rugby**
sneakers **les chaussures** *(f)* **de sport, les baskets** *(f)*
swimming trunks **le maillot de bain**
track suit **le survêtement**
waterproof jacket **la veste imperméable**
Wellington boots **les bottes** *(f)* **en caoutchouc**
wet suit **la combinaison de plongée**

Leisure and sport equipment

arrow   **la flèche**
backpack   **le sac à dos**
ball   **la balle**
bat *(cricket, baseball)*   **la batte**
bat (table tennis)   **la raquette de tennis de table**
binoculars   **les jumelles** *(f)*
boxing gloves   **les gants** *(m)* **de boxe**
bow   **l'archet** *(m)*
camera   **l'appareil** *(m)* **photo**
crash helmet   **le casque**
equipment   **le matériel**
exercise bike   **le vélo de santé/d'appartement**
fishing rod   **la canne à pêche**
headphone   **le casque (à écouteurs)**
hi-fi   **la chaîne hi-fi**
knapsack   **le sac à dos**
knitting needles   **les aiguilles** *(f)* **à tricoter**
javelin   **le javelot**
mountain bike   **le vélo tout terrain (VTT)**
net   **le filet**

outrigger   **l'outrigger** *(m)*
pruning shears   **les sécateurs** *(m)*
puck   **le palet**
racket *(tennis)*   **la raquette**
rifle   **le fusil**
roller skates   **les patins** *(m)* **à roulettes**
rowing machine   **la machine à ramer**
rowing boat   **le canot (à rames)**
sailboat   **le voilier**
sewing kit   **la boîte à couture**
skate   **le patin**
skis   **les skis** *(m)*
ski boots   **les chaussures** *(f)* **de ski**
ski sticks/poles   **les bâtons** *(m)* **de ski**
spinning wheel   **le rouet**
sports bag   **le sac de sport**
stick *(hockey)*   **le crosse (de hockey)**
surfboard   **la planche de surf**
stopwatch   **le chronomètre**
weights   **les poids** *(m)*
yacht   **le yacht**
zoom lens   **le zoom**

– Did you watch the game?

– No, I had to leave before the end. Who won?

– We lost 3 to 1. I still cannot understand how such a capable team could lose so disastrously after a brilliant season.

All sports commentators agree that they were particularly unlucky when the referee insisted on the penalty.

– **As-tu regardé le match?**

– **Non, j'ai dû partir avant la fin. Qui a gagné?**

– **Nous avons perdu 3 à 1. Je ne peux toujours pas comprendre comment une équipe aussi compétente a pu perdre de façon aussi désastreuse après une saison remarquable.**

Tous les commentateurs sportifs sont d'accord pour dire qu'ils n'ont surtout pas eu de chance quand l'arbitre a insisté sur le penalty.

➤ FARMING AND GARDENING 24c; TOOLS App.8b; PHOTOGRAPHY App.16a

17 The arts

17a Appreciation and criticism

abstract **abstrait**
abstruse **obscur, abstrus**
action **l'action** *(f)*
aesthete **l'esthète** *(m)*
aesthetics **l'esthétisme**
I appreciate **j'apprécie**
appreciation **l'appréciation** *(f)*
art **l'art** *(m)*
artist **l'artiste** *(m)*
artistic **artistique**
atmosphere **l'atmosphère** *(f)*
atmospheric **atmosphérique**
author **l'auteur** *(m)*
award **le prix**
I analyze **j'analyse**
avant-guarde **d'avant-garde**
believable **croyable**
character **le personnage**
characterization **la description des personnages**
characteristic **caractéristique**
climax **le point culminant**
it closes **il termine**
comic **comique, drôle**
commentary **le commentaire**
conflict **le conflit**
contemporary **contemporain**
contrast **le contraste**
it creates **il crée**
creativity **la créativité**
credible **crédible**
critic **le critique**
criticism **la critique**
cultivated **cultivé**
culture **la culture**
it deals with **il traite de**
it describes **il décrit**
it develops **il développe**
development **le développement**
device **la technique**

dialogue **le dialogue**
disturbing **inquiétant**
empathy **l'empathie** *(f)*
ending **la fin**
endless **interminable**
it ends **il se termine**
entertaining **distrayant**
entertainment **la distraction**
epic **l'aventure** *(f)* **épique**
event **l'événement** *(m)*
eventful **plein d'aventures**
example **l'exemple** *(m)*
exciting **palpitant, passionnant**
I explain **j'explique**
explanation **l'explication** *(f)*
it explores **il explore**
it expresses **il exprime**
extravagant **extravagant, excessif**
fake *(adj)* **faux [-se]**
fantastic **fantastique**
fantasy **la fantaisie**
figure **le personnage, la figure**
funny **amusant, drôle**
image **l'image** *(f)*
imaginary **imaginaire**
imagination **l'imagination** *(f)*
inspiration **l'inspiration** *(f)*
inspired (by) **inspiré (de)**
intense **intense**
intensity **l'intensité** *(f)*
interpretation **l'interprétation** *(f)*
invention **l'invention** *(f)*
inventive **inventif [-ve]**
ironic **ironique**
irony **l'ironie** *(f)*
issue **le problème**
life **la vie**
long-winded **long[ue] et laborieux [-se]**

lyrical **lyrique**
modern **moderne**
mood **l'humeur** *(f)*
moral **la morale**
  moral *(adj)* **moral**
morality **la moralité**
moving **émouvant**
mystery **le mystère**
mysterious **mystérieux [-se]**
mystical **mystique**
mysticism **le mysticisme**
nature **la nature**
obscure **obscur**
obscene **obscène**
obscenity **l'obscénité** *(f)*
opinion **l'opinion** *(f)*
optimism **l'optimisme** *(m)*
optimistic **optimiste**
parody **la parodie**
passion **la passion**
passionate **passionné**
pessimistic **pessimiste**
pessimism **le pessimisme**
poetic **poétique**
it portrays **il dresse le portrait (de)**
portrayal **le portrait**
precious **précieux [-se]**
protagonist **le protagoniste**

I read **j'étudie**
reader **le lecteur, la lectrice**
realistic **réaliste**
reference **la référence**
I reflect **je réfléchis**
reflection **la réflexion**
relationship **les rapports** *(m)*
review **la revue**
sad **triste**
satire **la satire**
it satirizes **il satirise**
satirical **satirique**
style **le style**
  in the style of . . . **à la manière
  de ...**
stylish **stylé, élégant**
subject **le sujet**
technique **la technique**
tension **la tension**
theme **le thème**
tone **le ton**
tragedy **la tragédie**
tragic **tragique**
true **vrai**
vivid **éclatant, vif [vive]**
viewpoint **le point de vue**
witty **spirituel[le], amusant**
work of art **l'œuvre** *(f)* **d'art**

Artistic styles and periods

Art Nouveau **l'art** *(m)* **nouveau**
Baroque **baroque**
Bronze Age **l'âge** *(m)* **de bronze**
Classical period **la période
  classique**
Dadaist **dada**
Enlightenment **le siècle des
  lumières**
expressionism
  l'expressionisme *(m)*
Futurist(ic) **futuriste**
Georgian **georgien[ne]**
Gothic **gothique**
Greek **grec[que]**
Middle Ages **le moyen âge**

moorish **mauresque, maure**
naturalistic **naturaliste**
Neolithic Age **l'âge néolithique**
Norman **normand**
Post- **post-**
realism **le réalisme**
Renaissance **la renaissance**
Rococo **rococo**
Roman Empire **l'empire** *(m)*
  romain
Romanesque **romanesque**
Romantic period **la période
  romantique**
structuralist **structuraliste**
surrealism **le surréalisme**
symbolism **le symbolisme**

THE ARTS

17b Art and architecture

antique   l'antiquité *(f)*
antiquity   l'antiquité *(f)*
architect   l'architecte *(m)*
art   l'art *(m)*
artifact   l'objet *(m)* d'art
artist   l'artiste *(m)*
art student   l'étudiant *(f)* des beaux-arts
auction sale   la vente aux enchères
auctioneer   le commissaire-priseur
balance   l'équilibre *(m)*
baroque   baroque
beam   la poutre
bronze   le bronze
brush   le pinceau
I build   je construis
building   le bâtiment
bust   le buste
caricature   la caricature
I carve   je sculpte, je taille
I cast   je moule, je coule
ceramics   la céramique
charcoal   le fusain
chisel   le ciseau
chiseled   ciselé
classical   classique
clay   l'argile *(f)*
collage   le collage
creative   créatif [-ve]
creativity   la créativité
decorated   orné, décoré
decoration   la décoration
decorative arts   les arts *(m)* décoratifs
I design   je crée
design   la création, le design, le motif
dimension   la dimension
I draw   je dessine
drawing   le dessin
easel   le chevalet
elevation   l'élévation *(f)*
enamel   l'émail *(m)*
I engrave   je grave
engraving   l'estampe *(f)*
I etch   je grave
etching   la gravure
exhibition   l'exposition *(f)*
figure   la figure
figurine   la figurine
fine arts   les beaux-arts *(m)*
flamboyant   flamboyant
form   la forme
free-hand   à main levée
fresco   la fresque
frieze   la frise
genre   le genre
graphic arts   les arts *(m)* graphiques
gravity   la gravité
holograph   l'hologramme *(f)*
interior   intérieur
intricate   compliqué
ironwork   la ferronnerie
landscape   le paysage
landscape architect   l'architecte

Here, we are probably in the best place. Look, in the foreground you can see the monastery, which dates back from 1279 and which is such a good example of religious architecture and in the background the medieval towers are still visible.

Ici, nous sommes sans doute au meilleur endroit. Regardez, au premier plan on peut voir le monastère, qui date de 1279 et qui est un si bel exemple d'architecture religieuse, et à l'arrière-plan on peut encore voir les tours médiévales.

(m) **paysagiste**
landscape painter   **le peintre paysagiste**
large-scale work   **l'œuvre** *(f)* **de grande échelle**
later works   **les œuvres** *(f)* **postérieures/plus récentes**
light   **la lumière**
   light *(adj)*   **clair**
lithography   **la lithographie**
luminosity   **la luminosité**
luminous   **lumineux [-se]**
masterpiece   **le chef-d'œuvre**
metal   **le métal**
miniature   **la miniature**
model   **le modèle**
monochrome   **monochrome**
mosaic   **la mosaïque**
museum   **le musée**
oil painting   **la peinture à l'huile**
ornate   **orné**
I paint   **je peins** *(peindre)*, **je fais de la peinture**
paint   **la peinture**
painting   **le tableau**
pastel   **le pastel**
portrait   **le portrait**
potter   **le potier**
pottery   **la poterie**
it represents   **il représente**
representation   **la représentation**
reproduction   **la reproduction**
restoration   **la restauration**
i restore   **je restaure**
restored   **restauré**

restorer   **le restaurateur**
roughcast   **l'ébauche** *(f)*
school   **l'école** *(f)*
I sculpt   **je sculpte**
sculptor   **le sculpteur**
sculpture   **la sculpture**
seascape   **le paysage marin**
shadow   **l'ombre** *(f)*
shape   **la forme**
I shape   **je forme**
sketch(ing)   **l'esquisse** *(f)*
I sketch   **j'esquisse**
stained glass   **le verre teint**
   stained-glass window   **le vitrail**
statuary   **la statuaire**
statue   **la statue**
still life   **la nature morte**
I stipple   **je pointille**
studio   **le studio**
style   **le style**
tapestry   **la tapisserie**
tempera   **la détrempe**
town planning   **l'urbanisme** *(m)*
traditional   **traditionnel**
translucent   **translucide**
transparent   **transparent**
visual arts   **les arts** *(m)* **plastiques**
water color   **l'aquarelle** *(f)*
weathering   **le vieillissement**
wood   **le bois**
wood carving   **la sculpture sur bois**
woodcut   **la sculpture sur bois**
wood engraving   **la gravure sur bois**

I have just been to the exhibition at the Academy, which has already attracted thousands of visitors. There is the most wonderful collection of drawings and sculptures.

Je viens de voir l'exposition à l'Académie, qui a déjà attiré des milliers de visiteurs. Il y a une collection vraiment merveilleuse de dessins et de sculptures.

THE ARTS

17c Literature

autograph l'autographe *(m)*
book le livre
bookshop/store la librairie
bookseller le libraire
character le personnage
   main character le/la protagoniste
comic comique
dialogue le dialogue
fictional fictif [-ve], fictionnel[le]
hardback *(adj)* relié
I imagine j'imagine
imagination l'imagination *(f)*
inspiration l'inspiration *(f)*
inspired by inspiré par/de
it introduces il introduit
introduction l'introduction *(f)*
I leaf through je feuillette
librarian le/la bibliothécaire
library la bibliothèque
   public library la bibliothèque municipale
   reference library la bibliothèque d'ouvrages à consulter
literal(ly) littéral(ement)
map la carte
myth le mythe
mythology la mythologie
it narrates il raconte, il narre
narrative le narratif
narrator le narrateur
page la page
paperback le livre de poche

poem le poème
poetic poétique
poetry la poésie
punctuation la ponctuation
quote la citation
I quote je cite
I read je lis *(lire)*
I recount je rapporte
rhyme la rime
it is set in il se situe en
text le texte
title le titre
verse le vers

Types of books

adventure story le roman d'aventure
atlas l'atlas *(m)*
autobiography l'autobiographie *(f)*
biography la biographie
children's literature la littérature enfantine
comic novel le roman comique
cookbook le livre de recettes/cuisine
crime novel le roman policier
dictionary le dictionnaire
   bilingual bilingue
   monolingual monolingue
diary le journal
encyclopedia l'encyclopédie *(f)*
epic poem le poème épique
essay l'essai *(m)*
fable la fable

– What are you all reading at the moment?

–A spine-chilling story with a tragic conclusion. It is set in contemporary Los Angeles.

– **Qu'est-ce que vous lisez en ce moment?**

– **Un récit à vous glacer le sang avec une conclusion tragique. Il se situe dans le Los Angeles d'aujourd'hui.**

fairy tale **le conte de fée**
feminist novel **le roman féministe**
fiction **la fiction**
Greek tragedy **la tragédie grecque**
horror story **le récit d'épouvante**
letters **les lettres, la correspondance**
manual **le manuel**
memoirs **les mémoires** *(m)*
modern play **la pièce moderne**
nonfiction **le documentaire**
novel **le roman**
picaresque **picaresque**
poetry **la poésie**
reference book **l'ouvrage** *(m)* **de référence**
satirical poem **le poème satirique**
science fiction **la science-fiction**
short story **la nouvelle**
spy story **le roman d'espionnage**
teenage fiction **la littérature pour les jeunes**
travel book **le guide/le récit de voyage**
war novel **le roman de guerre**

Publishing

abridged version **la version abrégée**
acknowledgements **les remerciements** *(m)*
appendix **l'appendice** *(m)*
artwork **les illustrations**
author **l'auteur** *(m)*
best-seller **le best-seller, le livre à succès**

bibliography **la bibliographie**
book fair **la foire du livre**
catalog **le catalogue**
chapter **le chapitre**
contract **le contrat**
copy **l'exemplaire** *(m)*
copyright **les droits** *(m)* **d'auteur**
cover (of book) **la couverture**
deadline **la date limite**
dedicated to **dédié à**
edition **l'édition** *(f)*
latest edition **l'édition la plus récente**
editor **le rédacteur**
copy editor **le rédacteur technique**
footnotes **les annotations** *(f)*
illustrations **les illustrations** *(f)*
manuscript **le manuscrit**
paperback **le livre de poche**
preface **la préface**
proofreading **la correction**
publication date **la date de publication**
publisher **l'éditeur** *(m)*
publishing house **la maison d'édition**
quote **la citation**
review **la critique**
reviewer **le critique**
subtitle **le sous-titre**
table of contents **la table des matières**
translation **la traduction**
version **la version**
with a forward by **préfacé par**

– A vivid account of life in the thirties. The writer explores the theme of lost innocence.

– Un tableau évocateur de la vie dans les années trente. L'auteur explore le thème de l'innocence perdue.

– I'm reading a collection of modern foreign fiction.

– Je lis un recueil d'ouvrages de fiction en langue étrangère.

➤ APPRECIATION AND CRITICISM 17a

THE ARTS

17d Music and dance

acoustics **l'acoustique** *(f)*
adjudicator **l'adjudicateur** *(m)*
agent **l'agent** *(m)*, **l'imprésario** *(m)*
album **l'album** *(m)*
amplifier **l'amplificateur** *(m)*
audience **le public, les spectateurs** *(m)*
audition **l'audition** *(f)*
auditorium **l'auditorium** *(m)*
ballet **la danse classique, le ballet**
band leader **le leader du groupe**
baton **la baguette**
brass band **la fanfare**
canned music **la musique d'ambiance**
cassette tape **la cassette audio**
cassette player **le lecteur de cassettes**
chamber music **la musique de chambre**
choir **le chœur**
choral **choral**
choreography **la chorégraphie**
chorister **le choriste**
chorus **le chœur**
classical music **la musique classique**
compact disk (CD) **le disque compact, le CD**
competition **la compétition**
compilation **le recueil**

I compose **je compose**
composer **le compositeur**
composition **la composition**
concert **le concert**
concert hall **la salle de concerts**
conductor **le chef d'orchestre**
I conduct **je dirige l'orchestre**
dance **la danse**
I dance **je danse**
dancer **le danseur, la danseuse**
dance music **la musique de ballet**
discotheque **la discothèque**
disc jockey **l'animateur** *(m)*, **le disc-jockey**
drummer **le batteur**
ensemble **l'ensemble** *(m)*
folk music **la musique folklorique**
group **le groupe**
harmony **l'harmonie** *(f)*
harmonic **harmonique**
hit (song) **le tube**
hit parade **le hit-parade**
I hum **je chantonne**
instrument **l'instrument** *(m)*
instrument maker **le luthier**
instrument repairer **le réparateur d'instruments de musique**
instrumental music **la musique instrumentale**
instrumentalist **le musicien instrumentaliste**
I interpret **j'interprète** *(interpréter)*

– Do you play an instrument?
– I play the viola.
– I never learned to play an instrument but I have just bought an electric guitar.

– I like traditional jazz.
– I prefer easy listening music.

– Jouez-vous d'un instrument?
– Je joue de l'alto.
– Je n'ai jamais appris à jouer d'un instrument mais je viens d'acheter une guitare électrique.

– J'aime le jazz traditionnel.
– Je préfère la musique d'ambiance.

interpretation **l'interprétation** *(f)*
jazz **le jazz**
jukebox **le juke-box**
key **la clé**
lesson **la leçon**
I listen to **j'écoute**
listening **l'écoute** *(f)*
microphone **le micro**
music **la musique**
musical(ly) **musical(ement)**
musician **le musicien, la musicienne**
note **la note**
orchestra **l'orchestre** *(f)*
orchestration **l'orchestration** *(f)*
it is performed **on joue**
performance **la représentation**
performed by **interprété par**
performer **un/une interprète**
pianist **le/la pianiste**
piano **le piano**
piece **le morceau**
I play **je joue**
player **le joueur, la joueuse**
popular music **la musique populaire**
portable **portatif [-ve]**
I practice **je m'entraîne**
promotional video **la vidéo promotionnelle**
I put on a record **je mets** *(mettre)* **un disque**
recital **le récital**
record **le disque**
I record **j'enregistre**

recording **l'enregistrement** *(m)*
recording studio **le studio d'enregistrement**
reed **l'anche** *(f)*
refrain **le refrain**
I rehearse **je répète** *(répéter)*
rehearsal **la répétition**
repertoire **le répertoire**
rhythm **le rythme**
rhythmic(ally) **rythmique(ment)**
rock **le rock**
show **le spectacle**
I sing **je chante**
singer **le chanteur, la chanteuse**
solo **le solo**
soloist **le/la soliste**
song **la chanson**
song writer **le compositeur**
string **les cordes** *(f)*
string quartet **l'ensemble** *(m)* **à cordes**
symphony **la symphonie**
tape **la bande (sonore)**
tour **la tournée**
  on tour **en tournée**
tune **l'air** *(m)*
  in tune **juste**
  out of tune **faux [-se]**
I tune **j'accorde**
vocal music **la musique vocale**
voice **la voix**
I whistle **je siffle**
whistling **le sifflement**
wind band **l'ensemble** *(m)* **d'instruments à vent**

– There is a rave concert at the Students' Union/college hall.
– What is the name of the band?
– I don't know. Their lyrics aren't bad but their music is dire.

Some people have perfect pitch.

– **Il y a un concert branché dans la salle des étudiants.**
– **Comment s'appelle ce groupe?**
– **Je ne sais pas. Les paroles ne sont pas mal mais la musique est nulle.**

Il y a des gens qui ont la voix très juste.

THE ARTS

17e Theater and film

act l'acte *(f)*
I act je joue
acting school le conservatoire de théâtre
actor l'acteur *(m)*
actress l'actrice *(f)*
I applaud j'applaudis
applause les applaudissements *(m)*
assistant director le régisseur
audience le public, les spectateurs *(m)*
auditorium la salle
balcony la galerie
I book je réserve
box la loge
box office le bureau des réservations
cabaret le cabaret
camera la caméra
camera crew l'équipe *(f)* de tournage
cameraman le caméraman
cartoons les dessins *(m)* animés
choreographer le /la choréographe
cinema/movies le cinéma
cinema/movie buff le/la cinéphile
circus le cirque
I clap j'applaudis
cloakroom les vestiaires *(m)*

comedian le comédien
comedienne la comédienne
curtain le rideau
I design je crée
designer le créateur
I direct je dirige
director le réalisateur
drama le drame
dress rehearsal la répétition générale
dubbed doublé
dubbing le doublage
expectation l'attente *(f)*
farce la farce
farcical ridicule
film/movie le film
film/moviemaker le cinéaste
filmstar/movie star la vedette de cinéma
film/movie producer le producteur de cinéma
first night la première
floor show le spectacle de variétés
flop le navet, le fiasco
gaffer l'éclairagiste *(m)*
intermission l'entracte *(m)*
interval l'entracte *(m)*
lights l'éclairage *(m)*
limelights les projecteurs *(m)*
in the limelight en vedette

Foreign films are usually dubbed, but some cinema/movie clubs show them in the original language.

Les films en langue étrangère sont en général doublés, mais certains ciné-clubs les passent en version originale.

Sci-fi films were popular in the sixties.

Les films de science-fiction étaient en vogue dans les années soixante.

The director has been nominated for an Oscar.

Le réalisateur a été désigné pour un Oscar.

lobby   **l'entrée** *(f)*
I make a film/movie   **je fais un film**
masterpiece   **le chef-d'œuvre**
matinée   **la séance en matinée**
melodrama   **le mélodrame**
mime   **le mime**
movie   **le film**
music hall   **le music-hall**
offstage   **dans les coulisses**
opening night   **la première**
ovation   **l'ovation** *(f)*
pantomime   **la pantomime**
performance   **la représentation, le spectacle**
photography   **la photographie**
play   **la pièce**
I play   **je joue**
playwright   **l'auteur** *(m)* **de pièces de théâtre**
premiere   **la première**
I produce   **je suis le producteur/la productrice**
producer   **le producteur, la productrice**
production   **la production**
public   **le public**
retrospective   **la rétrospective**
role   **le rôle**
row   **la rangée**
scene   **la scène**
scenery   **le décor**
screen   **l'écran** *(m)*

screen test   **l'audition** *(f)*
screening   **la projection**
I shoot *(a film/movie)*   **je tourne**
script   **le script**
scriptwriter   **l'auteur** *(m)* **du script**
seat   **le siège**
    seat *(cinema/movies)*   **le fauteuil**
sequel   **la suite**
sequence   **la séquence**
set *(cinema/movie)*   **le plateau**
I show *(film/movie)*   **je montre, je passe**
it is shown at   **on le passe à**
it is sold out   **c'est complet**
soundtrack   **la bande sonore**
special effects   **les effets** *(m)* **spéciaux**
stage *(theater)*   **la scène**
stage directions   **les indications** *(f)* **scéniques**
stage effects   **les effets** *(m)* **de scène**
stage fright   **le trac**
stalls   **places** *(f)* **d'orchestre**
stunt person   **le cascadeur, la cascadeuse**
trailer   **la présentation d'un nouveau film**
understudy   **la doublure**
usherette   **l'ouvreuse** *(f)*
I zoom   **je zoome**

He is playing one of the most demanding roles of his career.

Il joue l'un des rôles les plus difficiles de sa carrière.

I want to see the latest production of her three-act play. All the critics will attend the opening night.

Je veux voir la production la plus récente de sa pièce en trois actes. Tous les critiques assisteront à la première.

The matinée is sold out.

La séance en matinée est complète.

 The media

18a General terms

admission **l'entrée** *(f)*	detailed **détaillé**
I admit **je laisse entrer**	it discriminates **il fait une**
I analyze **j'analyse**	**discrimination**
analysis **l'analyse** *(f)*	disaster **le désastre**
I appeal to **je fais appel à**	disinformation **la désinformation**
I argue **j'argumente**	educational **pédagogique**
argument **la dispute**	I entertain **je divertis**
attitude **l'attitude** *(f)*	ethical **moral**
biased **partial**	event **l'événement** *(m)*
campaign **la campagne**	example **l'exemple** *(m)*
censorship **la censure**	expectations **les attentes** *(f)*
cogent **convaincant**	I exploit **j'exploite**
comment **le commentaire**	fallacious **trompeur**
conspiracy **la conspiration**	fallacy **l'illusion** *(f)*
criticism **la critique**	freedom **la liberté**
critique **la critique**	full/detailed **rempli**
cultural **culturel[le]**	gullible **crédule**
culture **la culture**	hidden **caché**
cultured **cultivé**	ignorance **l'ignorance** *(f)*
current events **l'actualité** *(f)*	I ignore **j'ignore**
declaration **la déclaration**	influential **influent**
it declares **il déclare**	information **l'information** *(f)*

During the recent elections it was difficult to find an example of unbiased reporting.

Pendant les récentes élections, il était difficile de trouver un exemple de reportage impartial.

In recent years many war correspondents have lost their lives while reporting from the front or have been taken hostage.

Ces dernières années, de nombreux correspondants de guerre ont péri alors qu'ils faisaient un reportage depuis le front ou ont été pris en otage.

informative   **informatif [-ve]**
it interferes   **il s'ingère** *(s'ingérer)*
interview   **l'entretien** *(m)*
intrusion   **l'intrusion** *(f)*
intrusive   **importun**
issue *(problem)*   **la question**
I keep up with (news)   **je me tiens** *(se tenir)* **au courant (des actualités)**
libel   **la diffamation**
libelous   **diffamatoire**
it is likely   **il est probable**
local interest news   **l'actualité** *(f)* **d'intérêt local**
material   **le matériel**
meddling   **indiscret [-ète]**
news   **les informations** *(f)*
news item   **l'information** *(f)*
partisan   **partisan**
persuasive   **persuasif [-ve]**
prejudice   **le préjugé**
political   **politique**
politics   **la politique**
press   **la presse**
privacy   **l'intimité** *(f)*
privacy law   **la loi sur la protection de la vie privée**
problem   **le problème**
review   **la revue**

I review   **je passe en revue**
scoop   **le scoop**
sensational   **sensationnel[le]**
sensationalism   **la recherche du sensationnel**
sexism   **le sexisme**
sexist   **sexiste**
silence   **le silence**
silent   **silencieux [-se]**
social   **social**
society   **la société**
specious   **spécieux [-se]**
summary   **le résumé**
   summary *(adj)*   **sommaire**
it takes place   **il a lieu**
trust   **la confiance**
I trust   **je fais confiance**
trustworthy   **digne de confiance**
truth   **la vérité**
truthful   **véridique**
unbiased   **impartial**
untrustworthy   **indigne de confiance**
up to date   **à jour**
violent   **violent**
violence   **la violence**
weekly *(adj)*   **hebdomadaire**

European current affairs are not always reported in the British press, though all quality papers have foreign correspondents in all the European capitals.

La presse britannique ne fait pas toujours un reportage sur l'actualité européenne, bien que tous les journaux de qualité aient des correspondants étrangers dans toutes les capitales européennes.

Media barons have dominated the press in many western countries.

Les magnats des médias ont dominé la presse dans de nombreux pays occidentaux.

THE MEDIA

article   l'article (m)
back page   la dernière page
barons   les magnats (m)
broadsheet   le journal plein format
cartoon   le dessin (humoristique)
chief editor   le rédacteur/la rédactrice en chef
circulation   le tirage
color supplement   le supplément illustré
column   la colonne
comic strip   la bande dessiné
correspondent   le correspondant, la correspondante
   foreign   à l'étranger
crossword puzzle   les mots (m) croisés
daily newspaper   le quotidien
I edit   je suis le rédacteur/la rédactrice en chef
edition   l'édition (f)
editor   le rédacteur, la rédactrice
editorial   l'éditorial (m)
forgotten   oublié
front page   la une
glossy magazine   le magazine de luxe

gutter press   la presse à scandales
headline   le (gros) titre, la manchette
heading   la rubrique
horoscope   l'horoscope (m)
illustration   l'illustration (f)
it is published   il est publié
journalist   le/la journaliste
layout   la mise en page
leader   l'article (m) de tête
local paper   la presse locale
magazine   le magazine
Miss Lonely Hearts   le/la journaliste responsable du courrier du cœur
monthly   la revue mensuelle, le mensuel
national newspaper   la grande presse
newsagent   le marchand/la marchande de journaux
newspaper   le journal
newsstand   le kiosque (à journaux)
page   la page
pamphlet   la brochure
periodical   le périodique

The gutter press has a surprisingly high readership.

La presse à scandales a un nombre étonnamment élevé de lecteurs.

The Sunday edition has so many supplements that I can't find the personal ads.

Il y a tellement de suppléments dans l'édition du dimanche que je ne peux pas trouver les petites annonces personnelles.

The leader in the *Examiner* breaks the sensational news. What a scoop!

L'article de tête de l'Examiner révèle la nouvelle sensationnelle. Quel scoop!

power **le pouvoir**
powerful **puissant**
press agency **l'agence** *(f)* **de presse**
press conference **la conférence de presse**
I print **j'imprime**
print **les caractères** *(m)*
printshop **l'imprimerie** *(f)*
problem page **le courier du cœur**
I publish **je publie**
publisher **un éditeur, une éditrice**
publishing company **la maison d'édition**
quality press **la presse sérieuse/ de qualité**
reader **le lecteur**
I report **je fais un reportage**
report **le reportage**
reporter **le/la journaliste**
short news item **l'information** *(f)* **brève**
small ad **la petite annonce**
special correspondent **un envoyé spécial, une envoyée spéciale**
special issue **le numéro spécial**
sports page **la page sportive**
I subscribe to **je m'abonne à**
subscription **l'abonnement** *(m)*
tabloid **le tabloïd**
type(face) **le caractère**

weekly **l'hebdomadaire** *(m)*

Newspaper sections

Announcements **Annonces** *(f)*
Arts **Arts** *(m)*
Classified ads **petites annonces** *(f)*
Economy **Economie** *(f)*
Editorial **Editorial** *(m)*
Entertainment **Divertissements** *(m)*
Food and drink **Nourriture** *(f)* **et Boissons** *(f)*
Games **Jeux** *(m)*
Gossip column **Echos** *(m)*
Home news **Nouvelles** *(f)* **nationales**
Horoscope **Horoscope** *(m)*
International news **Nouvelles** *(f)* **internationales**
Obituary **Notices, nécrologiques** *(f)*, **Nécrologie** *(f)*
Finance **Finances** *(f)*
Problems page **Courrier** *(m)* **du cœur**
Property **Immobilier** *(m)*
Real estate **Immobilier**
Sports section **Sport** *(m)*
Travel **Voyage** *(m)*
Weather **Météo** *(f)*
Women's page **Page** *(f)* **des lectrices**

When is the color supplement published?

– What is the frequency, circulation, and readership of the magazine?

– It's published monthly, is aimed at motorbike enthusiasts and has over 30,000 subscribers worldwide.

Quand est-ce qu'on publie le supplément illustré?

– Quels sont la fréquence et le tirage de ce magazine, et qui sont les lecteurs?

– C'est un mensuel qui vise les fanas de la moto et qui compte plus de 30.000 abonnés dans le monde entier.

THE MEDIA

18c Television and radio

aerial **l'antenne** *(f)*
anchorman **le présentateur**
anchorwoman **la présentatrice**
announcer **le speaker, la speakerine**
audience **le public**
I broadcast **je diffuse**
broadcasting station **la station de radio**
cable TV **la télévision par câble, le câble**
cameraman **le cadreur, le cameraman**
channel **la chaîne**
commercial **la publicité**
couch potato **le lézard**
dubbed **doublé**
earphones **les écouteurs** *(m)*
episode **l'épisode** *(m)*
high frequency **à haute fréquence**
interactive **conversationnel[le], interactif [-ve]**
listener **un auditeur, une auditrice**

live broadcast **la diffusion en direct**
live coverage/commentary **le reportage en direct**
loudspeaker **le haut-parleur**
low frequency **à basse fréquence**
microphone **le microphone**
body mike **le micro portatif**
newsreader **le présentateur, la présentatrice**
personal stereo **le baladeur, le Walkman**
production studio **le studio de production**
program **le programme**
radio **la radio**
on radio **à la radio**
I record **j'enregistre**
recording **l'enregistrement** *(m)*
remote control **la télécommande**
repeat **la rediffusion**
satellite dish **l'antenne** *(f)* **parabolique**

– What! Still glued to the set? You have been watching the box all evening! You have become a real couch potato!

– **Quoi! Encore cloué devant la télé? Tu as regardé la télé toute la soirée! Tu es devenu un vrai lézard!**

– I'm just going to record this film/movie, then I'll join you. Have we got a blank videocassette?

–**Je vais juste enregistrer ce film et je te rejoins. Est-ce que tu as des videocassettes vierges?**

Was the Pavarotti concert broadcast live from Venice?

Est-ce que le concert avec Pavarotti a été diffusé en direct de Venise?

Until recently most TV spots portrayed women in exclusively traditional roles.

Jusqu'à ces derniers temps, la plupart des publicités à la télévision représentaient les femmes dans des rôles exclusivement traditionnels.

satellite TV   **la télévision satellite**
screen   **l'écran** *(m)*
I show   **je montre**
signal   **le signal**
station   **la station**
subtitles   **les sous-titres** *(m)*
I switch off   **j'éteins** *(éteindre)*
I switch on   **j'allume**
teletext   **le télétexte**
television   **la télévision**
    on television   **à la télévision**
TV   **la télé**
I transmit   **je transmets
    (transmettre)**
TV film/movie   **le téléfilm**
TV set   **le téléviseur**
TV studio   **le studio de télévision**
video clip   **le clip vidéo**
videogame   **le jeu vidéo**
video library   **la vidéothèque**
video recorder   **le magnétoscope**
viewer   **le téléspectateur, la
    téléspectatrice**
I watch   **je regarde**

TV and radio programs

cartoons   **les dessins** *(m)* **animés**
chat show   **le talk-show**
children's program   **l'émission** *(f)*
    pour enfants
comedy   **la comédie**
current affairs   **les actualités** *(f)*
drama   **le drame**
documentary   **le documentaire**
feature film   **le long métrage**
game show   **le jeu télévisé**
light entertainment   **les
    divertissements** *(m)* **légers**
news   **les informations** *(f)*
quiz programs   **le quiz, le jeu-
    concours**
regional news   **les informations** *(f)*
    régionales
soap   **le feuilleton (à l'eau de rose)**
series   **la série**
show   **le spectacle**
sitcom   **le sitcom**
sports program   **l'émission** *(f)*
    sportive
weather report   **le bulletin météo**

There should be a program on
student grants on this channel, but
perhaps the children would prefer
watching the cartoons. Where is
the TV listings?

**Il devrait y avoir un programme
sur les bourses d'étudiants, sur
cette chaîne, mais les enfants
préfèrent peut-être regarder les
dessins animés. Où est le
programme de télé?**

During the summer the traffic
bulletin is broadcast every hour in
four languages for the benefit of
foreign visitors.

**Pendant l'été, le bulletin de la
circulation est diffusé toutes les
heures en quatre (inv) langues au
bénéfice des touristes étrangers.**

– What are you watching now?
– Nothing, but I can't find the
remote control to switch the TV off.

**– Qu'est-ce que tu es en train de
regarder? – Rien, mais je ne
trouve pas la télécommande
pour éteindre la télé.**

– There's a good program on this
channel at 9 o'clock.

**– Il y a un bon programme sur
cette chaîne à neuf heures.**

18d Advertising

I advertise   **je fais de la publicité**
advertisment   **la publicité**
advertising   **la publicité**
advertising industry   **l'industrie** *(f)* **de la publicité**
appeal   **l'attrait** *(m)*
it appeals to   **il plaît** *(plaire)* **à, il attire**
billboard   **le panneau d'affichage**
brochure   **le prospectus, la brochure**
campaign   **la campagne**
catalog   **la brochure**
it catches the eye   **il attire l'attention**
commercial   **la publicité**
　commercial *(adj)*   **commercial**
competition *(rival)*   **la concurrence**
competition *(game)*   **le concours**
consumer   **le consommateur, la consommatrice**
consumer society   **la société de consommation**
copywriter   **le rédacteur/la rédactrice publicitaire**

I covet   **je convoite**
it creates a need   **il crée un besoin**
demand   **la demande**
direct mail   **le mailing, le publipostage**
disposable income   **le revenu net**
distributor   **le concessionnaire**
ethical   **éthique**
goods   **la marchandise**
hidden persuasion   **la persuasion cachée**
image   **l'image** *(f)*
junk mail   **les prospectus** *(m)* **adressés par la poste**
I launch   **je lance**
life style   **le mode de vie**
market   **le marché**
　bear market   **bas de gamme**
　bull market   **haut de gamme**
market research   **l'étude** *(f)* **de marché**
materialism   **le matérialisme**
model   **le modèle**
I motivate   **je motive**

This has been his least successful campaign: next time we will use another agency or perhaps a freelance copywriter.

Cette campagne a été la plus désastreuse pour lui: la prochaine fois, nous utiliserons une autre agence ou peut-être un rédacteur indépendant.

– Do you think that TV advertisements are more effective than advertisements in newspapers?

– Pensez-vous que les publicités à la télévision ont plus d'effet que les publicités dans les journaux?

– National TV reaches many more potential consumers but is extemely expensive.

– Les grandes chaînes de télévision touchent un plus grand nombre de consommateurs potentiels mais elles coûtent extrêmement cher.

need **le besoin**
persuasion **la persuasion**
poster **l'affiche** *(f)*
product **le produit**
I promote/publicize **je fais de la publicité (pour)**
promotion **la promotion**
publicity **la publicité**
public relations **les relations** *(f)* **publiques**
purchasing power **le pouvoir d'achat**
radio advertisements **les spots** *(m)* **publicitaires à la radio**
it sells **il (se) vend**
slogan **le slogan**
status symbol **le signe de prestige/richesse**
stunt **l'exploit** *(m)*
I target **je vise**
target group **le groupe cible**
I tempt **je tente**
trend **la mode**
trendy **dernier cri, à la dernière mode**
truthful **véridique**
TV advertisements **les spots** *(m)*

publicitaires à la télévision, la «pub»
unethical **immoral**

Small ads

accommodation **les logements** *(m)*
appointments **les offres** *(f)* **d'emplois**
births **les naissances** *(f)*
courses and conferences **les cours** *(m)* **et les conférences** *(f)*
deaths **les décès** *(m)*
engagements **les fiançailles** *(f)*
exchange **l'échange**
exhibitions **les expositions** *(f)*
for sale **à vendre**
health **la santé**
holidays **les vacances** *(f)*
lonely hearts **les cœurs** *(m)* **à prendre**
marriages **les mariages** *(m)*
personal services **les services** *(m)* **personnels**
property/real estate **l'immobilier** *(m)*
travel **le voyage**
wanted **les demandes** *(f)*

Our market survey shows that customers tend to buy items at supermarket checkouts on impulse.

Notre enquête montre que les clients ont tendance à faire des achats d'impulsion aux caisses de supermarché.

SPECIAL OFFER! For one week only! Buy 2 and get 1 free! Plus 20% discount on your next purchase!

OFFRE SPECIALE! Pendant une semaine seulement! Achetez deux produits et le troisième vous est offert gratuitement! Plus 20% de réduction sur votre prochain achat!

This publicity can be offensive to some ethnic groups.

Cette publicité peut être blessante pour certains groupes ethniques.

➤ THE PRESS 18b; TELEVISION AND RADIO 18c

⟦19⟧ Travel

19a General terms

I accelerate/speed up   **j'accélère**
   (accélérer)
accident   **l'accident** *(m)*
adult   **un/une adulte**
announcement   **l'annonce** *(f)*
arrival   **l'arrivée** *(f)*
I arrive (at)   **j'arrive (à)**
assistance   **l'aide** *(f)*
I ask for assistance   **je demande**
   de l'aide
bag   **le sac**
baggage   **les bagages** *(m)*
I book   **je réserve**
booking office   **le guichet des**
   réservations
business trip   **le voyage d'affaires**
I buy a ticket   **j'achète** *(acheter)* **un**
   billet
I call at   **je me présente à**
I cancel   **j'annule**
I carry   **je porte**
I catch   **j'attrape**
I check *(tickets)*   **je contrôle**
child   **l'enfant** *(m)*
class   **la classe**
I confirm   **je confirme**
connection   **la correspondance**
I cross   **je traverse**
delay   **le retard**
I am delayed   **je suis retardé**
I depart   **je pars** *(partir)*
departure   **le départ**
destination   **la destination**
direct   **direct**
direction   **la direction**
disabled   **handicapé**
distance   **la distance**
documents   **les papiers** *(m)*
   d'identité
driver *(car)*   **le chauffeur**

early   **tôt**
emergency   **l'urgence** *(f)*
emergency call   **l'appel** *(m)*
   d'urgence
I enquire   **je me renseigne**
enquiry   **le renseignement**
en route   **en route**
entrance   **l'entrée** *(f)*
exit   **la sortie**
extra charge   **le supplément**
fare   **le tarif**
   fare reduction   **la réduction sur**
   le prix du billet
   reduced fare   **le tarif réduit**
fast   **rapide**
I fill a form   **je remplis un**
   formulaire
free   **gratuit**
information   **les renseignements**
   (m)
information office   **le bureau**
   d'information, des
   renseignements
insurance   **l'assurance** *(f)*
help   **l'aide** *(f)*
helpful (un-)   **(in)utile**
late   **tard**
I leave *(place)*   **je quitte**
I leave *(person/object)*   **je laisse**
I leave at   **je pars** *(partir)* **à**
left-luggage office   **la consigne**
lost   **perdu**
lost and found office   **les objets**
   (m) **trouvés**
loudspeaker   **le haut-parleur**
luggage   **les bagages** *(m)*
message   **le message**
I miss the train   **je rate le train**
nonsmoker   **le non-fumeur**
notice   **l'avis** *(m)*

nuisance   l'ennui *(m)*
occupied   **occupé**
on board   **à bord**
on time   **à l'heure**
I pack   **je fais mes valises**
passenger   **le passager, la passagère**
porter *(hotel)*   **le portier**
perfect timing   **juste au bon moment**
reduction   **la réduction**
rescue   **les secours** *(m)*
reservation   **la réservation**
I reserve   **je réserve**
I return   **je reviens** *(revenir)*
return   **le retour**
return/round-trip ticket   **le billet aller-retour**
safe   **sûr**
safety   **la sécurité**
season ticket (weekly/monthly)   **la carte de transport (hebdomadaire/mensuelle)**
seat   **le siège, la place**
seatbelt   **la ceinture de sécurité**
I set off   **je pars** *(partir)*
signal   **le signal**
single/one-way ticket   **un aller simple**
slow   **lent**
I slow down   **je ralentis**
smoking   **fumeur**
speed   **la vitesse**
staff   **le personnel**
I start from   **je pars** *(partir)* **de**
stop   **l'arrêt** *(m)*
I stop   **je m'arrête**

on strike   **en grève**
I take *(the bus, train)*   **je prends**
ticket   **le billet**
ticket desk   **la billetterie**
ticket office   **le guichet**
timetable   **l'horaire** *(m)*
toilet   **les toilettes** *(f)*
I travel   **je voyage**
travel   **le voyage**
travel agent/agency   **un agent/une agence de voyage**
travel documents   **les documents** *(m)* **de voyage**
travel information   **les informations** *(f)* **routières**
travel pass   **la carte d'abonnement**
travel sickness   **le mal des transports**
traveler   **le voyageur, la voyageuse**
tunnel   **le tunnel**
turn   **le virage**
I turn   **je tourne**
I unpack   **je défais** *(défaire)* **mes bagages**
valid   **valable**
via/through   **par, via**
visitor   **le visiteur, la visiteuse**
warning   **la mise en garde**
weekdays   **les jours** *(m)* **de la semaine**
weekend   **la fin de la semaine, le week-end**
window   **la fenêtre**
window seat   **le fauteuil côté fenêtre**

Does public transport operate after midnight?

Y a-t-il des transports en commun après minuit?

Have a pleasant journey.

Faites un bon voyage.

Where is the lost and found office?
I have lost my suitcase.

Où est le bureau des objets trouvés? J'ai perdu ma valise.

19b Going abroad and travel by boat

Going abroad

I cross (the English Channel) **je traverse (la Manche)**
currency **la devise**
currency exchange office **le bureau de change**
customs **la douane**
customs control **le contrôle douanier**
customs officer **l'officier** *(m)* **des douanes**
customs regulations **les règlements** *(m)* **douaniers**
declaration **la déclaration**
I declare **je déclare**
duty **la taxe douanière**
duty-free goods **les produits** *(m)* **détaxés**
duty-free shop **le magasin de produits détaxés**
English Channel **la Manche**
Channel Tunnel **le Tunnel sous la Manche**
exchange rate **le taux de change**
expired *(document)* **périmé**
foreign currency **la devise étrangère**
frontier **la frontière**
I go through customs **je passe la douane**
I go through passport control **je passe le contrôle des passeports**
immigration office **le bureau d'immigration**
immigration rules **les lois** *(f)* **sur l'immigration**
passport **le passeport**
I pay duty on **je paie** *(payer)* **la taxe sur**
smuggler **le contrebandier, la contrebandière**
smuggling **la contrebande**
visa **le visa**

– Here are my documents. My final destination is Palermo.
– Thank you. Have a good trip!

I have nothing to declare.
This is for my personal use.

For your comfort and safety, please fasten your seatbelts.

– **Voici mes papiers. Je descends à Palerme.**
– **Merci, et bon voyage!**

Je n'ai rien à déclarer.
C'est pour mon usage personnel.

Pour votre confort et votre sécurité, veuillez attacher vos ceintures.

Travel by boat

boat/ship **le bateau**
bridge **le pont**
cabin **la cabine**
calm sea **la mer calme**
captain **le capitaine**
car-ferry **le bac, le ferry**
coast **la côte**
crew **l'équipage** *(m)*
crossing **la traversée**
cruise **la croisière**
deck **le pont**
   lower deck **le pont inférieur**
   upper deck **le pont supérieur**
deck chair **la chaise longue**
I disembark **je débarque**
disembarkation **le débarquement**
dock **les docks** *(m)*
I embark **j'embarque**
embarkation card **la carte d'embarquement**
I go on board **je monte à bord**
harbour **le port**
life jacket **le gilet de sauvetage**
lifeboat **le canot de sauvetage**
lounge **le salon**
officer **l'officier** *(m)*

offshore **au large**
on board **à bord**
overboard **par-dessus bord**
port **le port**
   port of call **le port d'escale**
on the port (side) **à bâbord**
purser **le commissaire de bord**
quay **le quai**
reclining seat **le siège inclinable**
sea **la mer**
   calm sea **la mer calme**
   choppy sea **la mer houleuse**
   heavy sea **la mer agitée**
   stormy sea **la mer houleuse**
seasickness **le mal de mer**
seaman **le marin**
shipping forecast **les prévisions** *(f)* **marines**
shipyard **la marina**
smooth **calme**
starboard **à tribord**
storm **l'orage** *(m)*
tide **la marée**
waves **les vagues** *(f)*
wind **le vent**
windy **venteux**
yachting **faire du yachting**

– Have you got any remedy against seasickness?
– Yes, I have some pills in my cabin. Meet me on C deck in 10 minutes.
– I don't think I'll survive that long.

– Avez-vous un remède contre le mal de mer?
– Oui, j'ai des comprimés dans ma cabine. Retrouvez-moi sur le pont C dans dix minutes.
– Je ne crois pas que je vais tenir jusque-là.

From which pier does the ship leave?

De quel quai part le bateau?

Are passports checked on board?

Les passeports sont-ils contrôlés à bord?

➤ SHIPS AND BOATS App.19b; THE WEATHER 24d

19c Travel by road

access **l'accès** *(m)*
I allow **j'autorise**
automatic **automatique**
I back up/reverse **je fais marche arrière**
bike/bicycle **le bicyclette, le vélo**
black (invisible) ice **le verglas**
bottleneck **le rétrécissement**
breathalizer **le ballon (de l'alcootest)**
breathalizer test **l'alcootest** *(m)*
breakdown **la panne**
I breakdown **je tombe en panne**
breakdown service **l'assistance** *(f)* **autoroute**
broken **cassé**
bus **l'autobus** *(m)*
bus fare **le tarif de bus**
bus stop **l'arrêt** *(m)* **de bus**
car/automobile **la voiture**
car rental **la location de voiture**
car park/parking lot **le parking**
multistoried **le parking à niveaux multiples**
car parts **les pièces** *(f)* **détachées**
car wash **le lavage de voiture**
careful driver **le chauffeur prudent**
careless driving **la conduite négligente**
caution **la prudence**
caution *(legal)* **la réprimande**

I change gear **je change de vitesse**
chauffeur **le chauffeur**
check **le contrôle**
I collide (with) **j'entre en collision (avec)**
collision **la collision**
company car **la voiture de service**
competent **qualifié**
conductor/conductress *(bus)* **le receveur, la receveuse**
I cross **je traverse**
dangerous **dangereux [-se]**
detour **la déviation**
diesel **le gas-oil, le diesel**
I do 30 mph **je roule à 30 mph**
I drive **je conduis**
drive **la conduite**
driver **le conducteur, la conductrice**
driving **conduire**
driving instructor **le moniteur, la monitrice**
driving lesson **la leçon de conduite**
driver's license **le permis de conduire**
driving school **l'auto-école** *(f)*
driving test **l'examen** *(m)* **de conduite**
drunk driving **la conduite en état d'ébriété**

I have a flat tire. Could you also have a look at the clutch?

J'ai un pneu crevé. Pouvez-vous aussi vérifier l'embrayage?

Fill it up with unleaded, please.

Le plein d'essence sans plomb, s'il vous plaît!

I had to stop on the shoulder. Fortunately, emergency phones are found on all expressways.

J'ai dû m'arrêter sur la bande d'arrêt d'urgence. Heureusement, on trouve des bornes télépho-niques sur toutes les autoroutes.

emergency stop   **l'arrêt** *(m)* **d'urgence**
engine trouble   **le problème de moteur**
I fasten the seatbelt   **j'attache la ceinture**
I fill up   **je fais le plein**
filling station   **la station-service**
fine   **la contravention**
I fix/repair   **je répare**
flat tire   **la crevaison, le pneu crevé**
forbidden   **interdit**
garage   **le garage**
gasoline   **l'essence** *(f)*
  super/four-star   **le super**
  two-star   **l'essence normale**
  unleaded   **l'essence sans plomb**
gear   **les vitesses** *(f)*
  I put the car in first gear   **je passe la première**
  neutral   **le point mort**
  reverse gear   **la marche arrière**
I get in the car   **je monte dans la voiture**
I get in lane   **je me mets** *(se mettre)* **dans la file**
I get out   **je sors** *(sortir)*
I give way   **je cède** *(céder)* **le passage**
highway code   **le code de la route**
highway police   **la police de la route**
I hitchhike   **je fais de l'auto-stop**

hitchhiking   **l'auto-stop** *(m)*
hitchhiker   **un auto-stoppeur, une auto-stoppeuse**
I honk   **je klaxonne**
insurance   **l'assurance** *(f)*
I am insured   **je suis assuré**
insurance policy   **la police d'assurance**
I keep my distance   **je garde mes distances**
key   **la clef**
keyring   **le porte-clefs**
line of cars   **la file de voitures**
logbook   **le journal de bord**
make of car   **la marque de voiture**
maximum speed   **la vitesse maximum**
mechanic   **le mécanicien, la mécanicienne**
mechanical   **mécanique**
motel   **le motel**
motorbike   **le vélo**
motor show   **le salon automobile**
motor vehicle certification   **le certificat de contrôle**
one-way only   **le sens unique**
I park   **je me gare**
parking   **le stationnement**
parking ban   **l'interdiction** *(f)* **de stationner**
parking fine   **la contravention**
parking meter   **le parcmètre**
parking ticket (fine)   **la contravention pour stationnement illégal**

– Here is my driver's license: as you can see it is still perfectly valid.

Voici mon permis de conduire, comme vous pouvez le voir, il est parfaitement valable.

I wonder how much the toll is for this expressway section?

Je me demande combien coûte le péage sur ce tronçon d'autoroute.

This new model has very low gas consumption.

Cette nouvelle voiture consomme très peu.

parking ticket *(permit)* **le ticket de stationnement**
I pass **je passe, je double**
passing **le dépassement**
passage **le passage**
passenger **le passager, la passagère**
pedestrian **le piéton, la piétonne**
picnic area **l'aire *(f)* de pique-nique**
police **la police**
police station **le commissariat**
private car **la voiture privée**
public transport **le transport public**
I put on my seat belt **j'attache ma ceinture**
recreational vehicle, camper **le camping-car**
registration papers **les papiers *(m)* d'immatriculation**
I rent **je loue**
rental car **la voiture de location**
rental charge **les frais de location**
repair **la réparation**
I repair **je répare**
I reverse **je fais marche arrière**
right of way **la priorité**
road **la route, le chemin**
    by road **par la route**
road accident **l'accident *(m)* de la route**
road block **le barrage routier**
road hog **le chauffard**
road map **la carte routière**
road sign **le panneau indicateur**
road signals **la signalisation**
road works **les travaux *(m)***
route **l'itinéraire *(m)***
I run over **j'écrase**
rush hour **les heures *(f)* de pointe**
second-hand car **la voiture d'occasion**
self-service **le libre-service**
semi, tractor trailer **le semi-remorque**
service **le service**

service area **l'aire *(f)* de service**
I set off **je me mets *(se mettre)* en route**
signal **le signal**
signpost **le poteau indicateur**
slippery **glissant, du verglacé**
slow **lent**
I slow down **je ralentis**
speed **la vitesse**
I speed up **j'accélère *(accélérer)***
speed limit **la limitation de vitesse**
I start (engine) **je démarre**
statement **la déclaration**
student driver **un élève conducteur, une élève conductrice**
I switch off **j'éteins *(éteindre)***
I switch on **j'allume**
taxi/cab **le taxi**
taxi/cab driver **le chauffeur de taxi**
taxi station **la station de taxis**
I test **je teste**
toll **le péage**
I tow away **je remorque**
town plan **le plan de la ville**
town traffic **le trafic urbain**
traffic **la circulation**
traffic jam **l'embouteillage *(m)***
traffic light **les feux *(m)* de signalisation**
traffic news **l'information *(f)* routière**
traffic police **la police de la route**
traffic violation **l'infraction *(f)* au code de la route**
traffic warden **l'agent *(m)* de la circulation**
traffic-free zone **la zone piétonne**
trailer **la caravane**
trip **le voyage**
truck **le camion**
truck driver **le routier**
I turn left **je tourne à gauche**
I turn right **je tourne à droite**
I turn off (engine) **j'arrête le moteur**
underground garage **le parking**

souterrain
U turn **le demi-tour**
vehicle **le véhicule**
I wait **j'attends**
warning **l'avertisseur** *(m)*
witness **le témoin**

Roads and streets

access road **la bretelle d'accès**
alley **l'allée** *(f)*
avenue **l'avenue** *(f)*
bend/curve **le virage**
bridge **le pont**
built-up area **l'agglomération** *(f)*
bump **la bosse**
bypass **la rocade**
central reservation **le terre-plein central**
closed *(road)* **barrée**
corner **le coin**
crossing **le croisement**
crossroad **le carrefour**
cul-de-sac **la voie sans issue, l'impasse** *(f)*
emergency lane, shoulder **la bande d'arrêt d'urgence**
highway, expressway **l'autoroute** *(f)*
  entry **l'entrée** *(f)* **de l'autoroute**
  exit **la sortie de l'autoroute**

inside lane **la voie de droite**
intersection **l'intersection** *(f)*
junction **la sortie**
lane **la voie**
level crossing **le passage à niveau**
main street **la rue principale**
one-way street **la rue à sens unique**
outside lane **la voie de gauche**
pedestrian crossing **le passage pour piétons**
pedestrian island **le refuge pour piétons**
ramp **la dénivellation**
rest stop **l'aire** *(f)* **de stationnement**
ring road **la rocade**
road **la route, le chemin**
rotary, traffic circle **le rond-point**
side street **la petite rue**
speed bump **le ralentisseur**
square **la place**
street **la rue**
underground passage **le passage souterrain**
white/yellow line **la ligne blanche/jaune**

There has been a serious accident on route A1 between exits 7 and 8. A truck traveling toward Paris has crashed against the central barrier. Three vehicles are involved and one of the drivers is seriously injured. I have put on the hazard lights.

Delays are expected at the next exit.

Il y a eu un sérieux accident sur l'autoroute A1 entre les sorties 7 et 8. Un camion qui voyageait vers Paris s'est écrasé contre la barrière de sécurité.
Trois véhicules sont impliqués et un des conducteurs est sérieusement bléssé. J'ai mis mes feux de détresse.

On s'attend à des encombrements à la prochaine sortie.

➤ PARTS OF THE CAR App.19c; DIRECTIONS 2b

19d Travel by air

airplane **l'aéroplane** *(m)*
aircraft **l'avion** *(m)*
airline **la ligne aérienne**
airline desk **le guichet de la ligne aérienne**
air travel **le voyage en avion**
airport **l'aéroport** *(m)*
I am airsick **j'ai le mal de l'air**
baggage **les bagages** *(m)*
body search **la fouille corporelle**
I board a plane **j'embarque à bord d'un avion**
boarding card **la carte d'embarquement**
business class **la classe affaires**
by air **par avion**
cabin **la cabine**
canceled flight **le vol annulé**
carousel baggage claim **le tapis roulant à bagages**
charter flight **le vol charter**
I check in **j'enregistre**
check-in desk **l'enregistrement** *(m)*
control tower **la tour de contrôle**

copilot **le copilote**
courier **accompagnateur**
crew **l'équipage** *(m)*
desk **le guichet**
direct flight **le vol direct**
domestic flights **le vol intérieur**
during the flight **pendant le vol**
duty-free goods **les produits** *(m)* **détaxés**
economy class **la classe économique**
emergency exit **la sortie de secours**
emergency landing **l'atterrissage** *(m)* **d'urgence**
excess baggage **le surplus de bagages**
I fasten **j'attache**
flight **le vol**
flight attendant **le steward, l'hôtesse** *(f)* **de l'air**
I fly **je vole**
I fly at a height of **je vole à une altitude de**
flying **l'aviation** *(f)*

Can I make a connection to Lyons? Do I have to change flight?

Puis-je avoir une correspondance pour Lyon? Est-ce que je dois changer d'avion?

– I have some excess luggage.

– J'ai un surplus de bagages.

– Have you packed your luggage yourself?

– Avez-vous fait vos bagages vous-même?

Will Mr and Mrs Lebrun traveling on flight AZ 131 to Paris-Orly please contact the Information desk immediately.

Monsieur et Madame Lebrun voyageant sur le vol AZ 131 à destination de Paris-Orly sont priés de contacter le bureau d'informations immédiatement.

Where do I check in for flight AZ 537?

Où dois-je enregistrer mes bagages pour le vol AZ 537?

fuselage **le fuselage**
gate **la porte**
instruction **les instructions** *(f)*
hand luggage **les bagages** *(m)* à **main**
headphones **les écouteurs** *(m)*
highjacker **le pirate de l'air**
immigrant **un immigré, une immigrée**
immigration **l'immigration** *(f)*
immigration rules **les lois** *(f)* **d'immigration**
I land **j'atterris**
landing **l'atterrissage** *(m)*
landing lights **les lumières d'atterrissage**
life jacket **le gilet de sauvetage**
no-smoking sign **le panneau non-fumeur**
nonstop **sans escale**
on board **à bord**
parachute **le parachute**
passenger **le passager, la passagère**

passenger lounge **la salle d'embarquement**
passport control **le contrôle des passeports**
pilot **le pilote**
plane **l'avion** *(m)*
refreshments **le repas (léger), les rafraîchissements** *(m)*
runway **la piste**
security measures **les mesures** *(f)* **de sécurité**
security staff **le personnel de sécurité**
steward **le steward**
stewardess **l'hôtesse** *(f)* **de l'air**
I take off **je décolle**
takeoff **le décollage**
terminal **le terminal, l'aérsgare** *(f)*
tray **le plateau**
turbulence **la perturbation**
view **la vue**
window seat **le fauteuil côté fenêtre**

There is some turbulence on the Alps. The expected landing time is at 11:40, local time.

Il y a des perturbations au-dessus des Alpes. L'atterrissage est prévu pour 11h40, heure locale.

Last call for passengers traveling on flight BZ 881 to Marseilles!

Dernier appel pour les passagers du vol BZ 881 à destination de Marseille!

My luggage has not yet been unloaded.

Mes bagages n'ont pas encore été déchargés.

How long is the delay?

Combien de temps va durer le retard?

What is the flight number?

Quel est le numéro du vol?

➤ HOLIDAYS AND VACATIONS 20

19e Travel by rail

announcement	**l'annonce** (f)
barrier	**la barrière**
buffet	**le buffet**
coach	**le wagon**
compartment	**le compartiment**
connection	**la correspondance**
dining car	**le wagon-restaurant**
exemption	**l'exemption** (f)
fare	**le prix du billet**
inspector	**le contrôleur**
I lean out	**je me penche à la fenêtre**
level crossing	**le passage à niveau**
luggage rack	**le porte-bagages**
I miss	**je rate**
nonrefundable	**non-remboursable**
nonsmoker	**le non-fumeur**

occupied	**occupé**
on time	**à l'heure**
platform	**le quai**
porter	**le porteur**
I punch (ticket)	**je poinçonne**
railroad	**le chemin de fer**
elevated railway	**le métro aérien**
railroad station	**la gare**
railroad tracks	**les rails**
ramp	**la rampe**
reduction	**la réduction**
reservation	**la réservation**
reserved	**réservé**
sleeper	**la couchette**
sleeping car	**le wagon-lit**
smoker	**le fumeur, la fumeuse**
snack car	**la voiture-bar**

A special announcement:
On Sundays and holidays the service to Toulon does not operate and on weekdays after 9 a.m. fares are subject to supplementary charges.
In addition, reservations are required for seats in the non-smoking compartments on the Bordeaux service.

We apologise for any inconvenience.

The 11:45 to Orleans is now leaving from platform 10.

The express train to Lille will depart from platform 4 in 5 minutes.

Une annonce spéciale:
Le service de Toulon ne circule pas les dimanches et jours fériés, et est sujet à supplément les jours de la semaine après neuf heures.
D'autre part, une réservation est obligatoire pour les places assises dans les compartiments non-fumeurs sur le service de Bordeaux.
Nous vous prions de nous excuser pour tout désagrément.

Le train de 11h45 à destination d'Orléans au départ quai numéro 10.

Le train express à destination de Lille partira dans 5 minutes, quai numéro 4.

speed **la vitesse**
stairs **les escaliers** *(m)*
stationmaster **le chef de gare**
stop **un arrêt**
subway **le métro**
supplement **le supplément**
ticket **le billet**
  first/second-class ticket **un billet de première/deuxième classe**
  group ticket **un billet de groupe**
  single/one-way ticket **un aller simple**
  return ticket **un aller-retour**
ticket collector **le contrôleur de billets**
ticket office **le guichet**
timetable **l'horaire** *(m)*
  summer/winter timetable **l'horaire d'été/d'hiver**
timetable changes **les changements** *(m)* **d'horaire**
track **la voie**
traveler **le voyageur, la voyageuse**
train **le train**
  direct train **le train direct**
  express train **l'express** *(m)*
  Intercity train **l'interurbain** *(m)*
  local train **le train de banlieue**
  night train **le train de nuit**
trolley/cart **le chariot**
underground **le métro**
user **l'usager** *(m)*
I wait **j'attends** *(attendre)*
waiting room **la salle d'attente**
warning **la mise en garde, un avertissement**
window **la fenêtre**

– Where do I have to change?
– To go to the Eiffel Tower, you need to change at the next stop. Take the line to Nation and get off at Champ de Mars.

– Où dois-je changer?
Pour aller à la tour Eiffel, il faut changer au prochain arrêt. Prenez la direction Nation et descendez à Champ de Mars.

Excuse me, this a nonsmoking compartment.

Excusez-moi, ceci est un compartiment non-fumeur.

This is a public announcement for all passengers traveling to Geneva. We are sorry to announce that this service is subject to delays. There will also be a platform change.

Ceci est un message pour tous les passagers à destination de Genève. Nous sommes désolés de vous annoncer que cette ligne sera sujette à des retards. Il y aura également un changement de quai.

There are no facilities for disabled travelers on this train.

Ce train n'est pas aménagé pour les handicapés.

Holidays and vacations

20a General terms

abroad **à l'étranger**
accommodation **le logement**
alone **seul**
area **la région**
arrival **l'arrivée** *(f)*
available **libre**
backpack/knapsack **le sac à dos**
beach **la plage**
camera **l'appareil-***(m)* **photo**
clean **propre**
climate **le climat**
closed **fermé**
clothes **les vêtements** *(m)*
cold **froid**
comfort **le confort**
comfortable **confortable**
congested **encombré**
cost **le coût**
country **le pays**
countryside **la campagne**
dirty **sale**
disadvantage **l'inconvénient** *(m)*
disorganized **désorganisé**
exchange **l'échange** *(m)*
fire **le feu**
folding chair **la chaise pliante**
folding table **la table pliante**
food **la nourriture**
free **gratuit**
full **plein**
I go **je vais** *(aller)*
group **le groupe**
group travel **le voyage en groupe**
guide **le/la guide**
guide book **le guide (de voyage)**
guided tour **la visite guidée**
guided walk **la promenade guidée**
holidays/vacation **les vacances** *(f)*
land **le terrain**
landscape **le paysage**

journey **le trajet**
mild *(climate)* **doux [-se]**
money **l'argent** *(m)*
no vacancy **complet**
open **ouvert**
organization **l'organisation** *(f)*
I organize **j'organise**
organized **organisé**
plan (town) **le plan (de la ville)**
I plan **j'envisage**
portable **portable**
I return (to a place) **je retourne (à un lieu)**
sea **la mer**
seascape **le panorama marin**
seaside resort **la station balnéaire**
show **un spectacle**
I show **je montre**
sight **la vue**
I spend time **je passe du temps à**
stay **le séjour**
I stay **je reste**
sun **le soleil**
sunny **ensoleillé**
I sunbathe **je prends** *(prendre)* **un bain de soleil**
I tan/go brown **je bronze**
tour **la visite**
tourism **le tourisme**
tourist **le/la touriste**
tourist menu **le menu touristique**
tourist office **l'office** *(m)* **du tourisme**
town **la ville**
town plan **le plan de la ville**
travel **le voyage**
I travel **je voyage**
travel adaptor **l'adaptateur** *(m)*
trip **l'excursion** *(f)*
I understand **je comprends**

I unpack **je défais** *(défaire)* **mes bagages**
visit **la visite**
I visit **je visite**
visiting hours **les heures** *(f)* **de visite**
visitors **les visiteurs** *(m)*
welcome **la bienvenue**
worth seeing **qui vaut la peine d'être vu**

Holiday and vacation activities

beach holiday/vacation **à la plage**
boating holiday/vacation **les vacances** *(m)* **en bateau**
camping **faire du camping**
canoing **faire du canoë**
coach holiday/vacation **les vacances** *(m)* **en car**
cruise **faire une croisière**
cycling **faire du vélo**
fishing **la pêche**

fruit picking **cueillir des fruits**
home exchange **l'échange** *(m)* **de maison**
hunting **la chasse**
motoring holiday/vacation **les vacances** *(f)* **en voiture/auto**
mountain climbing **l'alpinisme** *(m)*
rock climbing **l'escalade** *(f)*
safari **faire un safari**
sailing **la voile**
shopping **les courses** *(f)*
sightseeing **le tourisme**
skiing **faire du ski**
study holiday/vacation **le voyage/ les vacances** *(f)* **d'études**
sunbathing **le bain de soleil**
trekking **le voyage-randonnée**
volunteer work **le travail bénévole**
walking **la marche**
wine tasting **la dégustation de vins**

Dear coworkers,

Having a wonderful holiday/ vacation. The weather is hot (I've a great tan), the campsite is clean, and the local food is excellent.

The kids are having a great time too, enjoying playing in the water, building sandcastles, and making lots of friends.

I'm not looking forward to coming home!

Best wishes, Sarah.

Chers collègues,

Vacances merveilleuses. Il fait chaud (je suis bien bronzée), le camping est propre, et la cuisine locale excellente.

Les enfants aussi s'amusent beaucoup, ils aiment jouer dans l'eau, faire des châteaux de sable et se sont fait beaucoup d'amis.

La perspective du retour ne me réjouit pas!

Meilleurs vœux, Sarah.

LEISURE 16a; ON THE BEACH App. 20a; THE WEATHER 24d **159**

20b Accommodation and hotel

Accommodation

apartment **l'appartement** *(m)*
bed and breakfast **la chambre d'hôte**
camper/trailer **la caravane**
campsite **le camping**
chalet **le chalet**
country cottage **le gîte rural**
farm **la ferme**
full board **la pension complète**
half board **la demi-pension**
home exchange **l'échange** *(m)* **de maison**
hotel **l'hôtel** *(m)*
mobile home **le mobile home**
inn **l'auberge** *(f)*, **l'hôtel** *(m)*
vacation rental property **le meublé, les vacances** *(f)* **en location**
villa **la villa** *(f)*
youth hostel **l'auberge** *(f)* **de jeunesse**

Booking and payment

affordable **qu'on peut se permettre**
all included **tout compris**
bill **la note**
I book **je réserve**
brochure **la brochure**
I cash **j'encaisse**
cheap **bon marché**
check **le chèque**
cost **le coût**
credit card **la carte de crédit**

credit **le crédit**
economical **économique, pas cher [chère]**
Eurocheque **l'eurochèque** *(m)*
expensive **cher [chère]**
excluding **non compris**
exclusive **en sus**
extra charge **le supplément**
extravagant **exorbitant**
fee **les droits** *(m)*
I fill in **je remplis**
form **le formulaire**
free **libre, gratuit**
inclusive **(y) compris**
I pay **je paie** *(payer)*
payment **le paiement**
price list **le tarif**
receipt **le reçu**
reduction **la réduction**
refund **le remboursement**
I reserve **je réserve**
reservation **la réservation**
I sign **je signe**
signature **la signature**
traveler's check **le chèque de voyage**

Hotel

air-conditioning **la climatisation**
amenities **les aménagements** *(m)*
balcony **le balcon**
bath **le bain**
bed **le lit**
bedding **la literie**

I'd like to complain.	**Je veux faire une réclamation.**
The hot water tap does not work and the elevator is out of order. There is only one coat hanger in the wardrobe; and I asked for a room with a view.	**Le robinet d'eau chaude ne fonctionne pas et l'ascenseur est en panne. Il n'y a qu'un porte-manteau dans l'armoire, et j'avais demandé une chambre avec vue.**

bedspread **le couvre-lit**
billiard room **la salle de billard**
board **la pension**
    full board **la pension complète**
    half board **la demi-pension**
breakfast **le petit déjeuner**
broken **cassé**
call **l'appel** *(m)*
I check in **je remplis une fiche**
I check out **je règle ma note**
comfortable **confortable**
I complain **je me plains**
complaint **la plainte**
conference **la conférence**
conference facilities **les falles pour,
les facilités pour conférence**
damage **les dégâts** *(m)*
dining room **la salle à manger**
early-morning call **le réveil matinal**
elevator **l'ascenseur** *(m)*
en-suite bathroom **la salle de
bains attenante**
evening meal **le dîner**
facilities **les locaux** *(m)*
fire exit **la sortie de secours**
fire extinguisher **l'extincteur** *(m)*
guest **le client, la cliente**
hairdresser **le coiffeur, la
coiffeuse**
hairdryer **le sèche-cheveux**
hall **le hall**
heating **le chauffage**
hotel **l'hôtel** *(m)*
laundry **le linge**
laundry bag **le bac à linge**
laundry service **le service de**

blanchisserie
meal **le repas**
night porter **le portier de service
de nuit**
noisy **bruyant**
overnight bag **le nécessaire de
voyage**
pants press **le presse-pantalon**
parking space **la place de parking**
plug *(bath)* **la bonde**
    plug *(electric)* **la prise**
porter **le porteur**
privacy **l'intimité** *(f)*
private toilet **les toilettes** *(f)*
privées
reception **la réception**
receptionist **le/la réceptionniste**
room **la chambre**
    double room **la chambre
double/pour deux personnes**
    family room **la chambre
familiale**
    room with twin beds **la
chambre à lits jumeaux**
room service **le service des
chambres**
service **le service**
shower **la douche**
showercap **le bonnet de
douche**
stay **le séjour**
I stay **je reste**
view **la vue**
water **l'eau** *(f)*
    hot water **l'eau chaude** *(f)*
welcome **la bienvenue**

I'd like to reserve a room with a
double bed and attached bathroom
for three days from March 4th.

**Je voudrais réserver une
chambre avec un lit pour deux
personnes et salle de bains pour
trois jours à partir du 4 mars.**

DO NOT DISTURB!
PRESS BUTTON!

**NE PAS DERANGER!
APPUYEZ SUR LE BOUTON!**

➤ THE HOUSE 8a; FURNISHINGS 8b, 8c; DRINKS AND MEALS 10a

20c Camping and vacation rentals

Camping

air bed	**le matelas pneumatique**
antihistamine cream	**la crème antihistaminique**
ants	**les fourmis** *(f)*
ashcan	**la poubelle**
barbeque	**le barbecue**
battery	**la pile**
camp bed	**le lit de camp**
camper	**le campeur, la campeuse**
camper/trailer	**la caravane**
camping equipment/gear	**l'équipement** *(m)* **de camping**
camping	**faire du camping**
camping gas	**le butane**
campsite	**le terrain de camping**
connected	**branché**
cooking facilities	**les cuisines** *(f)*
disconnected	**débranché**
drinking water	**l'eau** *(f)* **potable**
extension lead	**la rallonge**
flashlight	**la lampe de poche**

forbidden	**interdit**
gas cooker	**la cuisinière à gaz**
gas cylinder	**la bouteille de gaz**
groundsheet	**le tapis de sol**
I camp	**je campe**
I pitch/put up my tent	**je plante/dresse la tente**
I take down my tent	**je démonte la tente**
in the dark	**dans le noir**
laundromat	**la laverie automatique**
mosquito bite	**la piqûre de moustique**
mosquito net	**la moustiquaire**
mosquitos	**les moustiques** *(m)*
pans	**les casseroles** *(f)*
potty chair	**le pot (de bébé)**
registration	**l'inscription** *(f)*
services	**les services** *(m)*
sheet	**le drap**
showers	**les douches** *(f)*

– Where shall we put up the tent?
– Away from the main block.
– I'll pitch it in the shade.
– No, it is a bit damp there. This is better here and there are no mosquitos.

– **Où va-t-on dresser la tente?**
– **Loin du pavillon principal.**
– **Je la planterai à l'ombre.**
– **Non, c'est un peu humide là. Ici c'est mieux; il n'y a pas de moustiques.**

– Where's the flashlight? It's not in the tent.
– It was in your knapsack just now.

– **Où est la lampe de poche? Elle n'est pas dans la tente.**
– **Elle était dans ton sac à dos à l'instant.**

– Keep your voice down, please, we are trying to sleep!

– **Taisez-vous un peu, s'il vous plaît, nous essayons de dormir!**

Do you have a few spare clothespegs?

Avez-vous des pinces à linge en trop?

Did you bring a bottle opener?

As-tu apporté un ouvre-boîtes?

site/space **l'emplacement** *(m)*
sleeping bag **le sac de couchage**
space **la place**
tent **la tente**
tent peg **le piquet**
tin opener **l'ouvre-boîtes** *(m)*
toilet/restroom **les toilettes** *(f)*
vehicles **les véhicules** *(m)*
washing facilities **les sanitaires**
  (m), **le bloc sanitaire**
water filter **le filtre d'eau**

Vacation rentals

agency **l'agence** *(f)*
agreement **l'accord** *(m)*
amenities **les aménagements** *(m)*
apartment **l'appartement** *(m)*
clean **propre**
I clean **je nettoie** *(nettoyer)*
I cook **je fais la cuisine**
damaged **endommagé**
damages **les dégâts** *(m)*
dangerous **dangereux**

electricity **l'électricité** *(f)*
equipment **le matériel**
farm **la ferme**
maid **la bonne**
meter *(electricity, etc.)* **le**
  compteur
owner **le/la propriétaire**
rent **le loyer**
I rent **je loue**
I rent out **je donne en location**
repair **la réparation**
I repair **je répare**
I return *(give back)* **je rends**
ruined **en ruine**
self-service **le libre-service**
set of keys **le jeu de clés**
I share **je partage**
shutters **les volets** *(m)*
smelly **malodorant**
spare keys **le double des clés**
water supply **la provision d'eau**
well **le puit**
well kept **bien entretenu**

The apartment is close to all amenities, just a few kilometers from the nearest shops and convenient to the swimming pool.

L'appartement est proche de tous les aménagements; il se situe à quelques kilomètres des magasins les plus proches, et est commode pour la piscine.

There are no blankets, the stove doesn't work, and there is a frog in the bathroom.

Il n'y a pas de couvertures, le four ne marche pas, et il y a une grenouille dans la salle de bains.

How do you lock the door?

Comment fermez-vous la porte à clé?

Are there any spare bulbs?

Y a-t-il des ampoules de rechange?

You will find the electricity meter under the stairs.

Vous trouverez le compteur d'électricité sous les escaliers.

Language

21a General terms

accuracy **la fidélité**
accurate **fidèle**
I adapt **j'adapte**
I adopt **je choisis**
advanced **supérieur**
aptitude **l'aptitude** *(f)*
artificial language **le langage artificiel**
based on **basé sur**
bilingual **bilingue**
bilingualism **le bilinguisme**
borrowing **l'emprunt** *(m)*
branch **le rameau**
classical languages **les langues** *(f)* **classiques**
it is derived from **il dérive de**
development **le développement**
difficult **difficile**
easy **facile**
error **l'erreur** *(f)*
foreign language **la langue étrangère**
    foreign language *(to learn)* **une langue d'apprentissage**
I forget **j'oublie**
French speaker **le francophone**
French-speaking countries **les**

pays *(m)* **francophones**
grammar **la grammaire**
grammatical **grammatical**
I improve **je fais des progrès**
influence **l'influence** *(f)*
known **connu**
language **la langue**
    language course **le cours de langues**
    language family **la famille linguistique**
    language school **l'école** *(m)* **de langues**
    language skills **les compétences** *(f)* **linguistiques**
Latin **le latin**
I learn **j'apprends** *(apprendre)*
learning **l'apprentissage** *(m)*
level **le niveau**
linguistics **la linguistique**
link **la liaison, le lien**
living **vivant**
major languages **les langues** *(f)* **principales**
it means **il signifie**
I mime **je mime**
minor languages **les langues** *(f)*

I am not very good at languages, but my sister is a gifted linguist.

She learned French and Italian in school, then she traveled extensively and picked up Bulgarian and Urdu while working as a volunteer.

Je ne suis pas très doué pour les langues, mais ma sœur est une excellente linguiste.
Elle a appris le français et l'italien à l'école, puis le bulgare et l'ourdou à l'occasion des nombreux voyages qu'elle a faits quand elle travaillait en tant que volontaire/bénévole.

secondaires
mistake **la faute**
modern languages **les langues** *(f)* **vivantes**
monolingual **monolingue**
mother tongue **la langue maternelle**
mutation **la mutation**
name **le nom**
nation **la nation**
national **national**
native speaker **le locuteur natif, la locutrice native**
natural **naturel[le]**
official **officiel[le]**
offshoot **la conséquence**
origin **l'origine** *(f)*
phenomenon **le phénomène**
I practice **je m'exerce**
preserved **entretenu**
question **la question**
register **le registre**
self-assessment **l'auto-évaluation** *(f)*
separate **distinct**
sign language **le langage par signes**
survival **la survivance**
it survives **il survit** *(survivre)*
target language **la langue cible**
I teach **j'enseigne**
teacher **un enseignant, une enseignante**

teaching **l'enseignement** *(m)*
test **l'interrogation** *(f)*
I test **j'interroge**
I translate **je traduis** *(traduire)*
translation **la traduction**
I understand **je comprends**
unknown **inconnu**
widely **généralement**

Words and vocabulary

antonym **l'antonyme** *(m)*
colloquial **familier [-ère]**
consonant **la consonne**
dictionary **le dictionnaire**
expression **l'expression** *(f)*
idiom **l'idiome** *(m)*
idiomatic **idiomatique**
jargon **le jargon**
lexicographer **le lexicographe**
lexicon **le lexique**
phrase **la locution**
phrase book **le guide de conversation**
sentence **la phrase**
slang **l'argot** *(m)*
syllable **la syllabe**
synonym **le synonyme**
vocabulary **le vocabulaire**
vowel **la voyelle**
witticism **le mot d'esprit**
word **le mot**
word game **le jeu de mots**

Lesser languages may disappear. However, thanks to the oral tradition in some communities, a few have been preserved.

Les langues moins importantes ont peut-être tendance à disparaître. Toutefois, grâce à la tradition orale de certaines communautés, quelques-unes ont pu être préservées.

21b Using language

Speaking and listening

accent **l'accent** *(m)*
   regional accent **l'accent régional**
articulate **bien articulé**
I articulate **j'articule**
clear **clair**
I communicate **je communique**
conversation **la conversation**
I converse **je converse**
dialect **le dialecte**
diction **la diction**
I express myself **je m'exprime**
fluent **qui parle couramment**
fluently **couramment**
I interpret **je fais l'interprète**
interpreter **un/une interprète**
intonation **l'intonation** *(f)*
lisp **le zézaiement**
I lisp **je zézaie**
I listen **j'écoute**
listener **un auditeur, une auditrice**
listening **l'écoute** *(f)*
listening skills **la compréhension orale**

I mispronounce **je prononce mal**
mispronunciation **la faute de prononciation**
oral(ly) **oral, à l'oral**
phonetics **la phonétique**
I pronounce **je prononce**
pronunciation **la prononciation**
rhythm **le rythme**
sound **le son**
he sounds French **il a un accent français**
I speak **je parle**
speaker **un interlocuteur, une interlocutrice**
speaking **parlant**
speaking skills **l'art** *(m)* **oratoire**
speech **l'élocution** *(f)*
speed **la vitesse**
spoken **parlé**
spoken language **le langage parlé**
stress **l'accentuation** *(f)*
stressed (un-) **(in)accentué**
I stutter/stammer **je bégaie *(bégayer)***
unpronounceable **imprononçable**
verbally **verbalement**

– I have no difficulty in reading French, but I don't understand it when people speak very fast or with a strong regional accent.

– Je lis le français sans problème, mais je ne le comprends pas quand on parle très vite ou avec un fort accent régional.

– Do you practice French with a native speaker?
– No, I prefer to attend a class.

– Pratiquez-vous le français avec un francophone?
– Non, je préfère suivre des cours.

Do you have any previous knowledge of Russian?

Connaissez-vous déjà le russe?

Writing & reading

accent l'accent *(m)*
  grave/acute/circumflex
  grave/aigu/circonflexe
alphabet **l'alphabet** *(m)*
alphabetically **par ordre**
  alphabétique
in bold **en gras**
Braille **braille**
character **le caractère**
code **le code**
I correspond (with) **je**
  corresponds (avec)
correspondence **la**
  correspondance
I decipher **je déchiffre**
graphic **graphique**
handwriting **l'écriture** *(f)*
icon **l'icône** *(f)*
ideogram/ideograph
  l'idéogramme *(m)*
illiterate **analphabète**
in italics **en italique**
I italicize **je mets** *(mettre)* **en**
  italique
letter *(of alphabet)* **la lettre**
literate **instruit, qui sait lire et**
  écrire

literature **la littérature**
note **la note**
paragraph **le paragraphe**
philology **la philologie**
philologist **le/la philologue**
pictograph **l'idéogramme** *(m)*
plain text **le texte simple**
I print **j'imprime**
I read **je lis** *(lire)*
reading **la lecture**
reading skills **l'aptitude** *(f)* **à lire**
I rewrite **je récris** *(récrire)*
scribble **la gribouillage**
I scribble **je gribouille**
sign **le signe**
I sign **je signe**
signature **la signature**
I spell **j'épelle** *(épeler)*
spelling **l'orthographe** *(f)*
text **le texte**
I transcribe **je transcris**
transcription **la transcription**
I underline **je souligne**
I write **j'écris** *(écrire)*
writing **l'écriture** *(f)*
writing skills **l'art** *(m)* **d'écrire**
written language **la langue écrite**

Which languages have a Cyrillic alphabet?

Quelles langues ont un alphabet slave?

– Which is the easiest language to learn for an English speaker? – French, of course!

– Quelle est la langue la plus facile à apprendre pour un anglophone? – Le français, naturellement!

Portuguese spoken here.

Ici on parle portugais.

Don't worry about spelling mistakes for the moment.

Ne vous souciez pas des fautes d'orthographe pour l'instant.

Education

22a General terms

achievement **la réussite**
admission **l'admission** *(f)*
    I am admitted to school **je suis admis** *(admettre)* à l'école
absent **absent**
age group **le groupe d'âge**
I am away **je suis absent**
aptitude **l'aptitude** *(f)*
I analyze **j'analyse**
answer **la réponse**
I answer **je réponds (à)**
I ask (a question) **je pose (une question)**
    I ask *(someone)* **je demande (à)**
I attend (a school) **je suis élève (à l'école)**
boring **ennuyeux [-se], barbant**
career **la carrière**
career advice **le conseil d'orientation**
caretaker **le/la concierge**
I catch up **je rattrape**
chapter **le chapitre**
cheat **le tricheur, la tricheuse**
class **la classe**
class council **le conseil de classe**
class representative **le délégué de classe**
class teacher **le professeur**
class trip **le voyage scolaire**
club **le club**
I complete **je termine**
comprehension **la compréhension**
compulsory schooling **la scolarité obligatoire**
concept **le concept**

I copy (out) **je recopie**
copy **l'exemplaire** *(m)*
course **des cours** *(m)*
I cut classes/play hooky **je sèche** *(sécher)* **les cours** *(fam)*, **je fais l'école buissonnière** *(fam)*
deputy head **le directeur-adjoint**
detention **la retenue, la colle**
    I am in detention **je suis en retenue, je suis collé**
difficult **difficile**
I discuss **je discute**
easy **facile**
education **l'éducation** *(f)*, **l'enseignement** *(m)*
educational system **le système pédagogique**
I encourage **j'encourage**
essay **la dissertation, la rédaction**
example **l'exemple** *(m)*
excellent **excellent**
favorite **préféré**
favorite subject **la matière préférée**
I forget **j'oublie**
governing body **l'administration**
guidance counselor **le conseiller/ la conseillère d'orientation professionnelle**
holidays/vacation **les vacances** *(f)*
homework **les devoirs** *(m)*
interesting **intéressant**
I learn **j'apprends** *(apprendre)*
I leave **je quitte**
lesson *(class)* **le cours**
    lesson *(chapter)* **la leçon**

I listen **j'écoute**

local education authority **le rectorat, l'académie** *(f)*

I look at **je regarde**

I misunderstand **je ne comprends pas**

mixed-ability group **le groupe de plusieurs niveaux**

modular **par module**

module **le module**

oral **oral**

outdoor **à l'extérieur, en plein air**

extracurricular activity **les activités** *(m)* **parascolaires**

parent-teacher meeting **la réunion parents-enseignants**

I pass/qualify **je suis qualifié**

pastoral care **l'éducation** *(f)* **religieuse**

I praise **j'admire**

principal *(n)* **le directeur, la directrice, le principal**

principal *(adj)* **principal**

project **la recherche**

punctual **ponctuel[le]**

I punctuate **je ponctue**

punctuation mark **la ponctuation**

I punish **je punis**

punishment **la punition**

pupil **un/une élève**

qualification **les qualifications** *(f)*

question **la question**

I question **je mets** *(mettre)* **en doute**

I read **je lis** *(lire)*

reading **la lecture**

I repeat a year **je redouble**

repeating a year **le redoublement**

report **le bulletin**

research **la recherche**

I research **je fais de la recherche**

resources center **le centre de documentation**

scheme of work **le plan de travail**

school book **le livre de classe**

school council **le conseil d'administration**

school friend **le/la camarade**

set **le groupe de niveau**

setted *(by ability)* **classés par groupes de niveau**

skill **l'aptitude** *(f)*

specialist teacher **le professeur** *(m)* **spécialisé**

spelling **l'orthographe** *(f)*

staff **le personnel (enseignant)**

I stay in **je reste**

I stay down *(a year)* **je ne passe pas**

stream **le groupe de niveau**

strict **sévère**

I study **j'étudie**

sum **la somme**

I summarize **je résume**

I work hard **je bûche** *(fam)*

syllabus, courses **les cours** *(m)*

task **l'exercice** *(m)*

I teach **j'enseigne**

teacher **l'enseignant** *(m)*, **l'enseignante** *(f)*

teaching **l'enseignement** *(m)*

term/semester **le trimestre**

I train **je suis** *(suivre)* **une formation (de)**

training **la formation**

I translate **je traduis**

translation **la traduction**

tutor **le tuteur**

I understand **je comprends**

understanding **la compréhension**

unit (of work) **le chapitre**

I work **je travaille**

I work hard (at) **je travaille dur, je bosse (sur)**

work experience **l'expérience** *(f)* **professionnelle**

I write **j'écris** *(écrire)*

written (work) **(le travail) écrit**

EDUCATION

22b School

blackboard   **le tableau**
book   **le livre**
break   **la récréation**
briefcase   **le cartable**
canteen   **la cantine**
cassette (audio/video)   **la cassette (audio/vidéo)**
cassette recorder   **le magnétophone**
classroom   **la salle de classe**
computer   **l'ordinateur** *(m)*
desk   **le bureau**
dormitory   **le dortoir**
gym(nasium)   **le gymnase**
headphone   **les écouteurs** *(m)*
interactive TV   **la télévision interactive**
(language) laboratory   **le laboratoire (de langues)**
library   **la bibliothèque**
lunch hour   **l'heure** *(f)* **du repas**
note   **le message**
office   **le bureau**
playground   **la cour de récréation**
radio   **la radio**
ruler   **la règle**
slide   **la diapositive**
satellite TV   **la télévision par satellite**
school hall   **le hall de réunion**
schoolbag/bookbag   **le cartable**
sports field   **le terrain de sport**

staff room   **la salle des professeurs**
studio   **le studio**
timetable   **l'emploi** *(m)* **du temps**
video camera   **le caméscope**
videocassette   **la vidéocassette**
video recorder   **le magnétoscope**
workshop *(place)*   **l'atelier** *(m)*
workshop *(course)*   **le cours**

Type of school

boarding school   **le pensionnat**
boarder   **le/la pensionnaire**
comprehensive school   **le collège**
day school   **le collège (pour externes)**
further education   **la formation continue**
grammar school   **l'école** *(f)* **primaire**
high school   **le lycée**
infant/nursery school   **l'école** *(f)* **maternelle**
playgroup   **la garderie**
primary school   **l'école** *(f)* **primaire**
school   **l'école** *(f)*
school type   **le type d'école**
of school age   **d'âge scolaire**
secondary   **secondaire**
secondary school/high school   **le lycée, l'école** *(f)* **secondaire**
senior year   **la términale**

– At what age do children start school?
– They have to go to school when they are six.
Our son already goes to the kindergarten and is looking forward to school.
Our daughter goes to the primary school/elementary school.

– **A quel âge les enfants commencent-ils l'école?**
– **Ils doivent aller à l'école dès l'âge de six ans.**
Notre fils va déjà à l'école maternelle et il lui tarde d'aller à l'école primaire.
Notre fille va à l'école primaire.

special school **l'école** (f) **spécialisée**
technical school **le collège technique**

Classroom commands

Answer the question! **Répondez à la question!**
Ask your friend a question! **Posez une question à votre camarade!**
Be careful! **Attention!**
Be quiet! **Silence!**
Be quick! **Dépêchez-vous!**
Bring me your work! **Apportez-moi votre travail!**
Clean the blackboard! **Effacez le tableau!**
Close the door! **Fermez la porte!**
Come here! **Venez ici!**
Come in! **Entrez!**
Copy these sentences! **Ecrivez ces phrases!**
Do your homework! **Faites vos devoirs!**
Don't talk/chatter! **Taisez-vous!**
Fast forward! *(tape)* **Faites avancer rapidement la bande!**
Go out! **Sortez!**
Learn by heart! **Apprenez par cœur!**
Learn the vocabulary! **Apprenez le vocabulaire!**
Listen carefully! **Ecoutez bien!**

Make less noise! **Faites moins de bruit!**
Make notes! **Prenez des notes!**
Open the window! **Ouvrez la fenêtre!**
Pay attention! **Ecoutez bien!**
Put on the headphones! **Mettez vos écouteurs!**
Read the text! **Lisez le texte!**
Rewind the tape! **Rembobinez la cassette!**
Take this to the office! **Apportez ceci au secrétariat!**
Show me your notebooks! **Montrez-moi vos cahiers!**
Sit down! **Asseyez-vous!**
Stand up! **Levez-vous!**
Switch off the cassette recorder! **Eteignez le magnétophone!**
Switch on the OHP! **Allumez le rétroprojecteur!**
Tick the boxes! **Cochez les cases!**
Work in pairs! **Travaillez par deux!**
Work in groups! **Travaillez en groupes!**
Write an essay! **Ecrivez une dissertation/rédaction!**
Write it down! **Ecrivez ceci!**
Write out in neat/neatly! **Ecrivez-le au propre!**
Write out in rough! **Ecrivez-le au brouillon!**

She reads to her teacher every day and can read well now.

Elle fait de la lecture en classe tous les jours et elle sait bien lire maintenant.

– Do you move up a class every year?
– No, last year I had to stay down a year.

– Est-ce que vous passez d'une classe à l'autre tous les ans?
– Non, l'année dernière j'ai dû redoubler.

➤ EXAMINATIONS 22c; STATIONERY App.22b

EDUCATION

22c School subjects and examinations

School subjects

arithmetic   **l'arithmétique** *(f)*
art   **le dessin**
biology   **la biologie**
business studies   **les études** *(f)*
   commerciales
careers education   **l'orientation** *(f)*
chemistry   **la chimie**
commerce   **le commerce**
compulsory subject   **la matière**
   obligatoire
computer studies   **l'informatique** *(f)*
cooking   **la cuisine**
design technology   **la technologie**
   (du design)
economics   **l'économie** *(f)*
foreign language   **la langue**
   étrangère
French   **le français**
geography   **la géographie**
gymnastics   **la gymnastique**
history   **l'histoire** *(f)*
home economics   **les arts** *(m)*

   ménagers
information technology
   l'informatique *(f)*
main subject   **la matière principale**
mathematics   **les mathématiques**
   (f)
music   **la musique**
needlework   **la couture**
option(al subject)   **la matière**
   facultative
philosophy   **la philosophie**
physical education   **l'éducation** *(f)*
   physique
physics   **la physique**
religious education   **l'éducation** *(f)*
   religieuse
science   **les sciences** *(f)*
sex education   **l'éducation** *(f)*
   sexuelle
social studies   **les études** *(f)*
   sociales
sociology   **la sociologie**
sport   **le sport**

– Which school do you go to?
– I go to the comprehensive/public school. I enjoy it a lot. There are lots of clubs and activities.
– Which is your favorite subject?

– I like math, but prefer physics. My favorite subject is PE. I don't like history, it is so boring.

I'm good at English, since I did an exchange. I work very hard at it.

– **A quelle école vas-tu?**
– **Je vais au collège. Je m'y plais beaucoup. Il y a beaucoup de clubs et d'activités.**
– **Quelle est ta matière préférée?**
– **J'aime bien les maths, mais je préfère la physique. Ma matière préférée, c'est l'éducation physique. Je n'aime pas l'histoire, c'est tellement barbant.**
Je suis fort en anglais depuis que j'ai fait un échange. Je travaille beaucoup dans cette matière.

SCHOOL SUBJECTS AND EXAMINATIONS 22c

subject **la matière**
subsidiary subject **la matière secondaire**
technical drawing **le dessin technique**
vocational training **les travaux manuels/pratiques**
woodwork **la menuiserie**

Examinations

I assess **j'évalue**
assessment **l'évaluation** *(f)*
certificate **le certificat**
degree **la licence**
  higher degree **la maîtrise, le doctorat**
diploma **le diplôme**
dissertation **la dissertation**
distinction **la mention**
doctorate **le doctorat**
examination **l'examen** *(m)*
  external **public/national**
  final **de fin d'études**
grade **la mention**
I grade **je classe**

grade system **le barème/le système de notation**
graduate (engineer) **(l'ingénieur) diplômé**
listening comprehension **l'examen** *(m)* **oral, la compréhension orale**
mark **la note**
masters **la maîtrise**
merit **la mention (bien/très bien)**
oral **oral**
postgraduate course **la maîtrise, le doctorat**
reading comprehension **l'explication** *(f)* **de texte**
I pass (an exam) **je suis reçu** *(recevoir)* **(à un examen)**
I take an exam **je passe un examen**
syllabus **le programme**
I test **je teste**
test **le contrôle**
thesis **la thèse**
trainee **le stagiaire**
written test **le contrôle écrit**

– Here are your marks!
Marie-Claire, you have done excellent work. Well done!
Jerome, you will need to work harder. Your spelling is very poor.

Anna, this is very satisfactory, but please improve your handwriting. Your work is so sloppily presented.

In June we are going on a class trip to the Vosges. You will do a project on the geography and wildlife of the area.

– **Voici vos notes!**
Marie-Claire, ton travail était excellent. Très bien!
Jérôme, il faut t'appliquer davantage, tu fais beaucoup de fautes d'orthographe.
Anna, c'est très satisfaisant, mais fais un effort pour améliorer ton écriture. Ton travail est si mal présenté.

En juin nous ferons un voyage scolaire dans les Vosges. Vous ferez un projet d'études sur la géographie et la faune de la région.

EDUCATION

22d Higher education

adult **adulte**
adult education **la formation continue**
alumnus **un ancien élève, une ancienne élève**
apprentice **un apprenti, une apprentie**
apprenticeship **l'apprentissage** *(m)*
chair **la chaire**
college **la faculté**
 college of further education **le centre de formation continue**
course of study **des études** *(f)*
diploma **le diplôme**
faculty **la faculté**
further education **des études** *(f)* **supérieures**
residence hall **la résidence/cité universitaire, le foyer**
higher education **les études** *(f)* **supérieures**
in-service training **le stage de formation**

lecture **la conférence**
lecture hall **l'amphithéâtre** *(m)*
lecturer **un (maître) assistant**
master's degree **la maîtrise**
part-time education **des études** *(f)* **à temps partiel**
postgraduate/graduate **le licencié/ la licenciée (de lettres/de sciences)**
professor/college professor **le professeur**
quota *(for university entry)* **le nombre de places à l'université**
research **la recherche**
retraining **le recyclage**
I retrain **je me recycle**
scholarship **la bourse**
seminar **le séminaire**
student **un étudiant, une étudiante**
student grant **la bourse d'étude**
student union **le syndicat des étudiants**
teacher training college **le centre**

I would like to go to college to study environmental science.

J'aimerais aller en faculté pour étudier les sciences de l'environnement.

We have increased the number of universities and are aiming for a broader provision.

Nous avons augmenté le nombre des universités et nous visons de plus amples effectifs.

The technical colleges now belong to the university sector and we now speak of a comprehensive university.

Les instituts techniques font maintenant partie de l'université et nous parlons maintenant d'études universitaires globales.

The course length is four years (eight semesters).

Les études prennent quatre ans (huit semestres).

Many students want job qualifications. They can easily transfer between courses.

De nombreux étudiants désirent une formation spécialisée. Ils peuvent facilement changer de filière.

de formation pédagogique
technical college   l'institut *(m)*
  technique
university/college   l'université *(f)*
university entrance qualification
  **les qualifications requises
  pour entrer à l'université**
vocational route   **la formation
  spécialisée**

Faculties and subjects

accountancy/accounting   **la
  comptabilité**
anthropology   l'anthropologie *(f)*
architecture   l'architecture *(f)*
business management   **la gestion**
catering   **la restauration**
classics   **les lettres classiques**
civil engineering   **le génie civil**
commerce   **le commerce**
computer studies   l'informatique
  (f)
construction   **la construction**
education   l'enseignement *(m)*
electronics   l'électronique *(f)*
electrical engineering   **(des études)**

d'ingénieur en électronique
economics   l'économie, les
  sciences économiques
engineering   **(des études)
  d'ingénieur**
environmental sciences   **les
  sciences de l'environnement**
geology   **la géologie**
history of art   l'histoire *(f)* de l'art
hotel management   l'hôtellerie *(f)*
languages   **les langues** *(f)*
law   **le droit**
leisure and tourism   **le tourisme et
  les loisirs** *(m)*
literature   **la littérature**
mechanical engineering   **le génie
  mécanique**
medicine   **la médecine**
pharmacy   **la pharmacie**
nuclear science   **les sciences** *(f)*
  nucléaires
philosophy   **la philosophie**
psychology   **la psychologie**
sociology   **la sociologie**
theology   **la théologie**

Financial support is of the greatest importance. Many students get a state grant.

Le financement des études est primordial. Beaucoup d'étudiants reçoivent une bourse d'état.

Many students apply for places, but they cannot all be admitted to university.

De nombreux étudiants posent leur candidature, mais ils ne peuvent pas tous être admis à l'université.

There is now an entrance restriction. The right to a place depends on marks in the *baccalauréat.* They require particularly high marks for medicine. Our results are always outstanding.

Il y a maintenant des restrictions pour l'entrée á l'université. Le droit d'entrée dépend des résultats au baccalauréat. Il faut de très bonnes notes surtout en médecine. Nos résultats sont toujours excellents.

23 Science: the changing world

23a Scientific method and life sciences

Scientific method

academic paper **l'exposé** *(m)*, **la communication**
I analyze **j'analyse**
authentic **authentique**
I challenge **je mets** *(mettre)* **en question**
I check **je vérifie**
classification **la classification**
I classify **je classe**
I conduct (an experiment) **je fais une expérience**
control **le cas témoin**
I discover **je découvre** *(découvrir)*
discovery **la découverte**
experiment **l'expérience** *(f)*
I experiment **je fais une expérience**
flask **le ballon**
hypothesis **l'hypothèse** *(f)*
I identify **j'identifie**
I investigate **j'examine, j'étudie**
laboratory **le laboratoire**
material **le matériau**
measurement **le mesurage**
I observe **j'observe**

origin **l'origine** *(f)*
pipette **la pipette**
process **le processus**
research **la recherche, les recherches**
I research **je fais des recherches**
result **le résultat**
I solve (a problem) **je résouds** *(résoudre)*
test **l'analyse** *(f)*
I test **je fais une analyse**
test tube **l'éprouvette** *(f)*
theory **la théorie**
I transfer **je transfère** *(transférer)*

Biology

bacteria **la bactérie**
botanical **botanique**
I breathe **je respire**
cell **la cellule**
chlorophyll **la chlorophylle**
it circulates **il circule**
decay **le pourrissement**
decline **le déclin**
it declines **il décline**
it excretes **il excrète** *(excréter)*, **il sécrète** *(sécréter)*

The researcher took a sample, mounted it on a slide and put it under the microscope for examination. All the results from the experiments support her hypothesis.

La chercheuse a pris un échantillon qu'elle a posé sur une plaquette. Elle l'a examiné sous le microscope. Tous les résultats des expériences confirment son hypothèse.

excretion   l'**excrétion** *(f)*, **la sécrétion**
it feeds   **il mange**
food chain   **la chaîne alimentaire**
gene   **le gène**
genetic   **génétique**
genetic disorder   **la maladie/ malformation d'origine génétique**
it grows   **il croît** *(croître)*
growth   **la croissance**
habitat   l'**habitat** *(m)*
it inherits   **il hérite**
membrane   **la membrane**
it mutates   **il subit une mutation**
nucleus   **le nucléus**
organic   **organique**
organism   l'**organisme** *(m)*
photosynthesis   **la photosynthèse**
population   **la population**
it reproduces   **il se reproduit** *(se reproduire)*
respiration   **la respiration**
sensitivity   **la sensibilité**
survival   **la survie**
it survives   **il survit** *(survivre)*
virus   **le virus**

Medical science and research

cosmetic/plastic surgery   **la chirurgie esthétique**
DNA   l'**ADN** *(m)*
donor   **le donneur, la donneuse**
embryo   l'**embryon** *(m)*

embryo research   **les recherches** *(f)* **sur l'embryon**
ethical consideration   **la considération éthique**
ethics of human reproduction   **la bioéthique**
experiments on animals   **les expériences** *(f)* **sur des animaux**
hereditary illness   **la maladie héréditaire**
IVF (in vitro fertilisation)   **FIV (la fécondation in vitro)**
I justify   **je justifie**
microorganism   **le micro-organisme**
organ transplant   **la greffe d'organe**
pacemaker   **le stimulateur (cardiaque)**
I permit   **je permets** *(permettre)*
prenatal tests *(on fetus)*   **le diagnostic prénatal (le DPN)**
psychology   **la psychologie**
recipient   **la personne qui reçoit**
I reject (an organ)   **je rejette**
risk   **le risque**
I risk   **je risque**
survival rate *(death rate)*   **le taux de mortalité**
test-tube baby   **le bébé-éprouvette**
transplant   **la greffe**
x-ray   **le rayon X**

A girl of seventeen was today given a new heart in a transplant operation that lasted ten hours.

Une jeune fille de dix-sept ans a reçu une greffe du cœur au cours d'une intervention qui a duré dix heures.

Research on human embryo tissue is likely to remain highly controversial.

La possibilité de faire des recherches sur l'embryon humain tend à rester un sujet de controverse.

➤ ANIMAL WORLD 24b; MEDICAL TREATMENT 11c; FARMING 24c

23b Physical sciences

Chemistry

acid l'acide *(m)*
air l'air *(m)*
alkali l'alcali *(m)*
alkaline alcalin
alloy l'alliage *(m)*
I analyze j'analyse
Bunsen burner le bec Bunsen
I calculate je calcule
chemical chimique
compound le composé
composition la composition
it dissolves il dissoud
  (dissoudre)
    it dissolves in water il se
    dissoud dans l'eau
element l'élément *(m)*
emulsion l'émulsion *(f)*
equation l'équation *(f)*
gas le gaz
inorganic inorganique
insoluble insoluble
liquid le liquide
  liquid *(adj)* liquide
litmus paper le papier de
  tournesol
matter la matière
metal le métal
natural gas le gaz naturel
opaque opaque
periodic table le tableau de
  classification périodique des
  élements
physical physique
pure pur
it reacts il réagit
reaction la réaction
salt le sel
solid *(adj)* solide
soluble soluble
solution la solution
stable stable
substance la substance
transparent transparent

Physics and mechanics

it accelerates il accélère
  (accélérer)
acceleration l'accélération *(f)*
acoustics l'acoustique *(f)*
analysis l'analyse *(f)*
artificial artificiel[le]
boiling point le point d'ébullition
circuit le circuit
conservation la conservation
density la densité
distance la distance
electron microscope le
  microscope électronique
energy input l'énergie *(f)*
energy output la puissance de
  sortie
it expands il se dilate
fiber la fibre
force la force
it freezes il gèle *(geler)*
formula la formule
freezing point le point de
  congélation
friction la friction
gravity la pesanteur
I heat je fais chauffer
it heats il chauffe
heat la chaleur
heat loss la perte calorifique
invention l'invention *(f)*
laser le laser
laser beam le rayon laser
light la lumière
light beam le rayon de lumière
magnetism le magnétisme
magneto la magnéto
mass la masse
I measure je mesure
mechanics la mécanique
metallurgy la métallurgie
microscope le microscope
microwave la micro-onde
mineral le minéral

missile   **le missile**
model   **le modèle (réduit)**
motion   **le mouvement**
observation   **l'observation** *(f)*
optics   **l'optique** *(f)*
pressure   **la pression**
property   **la propriété**
proportional   **proportionnel[le]**
ray   **le rayon**
reflection   **la réflexion**
refraction   **la réfraction**
relativity   **la relativité**
resistant   **résistant**
solid   **le solide**
I sort   **je trie, je classe**
sound   **le son**
speed   **la vitesse**
structure   **la structure**
synthetic   **synthétique**
temperature   **la température**
theory   **la théorie**
time   **le temps**
transmission   **la transmission**
vapor   **la vapeur**
it vibrates   **il vibre**
vibration   **la vibration**
wave   **l'onde** *(f)*
  long waves   **grandes ondes**
  medium/short waves   **ondes**
  moyennes/courtes
wavelength   **la longueur d'ondes**

Electricity

battery *(large)*   **la batterie**
  battery *(small)*   **la pile**
charge   **la charge**

I charge the battery   **je mets**
  (mettre) la batterie en charge
current   **le courant**
electrical   **électrique**
electricity   **l'électricité** *(f)*
electricity grid   **le réseau**
  électrique
electrode   **l'électrode** *(f)*
electron   **l'électron** *(m)*
electronic   **électronique**
electronics   **l'électronique** *(f)*
negative   **négatif [-ve]**
positive   **positif [-ve]**
pylon   **le pylône**
resistance   **la résistance**
voltage   **le voltage, la tension**

Nuclear physics

atom   **l'atome** *(m)*
atomic   **atomique**
electron   **l'électron** *(m)*
fission   **la fission**
fusion   **la fusion**
molecular   **moléculaire**
molecule   **la molécule**
neutron   **le neutron**
nuclear   **nucléaire**
nuclear energy   **l'énergie** *(f)*
  nucléaire
nucleus   **le noyau**
particle   **la particule**
proton   **le proton**
quantum theory   **la théorie des**
  quanta
radiation   **la radiation**
reactor   **le réacteur**

Water has a boiling point of 100 degrees centigrade. It freezes at zero degrees.

Le point d'ébullition de l'eau est de cent degrés Celsius. Elle gèle à zéro degré Celsius.

What is the voltage of this equipment?

Quel est le voltage de cet appareil?

▶ MEASURING 4b; DESCRIBING THINGS 5c; ENERGY AND FUELS 23c

SCIENCE: THE CHANGING WORLD

23c The earth and space

Geology and minerals

bauxite   la bauxite
carbon dating   la datation au carbone 14
chalk   la craie
chalky   crayeux [-se], calcaire
clay   l'argile (f)
diamond   le diamant
geologist   le géologue
gemstone   la pierre gemme
granite   le granit
graphite   le graphite, la mine de plomb
layer   la couche
lime   la chaux
limestone   le calcaire
loam   le terreau
marble   le marbre
mine   la mine
I mine   j'extrais (extraire)
ore   le minerai
quartz   le quartz
quarry   la carrière
sand   le sable
sandstone   le grès
sediment   le sédiment
silica   la silice
slate   l'ardoise (f)
soil   le sol
stalactite   la stalactite
stalagmite   la stalagmite

Energy and fuels

atomic energy   l'énergie (f) atomique
coal   le charbon, la houille
concentration   la concentration
consumption   la consommation
energy   l'énergie (f)
energy conservation   les économies (f) d'énergie
energy consumption   la consommation d'énergie
energy crisis   la crise d'énergie

energy saving   qui économise l'énergie
energy source   la source d'énergie
fossil fuels   le combustible fossile
fuel   le combustible
fuel consumption   la consommation de combustibles
gasoline   l'essence (f)
it generates   il produit (produire)
geothermal energy   l'énergie (f) géothermique
global warming   le réchauffement de l'atmosphère
greenhouse effect   l'effet (m) de serre
hydroelectric dam   le barrage (m) hydro-électrique
hydroelectric power   l'énergie (f) hydro-électrique, la houille blanche
insulation   l'isolation (f)
natural gas   le gaz naturel
nuclear power station   la centrale nucléaire
nuclear reactor   le réacteur nucléaire
oil   le pétrole, l'huile (f)
oil production   la production de pétrole
oil-producing countries   les pays (m) producteurs de pétrole
petroleum   le pétrole
raw materials   la matière première
solar cell   la pile solaire
solar energy   l'énergie (f) solaire
thermal energy   l'énergie (f) thermique
wave power   l'énergie (f) des vagues
tidal power station   l'usine (f) marémotrice
wind energy/power   l'énergie (f) éolienne

Space

asteroid **l'astéroïde** *(m)*
big bang theory **la théorie du big-bang**
eclipse **l'éclipse** *(f)*
it eclipses **il éclipse**
galactic **galactique**
galaxy **la galaxie**
gravitational pull **la gravitation**
light-year **l'année-lumière** *(f)*
meteorite **le météore**
moon **la lune**
  full moon **la pleine lune**
  new moon **la nouvelle lune**
orbit **l'orbite** *(f)*
planet **la planète**
solar system **le système solaire**
solstice **le solstice**
star **l'étoile** *(f)*
sun **le soleil**
sunspot **la tache solaire**
the heavens **le ciel**
universe **l'univers** *(m)*

Space research and travel

antenna **l'antenne** *(f)*
astrologer **l'astrologue** *(m)*
astronomer **l'astronome** *(m)*
astronaut **l'astronaute** *(m)*
cosmonaut **le cosmonaute**
I launch **je lance**
launch pad **la rampe de lancement**
lunar module **le module lunaire**
moon buggy **la jeep lunaire**
moon walk **la marche lunaire**
observatory **l'observatoire** *(m)*
orbit **l'orbite** *(f)*
planetarium **le planétarium**
it reenters **il rentre (dans l'atmosphère)**
relativity **la relativité**
rocket **la fusée (interplanétaire)**
rocket fuel **le combustible**
satellite **le satellite**
  communications **le satellite de télécommunications**
  spy **le satellite d'espionnage**
  weather **le satellite météorologique**
sky lab **le laboratoire spatial**
space **l'espace** *(m)*
spaceflight **le voyage spatial**
space probe **la sonde spatiale**
space shuttle **la navette spatiale**
spacecraft **le vaisseau spatial**
space-suit **le scaphandre**
stratosphere **la stratosphère**
telescope **le télescope**
time warp **la distorsion du temps**
touchdown on land **l'atterrissage** *(m)*
  on sea **l'amerrissage** *(m)*
  on moon **l'alunissage** *(m)*
zodiac **le zodiaque**

By studying the light received from stars many millions of light years away, scientists hope to discover the origins of the universe.

Les scientifiques espèrent découvrir les origines de l'univers en étudiant la lumière qui provient des étoiles distantes de plusieurs millions d'années-lumière.

The earth orbits the sun.

La terre reste en orbite autour du soleil.

24 The environment: the natural world

24a Geography

archipelago **l'archipel** *(m)*	foothills **les contreforts** *(m)*
area **la région**	forest **la forêt**
bank (river) **le bord**	friendly **accueillant**
bay **la baie**	geographical **géographique**
beach **la plage**	geography **la géographie**
bog **le marais**	geyser **le geyser**
bottom **le fond**	globe **le globe**
canyon **le cañon, la gorge**	gradient **la pente, l'inclinaison** *(f)*
clean **propre, net[te]**	hemisphere **l'hémisphère** *(f)*
cliff **la falaise, l'escarpement** *(m)*	high **haut**
coast **la côte**	hill **la colline**
coastline **le littoral**	incline/slope **la déclivité**
continent **le continent**	it is situated **il est situé**
coppice, copse **le taillis, le boqueteau**	island **l'île** *(f)*
	jungle **la jungle**
country **le pays**	lake **le lac**
in the country **à la campagne**	land **la terre**
countryside **le paysage**	it is located **il se trouve**
creek **le ruisseau**	location **l'emplacement** *(m)*, **la situation**
crest **la crête**	
dangerous **dangereux [-se]**	map **la carte**
deep **profond**	marsh **le marais, le marécage**
delta **le delta**	meridian **le méridien**
desert **le désert**	mountain **la montagne**
dirty **sale**	mountain range **la chaîne de montagnes**
dune **la dune**	
earth tremor **la secousse sismique**	national **national**
	national park **le parc national**
earthquake **le tremblement de terre**	nature **la nature**
	nice/pleasant **agréable**
equator **l'équateur** *(m)*	ocean **l'océan** *(m)*
equatorial **équatorial**	ocean floor **le fond sous-marin**
eruption **l'éruption** *(f)*	peaceful **paisible**
it erupts **il entre en éruption**	peak **le pic, le sommet**
escarpment **l'escarpement** *(m)*	peninsula **la péninsule**
estuary **l'estuaire** *(m)*	plateau **le plateau**
field **le champ**	pole **le pôle**
fjord **le fjord**	province **la province**
flat **plat**	reef **le récif**
it flows **il coule**	region **la région**

regional **régional**
ridge **l'arête** *(f)*, **la crête**
river **la rivière**
river (major) **le fleuve**
riverbed **le lit de la rivière/du fleuve**
rockpool **la flaque d'eau (dans les rochers)**
sand **le sable**
scenery **le paysage**
sea **la mer**
seaside **le bord de la mer**
shore **le rivage, le bord**
spring **le printemps**
steep **raide**
steppe **la steppe**
stream **le ruisseau**
summit **le sommet**
tall **haut, élevé**
territory **le territoire**
top **le sommet**
the tropics **les tropiques** *(m)*
tundra **la toundra**
unfriendly **froid, hostile**
valley **la vallée**
volcano **le volcan**
water **l'eau** *(f)*
  freshwater **l'eau** *(f)* **douce**
waterfall **la chute d'eau**
wood **le bois**
woodland **la région boisée**

zenith **le zénith**
zone **la zone**

Man-made features

aqueduct **l'aqueduc** *(m)*
bridge **le pont**
canal **le canal**
capital (city) **la capitale**
city **la ville, la cité**
country road **la petite route de campagne**
dam **le barrage**
embankment/levee **le talus, le remblai**
factory **l'usine** *(f)*, **la fabrique**
farm **la ferme**
farmland **les terres** *(f)* **cultivées**
hamlet **le hameau**
harbor **le port**
industry **l'industrie** *(f)*
marina **la marina**
nature trail **l'itinéraire** *(m)* **aménagé pour amateurs de la nature**
oasis **l'oasis** *(f)*
reclaimed land **le terrain asséché**
reservoir **le réservoir**
town **la ville**
track **la trace**
village **le village**
well **le puits**

Wallonia, in the south of Belgium, is dominated by the forest uplands of the Ardennes.

La Wallonie, dans le sud de la Belgique, est une région dominée par les collines boisées des Ardennes.

The Water Authority plans to create a new reservoir. This will involve submerging several dwellings.

Le service des eaux a un projet pour créer un nouveau réservoir. Il faudra submerger plusieurs habitations.

The area was marshy and unsuitable for development.

La région était marécageuse et inadaptée au développement.

➤ ANIMAL WORLD 24b; FARMING 24c; THE WEATHER 24d; POLLUTION 24e

THE ENVIRONMENT: THE NATURAL WORLD

24b The animal world

Animals

animal   l'animal *(m)*
it barks   il aboie *(aboyer)*
it bites   il mord *(mordre)*
it bounds   il bondit
it breeds   il se reproduit
   (se reproduire)
burrow/hole   le terrier
cage   la cage
carnivore   le carnivore
cat   le chat
it crawls   il rampe
den   la tanière
dog   le chien
I feed   je donne à manger à
it feeds   il se nourrit
food   la nourriture
fox   le renard
frog   la grenouille
gerbil   la gerbille
goldfish   le poisson rouge
guinea pig   le cochon d'Inde
habitat   l'habitat *(m)*
hamster   le hamster
hare   le lièvre
hedgehog   le hérisson
herbivore   l'herbivore *(m)*
it hibernates   il hiberne
it howls   il hurle
hut/hutch   le clapier
I keep a cat   j'ai un chat
kitten   le chaton
lair   le repaire
it leaps   il saute
litter   la portée
mammal   le mammifère
it miaows   il miaule
mole   la taupe
mouse   la souris
omnivore   l'omnivore *(m)*
pack   la meute
parakeet   la perruche
pet   l'animal *(m)* familier
predator   le prédateur
prey   la proie

puppy   le chiot
rabbit   le lapin
rabies   la rage
reptile   le reptile
it roars   il rugit
safari park   la réserve
snake   le serpent
it squeaks   il couine
squirrel   l'écureuil *(m)*
I stroke   je caresse
toad   le crapaud
tortoise   la tortue
I walk (the dog)   je promène
   (promener) (le chien)
wildlife park   la réserve naturelle
wolf   le loup
zoo   le zoo

Birds

claw   la griffe
it crows   il chante
it flies   il vole
flock   la volée
it hovers   il plane
it migrates   il migre
nest   le nid
it nests   il se niche
it pecks at   il picore

Sealife/Waterlife

alligator   l'alligator *(m)*
anemone   l'anémone *(f)*
angling   la pêche (à la ligne)
coral   le corail
crab   le crabe
crocodile   le crocodile
dolphin   le dauphin
fish   le poisson
I fish   je vais à la pêche
harpoon   le harpon
hook   l'hameçon *(m)*
marine   marin
mollusc   le mollusque
net   le filet

octopus **la pieuvre, le poulpe**
plankton **le plancton**
rod **la canne (à pêche)**
seal **le phoque**
shark **le requin, le squale**
shoal **le banc (de poissons)**
starfish **l'étoile** *(f)* **de mer**
it swims **il nage**
turtle **la tortue marine**
whale **la baleine**
whaling **la pêche à la baleine**

Insects

ant **la fourmi**
bee **l'abeille** *(f)*
   queen bee **la reine, la repro-ductrice**
   worker bee **l'ouvrière** *(f)*
bedbug **la punaise**
beetle **le scarabée** *(m)*
bug **l'insecte** *(m)*, **la bestiole**
butterfly **le papillon**
it buzzes **il bourdonne**
caterpiller **la chenille**
cocoon **le cocon**
cockroach **le cafard**
cricket **le grillon**

dragonfly **la libellule**
flea **la puce**
fly **la mouche**
grasshopper **la sauterelle**
hive **la ruche**
insect **l'insecte** *(m)*
invertebrate **l'invertébré** *(m)*
ladybird/ladybug **la coccinelle, la bête à bon Dieu**
larva **la larve**
locust **la locuste**
it metamorphoses **il se métamor-phose**
mosquito **le moustique**
moth **le papillon de nuit**
scorpion **le scorpion**
silkworm **le ver à soie**
slug **la limace**
snail **l'escargot** *(m)*
spider **l'araignée** *(f)*
it spins (a web) **il tisse la toile**
it stings **il pique**
termite **le termite**
tick **la tique**
web **la toile**
wasp **la guêpe**
worm **le ver**

Guinea pigs and hamsters are popular pets in Britain.

Le cochon d'Inde et le hamster sont très populaires comme animaux familiers en Grande-Bretagne.

Don't forget to walk the dog and feed the cat!

N'oublie pas de promener le chien et de donner à manger au chat!

The campaign to save the whale is increasing in popularity.

La campagne pour la sauve-garde de la baleine devient de plus en plus populaire.

The panda is in danger of extinction in the wild.

Le panda est en danger d'extinction à l'état sauvage.

24c Farming and gardening

Farm animals

bull   le taureau
cattle   le bétail
chicken   la poule
cock   le coq
cow   la vache
it crows   il chante
dairy (adj)   laitier [-ère]
duck   le canard, la cane
it eats   il mange
feed   la nourriture
it feeds   il se nourrit
foal   le poulain
fodder   le fourrage
food (for animals)   l'aliment (m)
it gallops   il galope
goat   la chèvre
goose   l'oie (f)
it grazes   il broute, il pâture
it grunts   il grogne
horse   le cheval
horseshoe   le fer à cheval
it kicks   il rue
kid   le chevreau
I milk   je trais (traire)
it moos   il meugle, il beugle
it neighs   il hennit
ox   le bœuf
pasture   le pâturage
it pecks   il picore
pig   le cochon
pony   le poney
poultry   la volaille
produce   les produits (m)
it quacks   il cancane
I ride (a horse)   je monte à cheval
rooster   le coq
I shear   je tonds (tondre)

sheep   le mouton
sheep dog   le chien de berger
I slaughter   j'abats (abattre)
stallion   l'étalon (m)
it trots   il trotte

On the farm

agricultural   agricole
agriculture   l'agriculture (f)
arable   arable
barn   la grange
combine harvester   la
   moissonneuse-batteuse
crop   la culture
   crop (amount)   la récolte
dairy   la laiterie
farm   la ferme
farmhouse   la maison de ferme
farm laborer   l'ouvrier (m) agricole
farmyard   la cour de ferme
fence   la barrière, la clôture
I groom   je panse
harvest   la moisson, la récolte
I harvest   je moissonne, je récolte
hay   le foin
haystack   la meule de foin
irrigate   j'irrigue
milk churn   le bidon à lait
milking machine   la trayeuse
   (mécanique)
orchard   le verger
pen   l'enclos (m)
pigsty   la porcherie
silage   le fourrage ensilé, l'ensi-
   lage (m)
slaughterhouse   l'abattoir (m)
stable   l'écurie (f)
stud farm   le haras

Agriculture and gardening

acorn **le gland**
allotment **le lopin de terre**
barley **l'orge** *(f)*
bloom **la fleur**
bouquet **le bouquet**
bud **le bouton**
bulb **le bulbe**
bush **le buisson**
cactus **le cactus**
compost **le compost**
corn **le maïs**
I cultivate **je cultive**
cutting **la bouture**
I dig **je creuse**
   I dig (with spade) **je bêche**
fir **le sapin**
flax **le lin**
flower **la fleur**
it flowers/blooms **il fleurit**
flowerbed **le parterre de fleurs**
foliage **le feuillage**
garden/yard **le jardin**
gardening **le jardinage**
I gather **je cueille** *(cueillir)*
grain **la céréale**
grass **l'herbe** *(f)*
I grow **je cultive**
it grows **il pousse**
hedge **la haie**
horticulture **l'horticulture** *(f)*
lawn **la pelouse**
leaf **la feuille**
maize **le maïs**
I mow **je fauche**
   I mow *(lawn)* **je tonds** *(tondre)*
oats **l'avoine** *(f)*
patio **le patio**

petal **le pétale**
I pick **je cueille** *(cueillir)*
pine **le pin**
pine forest **la pinède**
I plant **je plante**
plant **la plante**
pond **l'étang** *(m)*
pollen **le pollen**
I reap **je moissonne**
ripe **mûr**
it ripens **il mûrit**
rockery **la rocaille**
root **la racine**
rotten **pourri**
rye **le seigle**
sap **la sève**
seed **le grain**
shed **l'abri** *(m)*
sorghum **le sorgho**
species **l'espèce** *(f)*
stem **la tige**
sweet chestnut **le marron, la**
   châtaigne
thorn **l'épine** *(f)*
I transplant **je transplante**
tree **l'arbre** *(m)*
tuber **le tubercule**
undergrowth **les broussailles** *(f)*
vegetable(s) **le légume**
vegetable garden **le potager**
vegetation **la végétation**
I water **j'arrose**
weed **la mauvaise herbe**
I weed **je désherbe**
wheat **le blé**
wild flower **la fleur sauvage**
it wilts **il se flétrit**

I must mow the lawn, plant some
bulbs, weed the flower bed and
trim the hedge.

**Il faut que je tonde la pelouse,
plante quelques bulbes,
désherbe le parterre de fleurs et
coupe la haie.**

➤ FLOWERS AND WEEDS, TREES App.24c; TOOLS App.8b

THE ENVIRONMENT: THE NATURAL WORLD

24d The weather

avalanche **l'avalanche** *(f)*
average temperature **la tempéra-ture moyenne**
bad weather **le mauvais temps**
bright **éclairci**
bright period **l'éclaircie** *(f)*
centigrade **Celsius**
changeable **variable**
climate **le climat**
climatic **climatique**
cloud **le nuage**
clouded over **couvert**
cloudless **sans nuages**
cloudy **nuageux [-se]**
cold **le froid**
it is cold **il fait froid**
cold front **le front froid**
it is cool **il fait frais**
daily temperature **la température**
damp **humide**
degree **le degré**
  above zero **au-dessus de zéro**
  below zero **au-dessous de zéro**
depression **la dépression**
drizzle **la bruine, le crachin**

dry **sec [sèche]**
dull (weather) **(le temps) maussade**
it's fine **il fait beau**
flash **l'éclair** *(m)*
fog **le brouillard, la brume**
it is foggy **il fait du brouillard**
it's freezing **il gèle** *(geler)*
freezing fog **le brouillard givrant**
frost **le givre**
frosty **glacial**
gale **le grand vent**
gale warning **l'avis** *(m)* **de coup de vent**
it's hailing **il grêle**
hailstones **des grêlons** *(m)*
heat **la chaleur**
heat wave **la vague de chaleur, la canicule**
high pressure **la haute pression (atmosphérique)**
highest temperature **la tempéra-ture maximale**
it's hot **il fait chaud**
ice **la glace**
Indian summer **l'été** *(m)* **indien/de la St Martin**

It will be cold tomorrow, maximum temperatures 4–6 Celsius (39–43 Fahrenheit).

Il fera froid demain, températures maximales de 4 à 6 degrés Celsius (39-43 Fahrenheit).

Freezing fog patches in parts of eastern Quebec should clear by midday.

Le brouillard givrant qu'on trouvera dans l'est du Québec devrait se dissiper avant midi.

The whole country will be affected by rain, turning to sleet in the mountains. Snow will fall in the west, drifting in places.

Sur tout le pays, il y aura de la pluie qui sera transformée en neige fondue en altitude. Il y aura des chutes de neige dans l'ouest, avec des amoncellements possibles.

lightning **l'éclair** *(m)*, **des éclairs**
low pressure **la basse pression**
lowest temperature **la température minimale**
mild **doux [-ce]**
mist **la brume**
misty **brumeux [-se]**
monsoon **la mousson**
moon **la lune**
occluded front **le front occlus**
rain **la pluie**
it's raining **il pleut** *(pleuvoir)*
rainy **pluvieux [-se]**
shade **l'ombre** *(f)*
it shines **il brille**
shower **l'averse** (f)
snow **la neige**
snowball **la boule de neige**
snowdrift **la congère, l'amoncelle-
 ment** *(m)* **de neige**
snowfall **la chute de neige**
snowflake **le flocon de neige**
snowman **le bonhomme de neige**
snow report *(for skiing)* **le bulletin
 d'enneigement**
it's snowing **il neige**
snowstorm **la tempête de neige**
star **l'étoile** *(f)*

storm **la tempête**
stormy **orageux [-se]**
sultry **lourd, étouffant**
sun/sunshine **le soleil**
sunny **ensoleillé**
thunder **le tonnerre**
it's thunder **il tonne**
thunderbolt **le coup de foudre**
thunderstorm **l'orage** *(m)*
torrent **le torrent**
torrential **torrentiel[le]**
tropical **tropical**
warm **chaud**
warm front **le front chaud**
weather **le temps qu'il fait**
weather conditions **les conditions
 (f) météorologiques**
weather forecast **la météo, les
 prévisions** *(f)* **de la météo**
weather report **le bulletin
 météorologique, la météo**
wet **pluvieux [-se]**
What's the weather like? **Quel
 temps fait-il?**
wind **le vent**
it is windy **il fait du vent, il vente**
wonderful **merveilleux [-se]**

The northeast monsoon is now well established over southeast Asia.

La mousson du nord-est est désormais bien établie sur l'Asie du Sud-Est.

Heavy rain has caused several rivers in southern Ohio to burst their banks.

Plusieurs rivières du sud de l'Ohio ont rompu leurs digues à cause des pluies abondantes.

The south of the country may be affected by tropical storms later tonight.

Sur le sud du pays, dans la soirée, il y aura une possiblité d'orages tropicaux.

Tomorrow's temperatures will rise to over 40°C (104°F) in the shade.

Demain les températures dépasseront les quarante degrés Celsius (104° F) à l'ombre.

THE ENVIRONMENT: THE NATURAL WORLD

24e Pollution

On the earth

artificial fertilizer l'engrais *(m)* chimique
balance of nature l'équilibre *(m)* de la nature
biodegradable bio-dégradable
conservation la préservation, la défense de l'environnement
conservationist le défenseur de l'environnement
deforestation le déboisement
disaster le désastre, la catastrophe
ecology l'écologie *(f)*
ecosystem l'écosystème *(m)*
environment l'environnement *(m)*
natural resources les ressources *(f)* naturelles
nature reserve la réserve naturelle
nitrates les nitrates *(m)*
pesticide le pesticide
quality of life la qualité de la vie
radioactive radioactif [-ve]
radioactive waste les déchets *(m)* radioactifs
rain forest la forêt tropicale humide
soil erosion l'érosion *(f)* du sol
weedkiller le désherbant, l'herbicide *(m)*

In the atmosphere

acid rain les pluies *(f)* acides
aerosol(system) l'aérosol *(m)*
aerosol can la bombe
air pollution la pollution atmosphérique
catalytic convertor le pot catalytique
CFCs les CFC
emission (of gas) l'émission *(f)*
skin cancer le cancer de la peau
unleaded gasoline l'essence *(f)* sans-plomb
waste gases les gaz *(m)* d'échappement

In the rivers and seas

detergent le détergent
drought la sécheresse
flooding l'inondation *(f)*
groundwater la nappe phréatique
oil slick la nappe de pétrole, la marée noire
phosphates les phosphates *(m)*
sea level le niveau de la mer
water level le niveau de l'eau
water pollution la pollution de l'eau
water suppply system le réseau hydrographiqe
water supply l'alimentation *(f)* en eau

Recent studies suggest the hole in the ozone layer will have serious consequences in the Northern Hemisphere.

Des études récentes suggèrent que le trou dans la couche d'ozone aura de graves conséquences dans l'hémisphère nord.

The city council provides facilities for recycling glass, cans, and newspapers.

Le conseil municipal offre l'opportunité de recycler verres, boîtes en métal, et vieux journaux.

Problems of pollution

it becomes extinct   **il disparaît** *(disparaître)*
I conserve   **j'économise**
I consume   **je consomme**
consumption   **la consommation**
I damage   **j'abîme**
danger (to)   **le danger (pour)**
I destroy   **je détruis** *(détruire)*
disposal   **l'enlèvement** *(m)* **(des ordures ménagères)**
I dispose of   **je me débarrasse de**
I do without   **je me prive de**
emission   **l'émission** *(f)*
it emits   **il émet** *(émettre)*, **il dégage**
I improve   **j'améliore**
I insulate   **j'isole**
I poison   **j'empoisonne**
pollutant   **le polluant**
I pollute   **je pollue**
pollution   **la pollution**
I predict   **je prédis** *(prédire)*, **je prévois** *(prévoir)*
I protect   **je protège** *(protéger)*
it runs out   **il s'épuise**
I store   **je mets** *(mettre)* **en réserve**
I throw away   **je jette** *(jeter)*

Waste and recycling

corrosion   **la corrosion**
damaging   **nuisible**
drainage   **le drainage**

exhaust pipe   **le tuyau d'échappement**
garbage dump   **la déchetterie, la décharge publique**
harmful   **nuisible**
incinerator   **l'incinérateur** *(m)*
industrial effluent   **l'effluent** *(m)* **industriel**
industrial waste   **les déchets** *(m)* **industriels**
litter   **les déchets** *(m)*, **les ordures** *(f)*
nuclear waste   **les déchets** *(m)* **nucléaires**
poison   **le poison**
recyclable   **recyclable**
I recycle   **je recycle**
recycled paper   **le papier recyclé**
recycling skip   **le conteneur de collecte de verre/papier etc.**
refuse   **les ordures** *(f)*
reprocessing   **le retraitement**
residue   **les restes** *(m)*
scrap metal   **la ferraille**
sewage   **les vidanges**
treatment   **le traitement**
waste (domestic)   **les ordures** *(f)* **(ménagères)**
waste disposal   **le traitement des ordures**
waste disposal unit   **le broyeur d'ordures**
waste products   **les déchets** *(m)*

– Do you think this awful weather is normal? Don't you think it's because of global warming?

– Well, I think it's a combination of the greenhouse effect and nuclear testing.

– Vous croyez que c'est normal, ce temps affreux? Vous ne croyez pas que ce soit à cause du réchauffement de l'atmosphère?
– Eh bien, moi je pense que c'est le résultat de l'effet de serre combiné avec les effets des essais nucléaires.

25 Government and politics

25a Political life

I abolish **je supprime**
act (of parliament) **la loi**
administration **l'administration** *(f)*
I appoint **je nomme**
appointment **la nomination**, la **désignation**
asylum seeker **le réfugié politique**
it becomes law **il devient** *(devenir)* **loi**
bill **le projet de loi**
I bring down **je fais tomber**
citizen **le citoyen, la citoyenne**
civil disobedience **la résistance passive**
civil servant **le fonctionnaire**
civil war **la guerre civile**
coalition **la coalition**
it comes into effect **il entre en vigueur**
common **commun**
constitution **la constitution**
cooperation **la coopération**
corruption **la corruption**
county **le comté**
coup **le coup d'état**
crisis **la crise**
debate **le débat**
decree **le décret**
delegate **le délégué**
I demonstrate **je manifeste**
demonstration **la manifestation**
I discuss **je discute de**
discussion **la discussion**
I dismiss **je congédie**
I dissolve **je dissouds** *(dissoudre)*
I draw up (a bill) **je rédige un projet de loi**
duty **le devoir**
I emigrate **j'émigre**
equality (in-) **l'(in)égalité** *(f)*

executive **l'exécutif** *(m)*
executive *(adj)* **exécutif [-ve]**
foreign policy **la politique extérieure**
I form a pact with **je signe un pacte avec**
freedom **la liberté**
freedom of speech **la liberté de parole**
I govern **je gouverne**
government **le gouvernement**
I immigrate **j'immigre**
immigration **l'immigration** *(f)*
I introduce (a bill) **je présente (un projet de loi)**
judiciary **le pouvoir judiciaire**
law **la loi**
I lead **je dirige**
legislation **la législation**
legislature **le législatif**
liberty **la liberté**
local affairs **les affaires** *(f)* **locales**
local government **l'administration** *(f)* **locale**
long-term **à long terme**
majority **la majorité**
meeting **le meeting, la réunion**
middle class **la bourgeoisie, la classe moyenne**
middle-class *(adj)* **bourgeois**
ministry **le ministère**
minority **la minorité**
moderate **modéré**
nation **la nation**
national **national**
national flag **le drapeau national**
French national flag **le drapeau tricolore**
I nationalize **je nationalise**
I oppose **je m'oppose à**

opposition   l'opposition *(f)*
I organize   j'organise
I overthrow   je renverse
pact   le pacte
I pass (a bill)   j'adopte (un projet de loi)
policy/politics   la politique
political   politique
power   le pouvoir
I privatize   je privatise
I protest   je proteste
public   le public
    public *(adj)*   public [-que]
public opinion   l'opinion *(f)* publique
I ratify   je ratifie
reactionary   réactionnaire
I reform   je réforme
reform   la réforme
I reject   je rejette *(rejeter)*
I repeal *(a law)*   j'abroge, je révoque
I represent   je représente
I repress   je réprime
I resign   je démissionne
responsible   responsable

responsiblity   la responsabilité
reunification   la réunification
revolt   la révolte
I rule   je gouverne
sanction   la sanction
seat   le siège (parlementaire)
short-term   à court terme
solidarity   la solidarité
speech   le discours
state   l'état *(m)*
statesman   l'homme *(m)* d'Etat
I support   je soutiens *(soutenir)*
I take power   je m'empare du pouvoir
(4-year) term of office   la durée/période (de 4 ans)
I throw out (a bill)   je rejette *(rejeter)* (un projet de loi)
unconstitutional   inconstitutionnel[le]
unilateral   unilatéral
unity   l'unité *(f)*
veto   le veto
I veto   j'exerce le droit de veto
welfare   le bien-être
working class   la classe ouvrière

The deputy introduced a bill to legalize the use of marijuana.

Le député a présenté un projet de loi pour légaliser l'usage de la marijuana.

The Lower Chamber voted on the question of immigration controls.

La Chambre des Députés a voté sur la question des contrôles de l'immigration.

The Treasury promised to cut the proportion of national income taken in taxes to 30 percent.

Le Ministère des Finances a promis de réduire la proportion de la taxe sur le revenu à trenté pour cent.

French government funding for the arts is to be cut next year.

Les subventions données par le gouvernement français aux arts doivent être réduites l'année prochaine.

GOVERNMENT AND POLITICS

25b Elections and ideology

Elections

ballot   **le scrutin**
ballot box   **les urnes** *(f)*
ballot paper   **le bulletin de vote**
by-election   **l'élection** *(f)* **partielle**
I hold an election   **je procède**
   (procéder) **à une élection**
campaign   **la campagne**
candidate   **le candidat**
constituency   **la circonscription**
count   **le dépouillement (des**
   votes d'un scrutin)
I elect   **j'élis**
election   **l'élection** *(f)*
electorate   **l'électorat** *(m)*
enfranchised   **admis au suffrage**
entitled to vote   **qui a le droit de**
   vote
floating vote   **le vote flottant**
general election   **les élections** *(f)*
   législatives

I go to the polls   **je me rends** *(se*
   rendre) **aux urnes**
opinion poll   **le sondage d'opinion**
poll   **le scrutin**
primary   **primaire**
recount   **le deuxième compte (des**
   suffrages)
I recount   **je compte de nouveau**
referendum   **le référendum**
right to vote   **le droit de vote**
seven-year term of office *(French*
   presidency)   **le septennat**
I stand for election   **je me présente**
   aux élections
suffrage   **le suffrage**
swing   **le revirement d'opinion**
universal suffrage   **le suffrage**
   universel
vote   **le vote**
I vote (for)   **je vote (pour)**
voter   **l'électeur** *(m)*

Parliamentary elections are held every five years. Presidential elections in the USA occur every four years.

Les élections législatives ont lieu tous les cinq ans. Les élections présidentielles aux Etats-Unis ont lieu tous les quatre ans.

The voters went to the polls today; it was a record turnout.

Aujourd'hui les électeurs se sont rendus aux urnes; c'était un scrutin record.

An opinion poll taken yesterday gave the Democrats a two-point lead over the Republicans.

Un sondage d'opinion effectué hier a révélé que les Démocrates ont deux points d'avance sur les Républicains.

In the local elections, the Liberal Democrat Party won a majority of seats on the town council.

Aux élections municipales, le Parti Libéral-Démocrate a gagné une majorité de sièges au conseil municipal.

Political ideology

anarchist **l'anarchiste** *(m)*, **l'anar** *(m) (fam)*

anarchy **l'anarchie** *(f)*

anti-Semitism **l'antisémitisme** *(m)*

anti-Semitic **l'antisémite** *(m)*

aristocracy **l'aristocratie** *(f)*

aristocrat **l'aristocrate** *(m)*

aristocratic **aristocrate**

capitalism **la capitalisme**

capitalist **capitaliste**

center ground **le centre**

communism **le communisme**

communist **communiste**

conservatism **le conservatisme**

conservative **le conservateur**

democracy **la démocratie**

democrat **le démocrate**

democratic **démocrate**

dictator **le dictateur**

dictatorship **la dictature**

duke **le duc**

empire **l'empire** *(m)*

emperor/empress **un empereur, une impératrice**

extremist **un/une extrémiste**

fascism **le fascisme**

fascist **le fasciste**

I gain independence **je gagne l'indépendance**

Green party **le parti des Ecologistes/Ecolos, les Verts**

ideology **l'idéologie** *(f)*

imperialism **l'impérialisme** *(f)*

imperialist **impérialiste**

independence **l'indépendance** *(f)*

independent **indépendant**

king **le roi**

Labor party **le parti Travailliste**

left **la gauche**

left-wing **de la gauche**

liberal **libéral**

Liberal Democrats **les Démocrates-Libéraux** *(m)*

liberalism **le libéralisme**

Liberals **les Libéraux** *(m)*

Marxism **le marxisme**

Marxist **le marxiste**

monarchy **la monarchie**

nationalism **le nationalisme**

nationalist **nationaliste**

patriotic **patriote**

patriotism **le pariotisme**

prince **le prince**

princess **la princesse**

queen **la reine**

racism **le racisme**

racist **raciste**

radicalism **le radicalisme**

radical **radical**

republic **la république**

republican **républicain**

republicanism **le républicanisme**

revolutionary **révolutionnaire**

right **la droite**

right-wing **de la droite**

royal **royal**

royalist **royaliste**

socialism **le socialisme**

socialist **socialiste**

Socialist **le/la socialiste**

French political parties

le Mouvement des Radicaux de Gauche (MRG) Radical Left

le Parti Communiste Français (PCF) Communist Party

le Parti Socialiste (PS) Socialist Party

le Rassemblement pour la République (RPR) Gaullist Republican Assembly

L'Union pour la Démocratie Française (UDF) Democrats

les Verts Green Party

le Front National National Front

26 Crime and justice

26a Crime

accomplice **le complice**

armed **armé**

assault **l'agression** *(f)*

assault and battery **coups** *(m)* **et blessures** *(f)*

battered baby **l'enfant** *(m)* **martyre**

burglar **le cambrioleur**

burglary **le cambriolage, le vol avec effraction**

I burglarize **je cambriole, je dévalise**

car theft **le vol de voiture**

theft *(from car)* **le vol à la roulotte**

child abuse **les mauvais traitements** *(m)* **infligés à un enfant**

I come to blows **j'en viens** *(venir)* **aux mains**

I commit **je commets** *(commettre)*

crime **le crime**

crime rate **le taux de la délinquance**

crime wave **la vague de criminalité**

criminal **le criminel, la criminelle**

I deceive **je trompe**

delinquency **la délinquance**

drug abuse **la toxicomanie**

drug addict **le toxicomane, le drogué**

drug barons **les gros trafiquants** *(m)*

drug dealer **le trafiquant**

drug pusher **le revendeur/la revendeuse de drogue**

drugs **la drogue**

drug-trafficking **le trafic de la drogue**

I embezzle **je détourne (de l'argent)**

embezzlement **le détournement de fonds**

extortion **l'extorsion** *(f)*

I fight **je me bats** *(se battre)*

fight **la bagarre**

firearm **une arme à feu**

I forge *(banknote)* **je contrefais** *(contrefaire)*

I forge *(signature)* **je falsifie**

forged **faux [fausse]**

forgery **la contrefaçon**

fraud **la supercherie, la fraude**

gang **la bande, le gang**

gang warfare **la guerre entre les bandes**

grievous bodily harm (GBH) **coups** *(m)* **et blessures** *(f)*

gun **le fusil**

handbag snatching **le vol à l'arraché**

handcuffs **les menottes** *(f)*

Help! **Au secours!**

hoax (call) **la mauvaise plaisanterie**

I hi jack **je détourne un avion**

hi jacker **le pirate de l'air**

hold up **le hold-up**

hooker **la putain** *(fam)*, **la prostituée**

hostage **l'otage** *(m)*

I importune **j'importune**

I injure/wound **je blesse**

I joyride **je fais une virée/une balade (dans une voiture volée)**

joyriding **la balade (dans une voiture volée)**

I kidnap **j'enlève** *(enlever)*

kidnapper **le kidnappeur, le ravisseur**

kidnapping   **le kidnapping, le rapt**
I kill   **je tue**
killer   **le tueur**
knifing   **l'agression** (f) **à coups de couteau**
legal (il-)   **(il)légal**
living off immoral earnings   **le proxénétisme**
mafia   **la mafia**
menace to society   **un danger public**
I mug   **j'agresse**
mugger   **l'agresseur** (m)
mugging   **l'agression** (f)
murder   **le meurtre**
I murder   **j'assassine**
murderer   **l'assassin** (m)
I offend   **je commets** (commettre) **une infraction**
pickpocket   **le voleur à la tire, le pickpocket**
pickpocketing   **le vol à la tire**
pimp   **le proxénète, le maquereau** (fam)

pimping   **le proxénétisme**
poison   **le poison**
I poison   **j'empoisonne**
procuring   **le proxénétisme**
prostitute   **la prostituée**
prostitution   **la prostitution**
public enemy No.1   **l'ennemi** (m) **public numéro un**
I rape   **je viole**
rape   **le viol**
receiver   **le receleur, la receleuse**
reprisals   **les représailles** (f)
shoplifting   **le vol à l'étalage**
I steal   **je vole**
stolen goods   **la marchandise volée**
terrorist   **le terroriste**
torture   **la torture**
thief   **le voleur**
traffic violation   **la contravention**
trafficking   **le trafic**
I traffick   **je trafique**
underworld   **le milieu**
victim   **la victime**

Pablo Escobar, the world's most infamous drug baron, was killed in a shootout with police and the army.

Pablo Escobar, le narco-trafiquant le plus infâme du monde, a été tué au cours d'une fusillade contre la police et l'armée.

He was stopped by the police for speeding in a residential area.

La police l'a arrêté pour excès de vitesse dans un quartier résidentiel.

Members of the public have begun to give information to the police about the rape of two teenage girls by a gang last week.

Le public a commencé à donner des informations à la police sur le viol de deux jeunes filles, commis la semaine dernière par une bande de voyous.

Many inner-city areas have seen an increase in crimes against the person as well as breakins.

Beaucoup de quartiers déshérités ont connu une augmentation de crimes contre la personne et des cambriolages.

➤ WEAPONS 27b; ADDICTION AND VIOLENCE 12d

CRIME AND JUSTICE

26b Trial

accusation   **l'accusation** *(f)*
I accuse   **j'accuse**
accused person   **l'accusé** *(m)*
I acquit   **j'acquitte**
I acquit for lack of evidence   **je
rends** *(rendre)* **une ordonnance
de non-lieu**
appeal   **le pourvoi, l'appel** *(m)*
I appeal   **je fais appel**
case for the defense   **les
arguments** *(m)* **en faveur de
l'accusé**
compensation   **la compensation,
la rémunération**
confession   **l'aveu** *(m)*
I confess   **je passe aux aveux**
I convince   **je convaincs**
(convaincre), **je persuade**
costs   **les dépens** *(m)*, **les frais**
(m) **judiciaires**
counsel for the defendant/defense
(l'avocat *(m)* **de) la défense**
court   **la cour, le tribunal**
court of appeal   **la cour d'appel**
courtroom   **la salle du tribunal**
criminal court   **le tribunal
correctionnel**
I cross-examine   **je fais subir un
interrogatoire à**
I debate   **le débat**
defense   **la défense**
I defend   **je défends**
I defend (myself)   **je me défends**
defendant   **un accusé, une
accusée**
diminished responsibility   **la
responsabilité atténuée**
I disagree   **je ne suis pas
d'accord**
I discuss   **je discute**
district attorney *(US)*   **le
représentant du ministère
public**
I enquire   **j'enquête sur**
evidence   **la preuve**

examining magistrate   **le juge
d'instruction**
extenuating circumstances   **des
circonstances** *(f)* **atténuantes**
I extradite   **j'extrade**
eye witness   **le témoin oculaire**
I find guilty   **je déclare coupable**
he was found guilty   **il a été
déclaré coupable**
I give evidence   **je témoigne**
I give evidence for the defense   **je
témoigne pour la défense**
guilt   **la culpabilité**
guilty   **coupable**
high court of appeal   **la cour de
cassation**
impeach   **je mets** *(mettre)* **en
accusation**
impeachment   **la mise en
accusation**
indictment   **l'acte** *(f)* **d'accusation**
indictment in court   **le
réquisitoire**
innocence   **l'innocence** *(f)*
innocent   **innocent, non coupable**
judge   **le juge**
juror   **le juré**
jury   **le jury**
jury box   **le banc des jurés**
justice   **la justice**
lawsuit   **le procès**
lawyer   **l'avocat** *(m)*
leniency   **la clémence**
life imprisonment   **la peine de
prison à vie, la réclusion à vie,
à perpétuité**
litigation   **le litige**
magistrate   **le magistrat**
magistrate's court   **le tribunal
d'instance**
mercy   **la pitié, l'indulgence** *(f)*
minor offense   **le délit mineur**
miscarriage of justice   **l'erreur** *(f)*
judiciaire
motive   **le motif, l'intention** *(f)*

not guilty **non coupable**
oath **le serment**
offence **le délit, l'infraction** *(f)*
on remand **en détention préventive, en prévention**
I pass judgment **je prononce, je rends** *(rendre)* **un jugement**
perjury **le faux serment, le parjure**
plea **la défense, l'argument** *(m)*
I plead (not) guilty **je plaide (non) coupable**
premeditation **la préméditation**
I prosecute **je poursuis** *(poursuivre)* **en justice**
prosecution **l'accusation** *(f)*
public prosecutor **le procureur (de la République)**
public prosecutor's office **le parquet**
I question **je questionne**
I interrogate **j'interroge**
retrial **le nouveau procès**
I rescue **je sauve**
reward **la récompense**
speech for the defense **le plaidoyer, la plaidoirie**

I stand accused **je suis accusé**
I stand bail for *(someone)* **je me porte garant pour**
statement **la déposition**
I sue/I take to court **j'intente un procès à**
summing up **le résumé**
summons **la citation**
I suspect **je soupçonne, je suspecte**
suspect **le suspect, la suspecte**
Supreme Court **la Cour suprême**
sustained! **accordée!**
I swear **je jure**
I take legal proceedings **je poursuis** *(poursuivre)* **en justice**
I take prisoner **je fais prisonnier**
trial **le procès**
unanimous **unanime**
verdict **le verdict**
I witness **je suis témoin de, j'assiste à**
witness **le témoin**
witness stand **le banc des accusés**
writ **l'acte** *(m)* **judiciaire**

The case against the accused was dismissed on grounds of insufficient evidence.

On a déclaré un non-lieu pour insuffisance de preuves.

The accused had strong connections in the underworld.

L'accusé avait des relations importantes dans le milieu.

The judge imposed a fine of 5,000 euros and ordered the accused to pay costs.

Le juge a imposé une amende de 5.000 euros et a condamné l'accusé aux dépens.

A man will appear in court today charged with the attempted murder of a 14-month-old baby boy.

Un homme, inculpé d'une tentative de meurtre d'un enfant de quatorze mois, comparaîtra ce matin devant la Cour d'Assises.

CRIME AND JUSTICE

26c Punishment and crime prevention

Punishment

confinement/imprisonment **la réclusion (criminelle)**
in solitary confinement **en isolement**
I convict **je déclare coupable**
convict **le détenu**
death penalty **la peine de mort**
I deport **je déporte**
I escape **je m'échappe, je m'évade**
fine **l'amende** *(f)*
I fine **je condamne à une amende**
I free **je libère** *(libérer)*
hard labor **les travaux** *(m)* **forcés**
I imprison **j'emprisonne, je mets** *(mettre)* **en prison**
jail sentence **la peine de prison**
life sentence **la réclusion à perpétuité**
prison **la prison**
prisoner **le détenu, la détenue, le prisonnier, la prisonnière**
I punish **je punis**
punishment **la punition, le châtiment**
I release on bail **je mets** *(mettre)* **en liberté provisoire sous caution**
I reprieve a condemned prisoner **j'accorde une remise de peine au condamné**

I sentence to death **je condamne à mort**
I serve a sentence **je purge une peine**
sentence **la sentence, la peine**
severity **la sévérité**
suspended sentence **la condamnation avec sursis**
a term of 10 years **une peine de dix ans**

Crime prevention

alarm **l'alarme** *(f)*
burglar/car alarm **la sonnerie d'alarme**
autopsy **l'autopsie** *(f)*
arrest **l'arrestation** *(f)*
I arrest **j'arrête**
baton **la matraque**
(hearing) in camera **à huis clos**
chief of police **le commissaire de police**
civil law **le code civil**
crime prevention **la lutte contre le crime**
criminal law **le droit pénal**
criminal record **le casier judiciaire**
clean *(record)* **vierge**
customs **la douane**
customs officer **le douanier**
deportation **la déportation**
detective **le détective**

– What was the verdict in the trial?

– He was sentenced to four years' imprisonment.

– Will he serve that long?

– No, nothing like it. He'd already spent 8 months awaiting trial. He'll probably be out in two years.

– Quel a été le verdict à la fin du procès?

– On l'a condamné à une peine de quatre ans.

– Et il en purgera autant?

– Pas du tout! Il avait déjà passé huit mois en détention préventive, avant le procès. Il en sortira probablement dans deux ans.

drug raid **la rafle, la saisie de drogues**

drug squad **la Brigade des Stupéfiants, les Stups** *(fam)*

enquiry/inquiry **l'enquête** *(f)*

error **l'erreur** *(f)*, **la bavure**

escape **la fuite, l'évasion** *(f)*

I escape (to) **j'échappe, je m'échappe (de)**

examination **l'examen** *(m)*

I examine **j'examine**

extradition **l'extradition** *(f)*

fingerprints **les empreintes** *(f)* **digitales**

fugitive **le fugitif, la fugitive**

guard dog **le chien de garde**

handcuff **les menottes** *(f)*

identikit/photofit picture **le portrait-robot**

informer **le délateur, la délatrice**

interview **l'entrevue** *(f)*

I interview **j'interroge**

I investigate **je fais une enquête**

investigation **l'enquête** *(f)*

investigator **un investigateur, une investigatrice**

   private investigator **le détective privé**

key **la clé, la clef**

law **la loi**

lock **la serrure**

I lock **je ferme à clef**

misdemeanor **l'infraction** *(f)*, **le délit**

padlock **le cadenas**

plainclothes *(adj)* **en civil**

police **la police**

police officer **l'agent** *(m)* **de police**

policewoman **la femme agent (de police)**

police badge **la plaque**

police constable *(UK)* **l'agent** *(m)*, **le gendarme**

police record **le casier judiciaire**

   clean *(record)* **vierge**

police station **le commissariat**

reward **la récompense**

riot police **les CRS (la Compagnie Républicaine de Sécurité)**

security **la sécurité**

security firm **la société de surveillance**

I set bail at $5,000 **je fixe la caution à $5.000**

speed trap **le piège de police pour contrôle de vitesse**

station **le commissariat**

traffic police **la police de la route/circulation**

traffic warden **le contractuel, la contractuelle**

truncheon **la matraque**

warrant **le mandat**

   search warrant **le mandat de perquisition**

– Did he plead guilty?
– Yes, to manslaughter on grounds of diminished responsibility/ insanity.

– Il a plaidé coupable?
– Oui, à l'homicide involontaire, pour raison de responsabilité atténuée.

He was convicted of breaking and entering and given a suspended sentence of two years.

Il a été déclaré coupable de vol avec effraction, et on l'a condamné à une peine de deux ans avec sursis.

➤ ADDICTION AND VIOLENCE 12d

27 War and peace

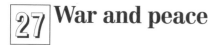

27a War

I abduct   **j'enlève** *(enlever)*
aggression   **l'agression** *(f)*
aerial bombing   **le bombardement aérien**
air force   **l'armée** *(f)* **de l'air**
I airlift   **l'évacue par pont aérien**
air-raid   **l'attaque** *(f)* **aérienne, le raid aérien**
air-raid shelter   **l'abri** *(m)*
air-raid warning   **l'alerte** *(f)* **(aérienne)**
ambush   **l'embuscade** *(f)*
anti-aircraft   **antiaérien[ne]**
army   **l'armée** *(f)*
I assassinate   **j'assassine**
assault   **l'assaut** *(m)*
atomic   **atomique**
atrocity   **l'atrocité** *(f)*
I attack   **j'attaque**
attack   **l'attaque** *(f)*
barracks   **la caserne**
battle   **la bataille**
battlefield   **le champ de bataille**
blast   **l'explosion** *(f)*, **le souffle**
I blockade   **je bloque**
blockade   **le blocus**
I blow up   **je fais sauter**
bomb alert   **l'alerte** *(f)* **à la bombe**
bombardment   **le bombardement**
brave   **courageux [-se]**
war breaks out   **la guerre éclate**
I call up   **j'appelle** *(appeler)* **sous les drapeaux**
camp   **le camp**
campaign   **la campagne**
I capture   **je capture**
causes of war   **les causes** *(f)*
I claim responsibility for   **je revendique**

I commit *(an act)*   **je commets** *(commettre)*
conflict   **le conflit**
confrontation   **l'affrontement** *(m)*
I contaminate   **je contamine**
conventional *(weapon)*   **classique**
court-marshal   **le conseil de guerre**
cowardly   **lâche**
the plane crashes   **l'avion** *(m)* **s'écrase**
I crush *(opposition)*   **j'écrase**
I declare (war)   **je déclare (la guerre)**
defeat   **la défaite**
I defeat   **je bats** *(battre)*
I am defeated   **je suis vaincu** *(vaincre)*
defense   **la défense**
I defend   **je défends**
I destroy   **je détruis** *(détruire)*
I detain   **je détiens** *(détenir)*
I detect   **je détecte, je découvre** *(découvrir)*
devastating   **dévastateur [-trice]**
enemy   **l'ennemi** *(m)*
espionage   **l'espionnage** *(m)*
ethnic cleansing   **le nettoyage/ l'épuration** *(f)* **ethnique**
I evacuate   **j'évacue**
evacuation   **l'évacuation** *(f)*
I fight a battle   **je livre bataille**
I fight off   **je repousse**
I flee   **je fuis** *(fuir)*, **je m'enfuis** *(enfuir)*
front   **le front**
genocide   **le génocide**
guerrilla warfare   **la guérilla**
harmful   **nuisible**

headquarters **le quartier général**
hostilities **les hostilités** *(f)*
I interrogate **j'interroge**
interrogation **l'interrogation** *(f)*
I intervene **j'interviens** *(intervenir)*
intervention **l'intervention** *(f)*
intimidation **l'intimidation** *(f)*
I invade **j'envahis**
invasion **l'invasion** *(f)*
I issue an ultimatum **je lance un ultimatum**
I liquidate **j'anéantis**
maneuvers **les manœuvres** *(f)*
massacre **le massacre**
missing in action **porté disparu**
military service **le service militaire**
mobilization **la mobilisation**
I mobilize **je mobilise**
morale **le moral**
multilateral **multilatéral**
navy **la marine**
nuclear **nucléaire**
occupation **l'occupation** *(f)*
I occupy **j'occupe**
offensive **l'offensive** *(f)*
I patrol **je fais une patrouille**
peace **la paix**
propaganda **la propagande**
I provoke **je provoque**
battle rages **la bataille fait rage**
raid **le raid**
rank **le grade, le rang**

reinforcements **les renforts** *(m)*
reprisals **les représailles** *(f)*
I resist **je résiste à**
resistance **la résistance**
review **la revue** *(f)*
I revolt **je me révolte**
revolution **la révolution**
riot **l'émeute** *(f)*
rubble **les décombres** *(f)*
shelter **l'abri** *(m)*
skirmish **l'accrochage** *(m)*
I spy **je fais de l'espionnage**
I start a war **je déclare la guerre**
strategy **la stratégie**
striking power **la force de frappe**
the vessel submerges **le vaisseau plonge/s'immerge**
the vessel surfaces **le vaisseau fait surface**
survival **la survie**
tactics **la tactique**
terrorist attack **l'attentat** *(m)* **terroriste**
I threaten **je menace**
trench **la tranchée**
underground **clandestin**
war **la guerre**
war crime **le crime de guerre**
warmongering **belliciste**
I win **je gagne, je suis victorieux [-se]**

Hitler invaded Poland on September 1, 1939. Two days later, Britain and France declared war on Germany.

Hitler envahit la Pologne le 1er septembre 1939. Deux jours après, la Grande-Bretagne et la France déclarèrent la guerre à l'Allemagne.

The Christmas truce was broken as hostilities broke out again in Bosnia.

La trêve de Noël a été rompue, alors que des hostilités ont de nouveau éclaté en Bosnie.

Civil wars are the bloodiest of all.

Les plus ensanglantées de toutes sont les guerres civiles.

WAR AND PEACE

27b Military personnel and weaponry

aggressor **l'agresseur** *(m)*
ally **un allié, une alliée**
archer **l'archer** *(m)*
assassin **l'assassin** *(m)*
casualty *(dead)* **le mort**
   casualty *(injured)* **le blessé**
cavalry **la cavalerie**
civilian **le civil, la civile**
commandos **les commandos** *(m)*
conscientious objector **l'objecteur**
   (m) **de conscience**
conscript **le conscrit, l'appelé** *(m)*
convoy **le convoi**
deserter **le déserteur**
division **la division**
foot soldier **le fantassin**
general **le général**
guard **le garde**
guerrilla **le guerrillero**
hostage **l'otage** *(m)*
infantry **l'infanterie** *(f)*
intelligence officer **l'officier** *(m)* **de**
   renseignements
marines *(UK)* **les fusiliers marins**
   (m)
marines *(US)* **les marines** *(m)*
NCO **le sous-officier**
orderly **le planton**
parachutist **le parachutiste**
prisoner of war **le prisonnier de**
   guerre
rebel **le/la rebelle**
recruit **la recrue**
regiment **le régiment**
seaman/sailor **le marin**
secret agent **l'agent** *(m)* **secret**
Secretary of Defense **le Ministre**
   de la Défense
sentry **la sentinelle**
sniper **le tireur isolé, le sniper**
soldier **le soldat**
spy **l'espion** *(m)*
squadron **l'escadron** *(m)*
staff **l'état-major** *(m)*

terrorist **le terroriste**
traitor **le traître**
troops **les troupes** *(f)*
victor **le vainqueur**

Weaponry and its effects

I aim (at) **je vise (sur)**
aircraft carrier **le porte-avions**
ammunition **les munitions** *(f)*
armaments **les armements** *(m)*
armored **blindé**
arms **les armes** *(m)*
arms manufacturer **le fabricant**
   d'armes
arms race **la course aux armements**
artillery **l'artillerie** *(f)*
bacteriologic **bactériologique**
barbed wire **les barbelés** *(m)*
bayonet **la baïonnette**
I bomb(ard) **je bombarde**
bomb **la bombe**
bombardment **le bombardement**
bomber *(aircraft)* **le bombardier**
bullet **la balle**
car bomb **la voiture piégée**
crossbow **l'arbalète** *(f)*
chemical **chimique**
destroyer *(ship)* **le contre-**
   torpilleur, le destroyer
I execute **j'exécute**
I explode a bomb **je fais exploser**
   une bombe
explosive **l'explosif** *(m)*
fallout **les retombées** *(f)*
fighter plane **l'avion** *(m)* **de**
   chasse, le chasseur
I fire (at) **je tire (sur)**
frigate **la frégate**
gas **le gaz**
gas attack **l'attaque** *(m)* **au gaz**
gun **le fusil**
handgrenade **la grenade**
H-bomb **la bombe-H**
it hits **il frappe, il atteint**

(atteindre) le but
jet *(plane)* le réacteur
I kill je tue
knife le couteau
laser le laser
letter bomb la lettre piégée
machine gun la mitrailleuse
minefield le champ de mines
mine sweeper le dragueur de mines
missile le missile
missile launcher le lance-missiles
mortar le mortier
neutron bomb la bombe à neutrons
nuclear test l'essai *(m)* nucléaire
nuclear warhead la tête *(f)* nucléaire, l'ogive *(f)* nucléaire
pistol le pistolet
poison gas le gaz toxique/asphyxiant
radar le radar
radar screen l'écran *(m)* du radar
radiation la radiation
radiation sickness le mal des rayons
radioactive radioactif [-ve]
revolver le revolver
rifle le fusil

rocket la fusée
rocket attack l'attaque *(f)* à la roquette
sabotage le sabotage
shell l'obus *(m)*
I shoot dead j'abats *(abattre)*
shotgun le fusil de chasse
shrapnel le shrapnel, les éclats *(m)* d'obus
siege le siège
I sink the ship je fais couler le navire
the ship sinks le navire coule/sombre
I stock-pile je constitue des réserves
submachine gun la mitraillette
submarine le sous-marin
tank le char
target la cible
I test je teste, j'examine
torpedo la torpille
torpedo attack une attaque à la torpille
I torpedo je torpille
warship le vaisseau de guerre
weapon l'arme *(f)*
wound la blessure, la plaie
I wound je blesse

Yesterday a man was shot dead by a sniper.

Hier, un homme a été abattu par un tireur isolé.

The explosion was several miles away, but it knocked everyone to the ground. Then the alert sounded for chemical weapons.

L'explosion s'est produite à plusieurs kilomètres de distance, mais la force a jeté tout le monde au sol. Puis, on a sonné l'alerte aux armes chimiques.

The event that has most marked the twentieth century is the Second World War.

L'événement qui a le plus marqué le vingtième siècle, c'est la Deuxième Guerre Mondiale.

WAR AND PEACE

27c Peace and international relations

Peace

ban-the-bomb campaign   **la campagne contre la bombe**
ceasefire   **le cessez-le-feu**
control   **le contrôle**
I demobilize   **je démobilise**
deterrent   **la force de dissuasion**
I diminish tension   **je travaille pour diminuer la tension**
disarmament   **le désarmement**
exchanges of information   **des échanges** *(m)* **d'informations**
free   **libre**
I free   **je libère** *(libérer)*
human rights   **les droits** *(m)* **de l'homme**
I make peace   **je conclus** *(conclure)* **la paix**
I mediate   **je sers** *(servir)* **d'intermédiaire**
national service   **le service national**
negotiable   **négociable, à débattre**
negotiation   **la négociation, les** *(m)* **pourparlers**
neutral   **neutre**
neutrality   **la neutralité**
pacifist   **le/la pacifiste**
pacifism   **le pacifisme**
peace agreement   **l'accord** *(m)*
peace plan   **le plan pour la paix**
peace protester   **le militant pour la paix**
peace talks   **les pourparlers** *(m)* **de paix**
peacekeeping force   **les forces** *(f)* **de maintien de la paix**
surrender   **la capitulation**
I surrender   **je me rends** *(se rendre)*, **je capitule**
test ban   **l'interdiction** *(f)* **des essais (nucléaires)**
treaty   **le traité**
uncommitted   **neutraliste**
victory   **la victoire**

International relations

aid   **l'aide** *(f)*
ambassador   **l'ambassadeur** *(m)*
arms reduction   **la réduction des armements**
attaché   **un attaché, une attachée**
citizen   **le citoyen, la citoyenne**
citizenship   **la citoyenneté**
consul   **le consul**
consulate   **le consulat**
developing countries   **les pays** *(m)* **en voie de développement**
diplomacy   **la diplomatie**
diplomat   **le/la diplomate**
diplomatic immunity   **l'immunité** *(f)* **diplomatique**

Emergency food aid was dropped on the mountains by UN Forces.

Les forces de l'ONU ont parachuté une aide alimentaire d'urgence dans les montagnes.

The French government was in danger of being embroiled in a diplomatic row.

Le gouvernement français risquait de se laisser entraîner dans une dispute diplomatique.

Importers continue to take advantage of the lowest possible tariff rates.

Les importateurs continuent de bénéficier des droits de douane les plus bas possibles.

embassy **l'ambassade** *(f)*
emergency **d'urgence**
envoy **un envoyé, une envoyée**
famine **la famine**
foreign **extérieur, étranger [-ère]**
foreigner **un étranger, une étrangère**
foreign relations **les relations** *(f)* **extérieures**
gap between rich and poor **l'écart** *(m)* **entre les riches et les pauvres**
I impose sanctions (against) **je prends** *(prendre)* **des sanctions** *(f)* **économiques (contre)**
international aid **l'aide** *(f)*
I join (organization) **je deviens** *(devenir)* **membre de**
national security **la sécurité nationale**
non aligned **non-aligné**
overseas **outre-mer**
partner **le/la partenaire**
relief organization **l'organisation** *(f)* **humanitaire**
relief supplies **les secours** *(m)*
I represent **je représente**
I ratify (treaty) **je ratifie**
sanctions **les sanctions** *(f)*
summit meeting **la rencontre au sommet**
Third World **le Tiers-Monde**

Trade

agricultural policy **la politique agricole**
balance of payments **la balance des paiements**
balance of trade **la balance commerciale**
currency **la monnaie, la devise**
customs **la douane**
customs union **l'union** *(f)* **douanière**
exchange rate **le taux de change**
exports **les exportations** *(f)*
floating currency **la devise flottante**
it floats **il flotte**
foreign investment **l'investissement** *(m)* **étranger**
free trade **le libre-échange**
free-trade zone **la zone franche**
import controls **les limites** *(f)* **sur les importations**
imports **les importations** *(f)*
tariff barriers **la barrière douanière**
tariffs **les tarifs** *(m)* **douaniers**
trade **le commerce**
trade gap **le déficit extérieur**
trade talks **les négociations** *(f)* **commerciales**
trading partner **la partenaire commercial**

The Secretary of State left this morning for a meeting with his opposite number in London.

Le Ministre des Affaires Etrangères est parti ce matin pour une entrevue avec son homologue à Londres.

The European Commission is looking into allegations of unfair trading practices/practises.

La Commission Européenne va faire une enquête sur certaines allégations de pratiques commerciales frauduleuse.

C

APPENDIXES

Appendixes

Appendixes are numbered by the vocabulary to which they most closely relate.

3b Clocks and watches

alarm clock   **le réveil**
clock   **la pendule l'horloge** *(f)*
cuckoo clock   **le coucou**
dial   **le cadran**
digital watch   **la montre à affichage numérique**
egg timer   **le sablier**
grandfather clock   **l'horloge** *(f)* **comtoise/de parquet**
hand (of a clock)   **l'aiguille** *(f)*
    second hand   **la trotteuse**
    minute hand   **la grande aiguille**
    hour hand   **la petite aiguille**
hourglass   **le sablier**
pendulum   **le balancier**
stopwatch   **le chronomètre**
sundial   **le cadran solaire**
timer *(cooker/lighting)*   **la minuterie**
watch   **la montre**
watch strap   **le bracelet de montre**
I wind up   **je remonte**

4d Mathematical and geometric terms

acute   **aigu**
algebra   **l'algèbre** *(f)*
algebraic   **algébrique**
Arabic numerals   **les nombres** *(m)* **arabes**
arithmetic   **l'arithmétique** *(m)*
arithmetical   **arithmétique**
average   **la moyenne**
axis   **l'axe** *(m)*
circumference   **la circonférence**
complex   **complexe**
constant   **la constante**
cube   **le cube**
cube root   **la racine cubique**
cubed   **au cube**
decimal   **la décimale**
equality   **l'égalité** *(f)*
factor   **le facteur**
I factor   **je factorise**
fraction   **la fraction**
function   **la fonction**
geometry   **la géométrie**
geometrical   **géométrique**
imaginary   **imaginaire**
integer   **le nombre entier**
irrational   **irrationnel**
logarithm   **le logarithme**
mean   **la moyenne**
median   **la médiane**
multiple   **le multiple**
nine is to three as . . .   **neuf est à trois ce que ...**
natural   **naturel**
numerical   **numérique**
obtuse   **obtus**
prime   **premier [-ère]**
product   **le produit**
probability   **la probabilité**
I raise to a power   **j'élève à la puissance**
    to the fifth power   **puissance cinq**
    to the *n*th power   **puissance** *n*
radius   **le rayon**
rational   **rationnel**
quotient   **le quotient**
real   **réel**
reciprocal   **réciproque**
Roman   **Romain**
set   **l'ensemble** *(m)*
square   **le carré**
square root   **la racine carrée**
symmetry   **la symétrie**
symmetrical   **symétrique**
table   **la table**

tangent   **la tangente**
trigonometry   **la trigonométrie**
variable   **la variable**
vector   **le vecteur**

5b Parts of the body

ankle   **la cheville**
arm   **le bras**
back   **le dos**
backbone   **la colonne vertébrale**
bladder   **la vessie**
blood   **le sang**
blood pressure   **la tension
   artérielle**
body   **le corps**
bone   **l'os** *(m)*
bowel   **l'intestin** *(m)*
brain   **le cerveau**
breast   **la poitrine, le sein**
buttock   **les fesses** *(f)*
cheek   **la joue**
chest   **la poitrine**
chin   **le menton**
ear   **l'oreille** *(f)*
elbow   **le coude**
eye   **l'œil** *(m)*, **les yeux**
eyebrow   **le sourcil**
eyelash   **le cil**
face   **le visage**
finger   **le doigt**
fingernail   **l'ongle** *(m)*
foot   **le pied**
forehead   **le front**
genitalia   **les organes** *(m)*
   génitaux
gland   **la glande**
hair   **les cheveux** *(m)*
hand   **la main**
head   **la tête**
heart   **le coeur**
hip   **la hanche**
hormone   **l'hormone** *(f)*
index finger   **l'index** *(m)*
jaw   **la mâchoire**
kidney   **le rein**
knee   **le genou**

knuckle   **l'articulation** *(f)*
leg   **la jambe**
lid   **la paupière**
lip   **la lèvre**
liver   **le foie**
lung   **le poumon**
mouth   **la bouche**
muscle   **le muscle**
nape of neck   **la nuque**
neck   **le cou**
nose   **le nez**
nostril   **la narine**
organ   **l'organe** *(m)*
part of body   **la partie du corps**
penis   **le pénis**
sex organs   **les organes** *(m)*
   sexuels
shoulder   **l'épaule** *(f)*
skin   **la peau**
stomach   **l'estomac** *(m)*
thigh   **la cuisse**
throat   **la gorge**
thumb   **le pouce**
toe   **l'orteil** *(m)*
tongue   **la langue**
tooth   **la dent**
vagina   **le vagin**
waist   **la taille**
womb   **l'utérus** *(m)*
wrist   **le poignet**

6a Human characteristics

absentminded   **distrait**
active   **actif [-ve]**
adaptable   **capable de s'adapter**
affection (-ate)   **l'affection** *(f)*,
   affectueux [-se]
aggression   **l'agression** *(f)*
aggressive   **agressif [-ve]**
ambition   **l'ambition** *(f)*
ambitious   **ambitieux [-se]**
amusing   **amusant**
anxious   **anxieux [-se]**
arrogant   **arrogant**
artistic   **artistique**
attractive   **attrayant**

211

6a Human characteristics (cont.)

bad-tempered **qui a mauvais caractère**	
bad/evil **méchant**	
boring **ennuyeux [-se]**	
brave **brave**	
care **le soin**	
careful **soigneux [-se]**	
careless **négligent**	
charm **le charme**	
charming **charmant**	
cheek **l'insolence** *(f)*	
cheeky **insolent**	
cheerful **joyeux [-se]**	
clever **intelligent**	
cold **froid**	
comic **comique**	
confidence **la confiance**	
confident **confiant**	
conscientious **consciencieux [-se]**	
courage **le courage**	
courtesy **la courtoisie**	
cowardly **lâche**	
creative **créatif [-ve]**	
critical **critique**	
cruel **cruel[le]**	
cruelty **la cruauté**	
cultured **cultivé**	
cunning **l'habileté** *(f)*	
curiosity **la curiosité**	
decisive (in-) **(in)décisif [-ve]**	
demanding **exigeant**	
dependence **la dépendance**	
dependent (in-) **(in)dépendant**	
dishonest **malhonnête**	
dishonesty **la malhonnêteté**	
disobedience **la désobéissance**	
distrustful **méfiant**	
eccentric **excentrique**	
energetic **énergique**	
envious **envieux**	
envy **l'envie** *(f)*	
extroverted **extraverti**	
faithful (un-) **(in)fidèle**	
faithfulness **la fidélité**	
friendly (un-) **(in)amical**	

frivolous **frivole**
generosity **la générosité**
generous **généreux [-se]**
gentle **gentil[le]**
gentleness **la gentillesse**
good-tempered **qui a bon caractère**
gluttony **la gourmandise**
greed *(for money)* **l'avidité** *(f)*
greedy **gourmand**
hardworking **travailleur**
helpful **serviable**
honest **honnête**
honesty **l'honnêteté** *(f)*
honor **l'honneur** *(m)*
humane (in-) **(in)humain**
humble **humble**
humorous **humoristique**
hypocritical **hypocrite**
idealistic **idéaliste**
imagination **l'imagination** *(f)*
imaginative **imaginatif [-ve]**
independence **l'indépendance** *(f)*
individualistic **individualiste**
innocence **l'innocence** *(f)*
innocent **innocent**
inquisitive **curieux [-se]**
intelligence **l'intelligence** *(f)*
intelligent **intelligent**
introverted **introverti**
ironic **ironique**
kind **gentil[le]**
kindness **la gentillesse**
laziness **la paresse**
lazy **paresseux [-se]**
liberal **libéral**
likable **sympathique**
lively **vivant**
lonely **seul**
lovable **adorable**
mad **fou [folle]**
madness **la folie**
malicious **méchant**
mature (im-) **(im)mature**
mean/stingy **avare**
modest **modeste**

modesty la **modestie**
moody **lunatique, ténébreux [-se]**
moral (im-) **(im)moral**
naive **naïf [-ve]**
naïvité la **naïveté**
natural **naturel[le]**
naughty **méchant**
nervous **nerveux [-se]**
nervousness la **nervosité**
nice **gentil[le]**
niceness la **gentillesse**
obedience l'**obéissance** *(f)*
obedient (dis-) **(dés)obéissant**
open **franc[he]**
openness la **franchise**
optimistic **optimiste**
original (-ity) **original**
originality l'**originalité** *(f)*
patience (im-) la **patience**
  (l'**impatience** *(f)*)
patient (im-) **(im)patient**
pessimistic **pessimiste**
pleasant **agréable**
polite (im-) **(im)poli**
politeness la **politesse**
possessive **possessif [-ve]**
prejudiced (un-) **(im)partial**
pride la **fierté**
proud **fier [-ère]**
reasonable (un-) **(de')raisonnable**
rebellious **rebelle**
reserved **réservé**
respect le **respect**
respectable **respectable**
respectful **respectueux [-se]**
responsible (ir-) **(dé)responsable**
rude **vulgaire**
rudeness la **vulgarité**
sad **triste**
sarcastic **sarcastique**
scornful **méprisant**
self-confident **sûr de soi**
self-esteem l'**amour** *(m)* **propre**
selfish (un-) **égoïste (généreux
  [-se])**
selfishness l'**égoïsme** *(m)*

self-sufficient **autosuffisant**
sensible **sensé**
sensitive (in-) **(in)sensible**
serious **sérieux [-se]**
shy **timide**
silent **silencieux [-se]**
silly **bête**
sincerity la **sincérité**
skilful **doué**
sociable (un-) **(in)sociable**
strange **bizarre**
strict **sévère**
stubborn **têtu**
stupid(ity) **stupide (la stupidité)**
suspicious **suspect**
sweet **adorable**
sympathetic (un-) **compatissant
  (peu compatissant)**
sympathy la **compassion**
tact le **tact**
he is tactful/tactless **il est plein de
  tact/il manque de tact**
talented **talentueux [-se]**
talkative **bavard**
temperamental **capricieux [-se]**
thoughtful **attentionné**
thoughtless **étourdi**
tidy (un-) **(dés)ordonné**
tolerance (in-) la **tolérance**
  (l'**intolérance** *(f)*)
tolerant (in-) **(in)tolérant**
traditional (un-) **(non-)
  traditionnel[le]**
trust la **confiance**
trusting **confiant**
vain **vaniteux [-se]**
vanity la **vanité**
violent **violent**
virtuous **virtueux [-se]**
warm **chaleureux [-se]**
well-adjusted **bien adapté**
well-behaved *(child)* **sage**
wisdom la **sagesse**
wise **sage**
wit l'**esprit** *(m)*
witty **spirituel[le]**

8b Tools

ax   **la hache**
bit   **le foret**
blade   **la lame**
bolt   **le boulon**
bucket   **le seau**
chainsaw   **la tronçonneuse**
chisel   **le ciseau**
crowbar   **la pince-monseigneur** *(m)*
drill   **le foret, la mèche**
file   **la lime**
garden gloves   **les gants** *(m)*
garden shears   **la cisaille de jardinier, le sécateur**
hammer   **le marteau**
hedge clippers   **le sécateur à haie**
hoe   **l'houe** *(f)*, **la binette**
hose   **le tuyau d'arrosage**
ladder   **l'échelle** *(f)*
lawnmower   **la tondeuse (à gazon)**
mallet   **le maillet**
nail   **le clou**
nut   **l'écrou** *(m)*
paint   **la peinture**
paintbrush   **le pinceau**
pick   **la pioche**
plane   **le rabot**
pliers   **la pince, la tenaille**
rake   **le râteau**
roller   **le rouleau de jardin**
sandpaper   **le papier de verre**
saw   **la scie**
screw   **la vis**
screwdriver   **le tournevis**
shovel   **la pelle**
spade   **la bêche**
spirit level   **le niveau à bulle**
stepladder   **l'escabeau** *(m)*
toolbox   **la boîte à outils**
trowel   **le déplantoir**
varnish   **le vernis**
vice   **l'étau** *(m)*
weedkiller   **le désherbant, l'herbicide** *(m)*

wrench (adjustable)   **la clé à molette**

9a Shops, stores, and services

antique shop   **(chez) l'antiquaire** *(m)*
art store   **la boutique d'objets d'art**
bakery   **la boulangerie**
bank   **la banque**
bookmaker's   **le PMU**
bookshop/store   **la librairie**
boutique   **la boutique**
butcher's   **la boucherie**
camera store   **le magasin de matériel photographique**
candy store   **le magasin de bonbons**
car parts store   **le magasin de pièces détachées**
clothes store   **la boutique de prêt-à-porter**
cosmetics shop/store   **la parfumerie**
covered market   **le marché couvert**
dairy   **la crèmerie**
delicatessen   **la charcuterie, le traiteur**
department store   **le grand magasin**
dress shop/store   **la boutique de prêt-à-porter**
drugstore   **le drugstore**
dry cleaners   **la blanchisserie**
electronics store   **le comptoir électrique**
fast-food restaurant   **le restaurant à service rapide**
fish store   **la poissonnerie**
fish-sellers stall   **le poissonnier (au marché)**
florist's   **chez le/la fleuriste**
furniture store   **le magasin de meubles**

garden center   **la pépinière**
greengrocer's   **le magasin de fruits et légumes**
grocer's   **l'épicerie** *(f)*
hairdresser   **le coiffeur, la coiffeuse**
hairdresser's   **le salon de coiffure**
hardware store   **la quincaillerie**
health-food store   **le magasin de diététique**
hypermarket   **l'hypermarché** *(m)*
indoor market   **le marché couvert**
jewelry store   **la bijouterie**
Laundromat   **la laverie**
lottery   **le kiosque de PMU**
mail-order house   **la maison de vente par correspondance**
market   **le marché**
men's wear store   **le magasin de prêt-à-porter masculin**
model (craft) store   **le magasin d'aéromodélisme**
music store   **le magasin de musique**
newsstand   **la maison de la presse, le kiosque à journaux**
optician's   **chez l'opticien**
outdoor market   **le marché en plein air**
pastry shop   **la patisserie**
pet store   **le magasin pour animaux domestiques**
pharmacy   **la pharmacie**
post office   **la poste**
pottery store   **le magasin de poterie**
shoe repair store (cobbler's)   **la cordonnerie**
shoe store   **le magasin de chaussures**
shop   **le magasin**

shopping mall/center/arcade   **le centre commercial, la galerie marchande**
souvenir shop   **le magasin de souvenirs**
sporting goods store   **le magasin de sport**
stationery store   **la papeterie**
store   **le magasin**
superstore   **la grande surface**
supermarket   **le supermarché**
take-out food store   **le magasin de plats à emporter**
thriftshop   **la boutique d'une œuvre de bienfaisance**
tobacconist   **le bureau de tabac**
toy store   **le magasin de jouets**
travel agent   **l'agence** *(f)* **de voyages**
vendor   **le vendeur, la vendeuse**
vending machine   **le distributeur**
video store   **le magasin de vidéocassettes**

9a Currencies

dollar   **le dollar**
euro   **l'euro** *(m)*
pence   **les pence**
penny   **le penny**
peso   **le peso**
pound sterling   **la livre sterling**
ruble   **le rouble**
swiss franc   **le franc suisse**

9c Jewelry

bangle   **le bracelet**
chain bracelet   **la gourmette**
brooch   **la broche**
carat   **le carat**
chain   **la chaînette**
charm   **la breloque**
cufflinks   **les boutons** *(m)* **de manchette**
earring   **les boucles** *(f)* **d'oreilles**
engagement ring   **la bague de fiançailles**
eternity ring   **la bague de fidélité**
jewel   **le bijou**
jewelry box   **le coffret à bijoux**
jewelry   **les bijoux** *(m)*
medallion   **le médaillon**
necklace   **le collier**
pendant   **le pendentif**
precious stone/gem   **la pierre précieuse**
real   **véritable**
ring   **la bague**
semiprecious   **la pierre fine/semi-précieuse**
tiara   **le diadème**
tie pin   **l'épingle** *(f)* **à cravate**
wedding ring   **l'alliance** *(f)*

9c Precious stones and metals

agate   **l'agate** *(f)*
amber   **l'ambre** *(m)*
amethyst   **l'améthyste** *(f)*
chrome   **le chrome**
copper   **le cuivre**
coral   **le corail**
crystal   **le cristal**
diamond   **le diamant**
emerald   **l'émeraude** *(f)*
gold   **l'or** *(m)*
gold plate   **plaqué or**
ivory   **l'ivoire** *(m)*
mother of pearl   **la nacre**
onyx   **l'onyx** *(m)*
opal   **l'opale** *(f)*

pearl   **la perle**
pewter   **l'étain** *(m)*
platinum   **le platine**
quartz   **le quartz**
ruby   **le rubis**
sapphire   **le saphir**
silver plate   **plaqué argent**
silver   **l'argent** *(m)*
topaz   **la topaze**
turquoise   **la turquoise**

10c Herbs and spices

aniseed   **l'anis** *(m)*
basil   **le basilic**
bay leaf   **la feuille de laurier** *(m)*
caper   **la câpre**
caraway   **le cumin**
chives   **la ciboulette**
cinnamon   **la cannelle**
clove   **le clou de girofle** *(m)*
dill   **l'aneth** *(m)*
garlic   **l'ail** *(m)*
ginger   **le gingembre**
marjoram   **la marjolaine**
mint   **la menthe**
mixed herbs   **les fines herbes** *(f)*
mustard   **la moutarde**
nutmeg   **la noix (de) muscade** *(f)*
oregano   **l'origan** *(m)*
parsley   **le persil**
pepper   **le poivre**
rosemary   **le romarin**
saffron   **le safran**
sage   **la sauge**
tarragon   **l'estragon** *(m)*
thyme   **le thym**

10d Cooking utensils

aluminum foil   **le papier d'aluminium**
baking tray   **la plaque à gâteaux**
carving knife   **le couteau à découper**
can opener   **l'ouvre-boîtes** *(m)*
colander   **la passoire**

food processor   **le robot de cuisine**
fork   **la fourchette**
frying pan   **la poêle**
grater   **la râpe**
grill   **le gril**
kettle   **la bouilloire**
knife   **le couteau**
lid   **le couvercle**
pot   **la marmite**
rolling pin   **le rouleau (à pâtisserie)**
saucepan/casserole dish   **la cocotte**
scales   **la balance**
sieve   **le tamis**
skewer   **la brochette**
spatula   **la spatule**
spoon   **la cuiller, la cuillère**
tablespoon   **la cuiller de service**
tablespoonful   **la cuillerée à soupe**
teaspoon   **la petite cuiller, la cuiller à thé/café**
teaspoonful   **la cuillerée à café**
tenderizer   **l'attendrisseur** *(m)*
wax paper   **le papier sulfurisé**

10d Smoking

ashtray   **le cendrier**
box of matches   **la boîte d'allumettes**
cigar   **le cigare**
cigarette   **la cigarette**
lighter   **le briquet**
matches   **les allumettes** *(f)*
pipe   **la pipe**
smoke   **la fumée**
I smoke   **je fume**
smoking   **fumer**
tobacco   **le tabac**
tobacconist's   **les bureaux** *(m)* **de tabac**

11c Hospital departments

admissions   **l'accueil** *(m)*
casualty/emergency   **les urgences** *(f)*
consulting room   **la salle de consultation**
coronary care   **la cardiologie**
dialysis unit   **le service de dialyse**
ear, nose and throat (ENT)   **ORL** *(f)*, **l'oto-rhino-laryngologie** *(f)*
eye clinic   **le service d'ophtalmologie**
geriatrics   **la gérontologie**
gynaecology ward   **le service de gynécologie**
infectious diseases   **les maladies** *(f)* **infectieuses**
intensive care   **les soins** *(m)* **intensifs**
intensive care unit   **la salle de réanimation**
maternity   **la maternité**
medical ward   **le service de médecine**
mortuary   **la morgue**
oncology   **l'oncologie** *(f)*
operating room   **le bloc opératoire**
orthopedic   **orthopédique**
outpatients department   **le service de consultations externes**
pediatrics   **la pédiatrie**
pathology   **la pathologie**
pharmacy   **la pharmacie**
psychiatry   **la psychiatrie**
reception   **la réception**
recovery room   **la salle de soins postopératoires**
surgery   **la chirurgie**
transfusion   **la transfusion**
treatment room   **la salle de soins**
ward   **la salle**
x-ray   **la radiographie**

11c Illnesses & diseases

AIDS   le SIDA
angina   l'infection *(f)* pulmonaire
appendicitis   l'appendicite *(f)*
arthritis   l'arthrose *(f)*
asthma   l'asthme *(m)*
bacillus   le bacille
bacteria   la bactérie
bronchitis   la bronchite
bubonic plague   la peste
   bubonique
cancer   le cancer
catarrh   le catarrhe
chickenpox   la varicelle
cholera   le choléra
colic   la colique
cold   le rhume
constipation   la constipation
corn   le cor
cough   la toux
deafness   la surdité
death   la mort
depression   la dépression
dermatitis   la dermatite
diabetes   le diabète
diarrhea   la diarrhée
diphtheria   la diphtérie
disease   la maladie
dizziness   le vertige,
   l'étourdissement *(m)*
earache   le mal d'oreille
eczema   l'eczéma *(m)*
epilepsy   l'épilepsie
fever   la fièvre
flatulence   la flatulence
flu   la grippe
food poisoning   l'intoxication *(f)*
   alimentaire
gallstone   le calcul biliaire
German measles   la rubéole
gingivitis   la gingivite
gonorrhea   la blennorragie
hemorrhoids   les hémorroïdes *(f)*
headache   le mal de tête
heart attack   la crise cardiaque
hepatitis   l'hépatite *(f)*

hernia   l'hernie *(f)*
high blood pressure
   l'hypertension *(f)*
HIV   le VIH, le HIV
illness   la maladie
incontinence   l'incontinence *(f)*
influenza   la grippe
infection   l'infection *(f)*
jaundice   la jaunisse
leukemia   la leucémie
malaria   le malaria, la paludisme
measles   la rougeole
meningitis   la méningite
mental illness   la maladie mentale
microbe   le microbe
migraine   la migraine
mumps   les oreillons
overdose   l'overdose *(f)*
piles   des hémorroïdes
pneumonia   la pneumonie
polio   la polio
pregnancy   la grossesse
rabies   la rage
rheumatism   le rhumatisme
rubella   la rubéole
salmonella   la salmonelle
scabies   la gale
seasickness   le mal de mer
sickness   la maladie
smallpox   la variole
stomachache   le mal à l'estomac
stomach upset   l'indigestion *(f)*
stroke   l'attaque *(f)*
sty   l'orgelet *(m)*
syphilis   la syphilis
temperature   la température
tetanus   le tétanos
thrombosis   la thrombose
tonsillitis   l'amygdalite *(f)*
toothache   le mal de dents, (avoir)
   mal aux dents
tuberculosis   la tuberculose
ulcer   l'ulcère *(m)*
urinary infection   l'infection *(f)*
   urinaire
venereal disease   la maladie
   vénérienne

whooping cough **la coqueluche**
yellow fever **la fièvre jaune**

11d Hairdresser

bangs **la frange**
bleach **la décoloration**
blow-dry **le brushing**
color chart **le nuancier**
color rinse **la coloration**
I cut **je coupe**
dye **la teinture**
hair **les cheveux** *(m)*
  dry **sec [sèche]**
  greasy/oily **gras[se]**
  gray **gris**
haircut **la coupe de cheveux**
I have my hair cut **je me fais**
  couper les cheveux
hairdresser **le coiffeur**
hairspray **la laque**
hairdo **la coiffure**
moustache **la moustache**
perm(anent wave) **la permanente**
setting lotion/gel **le fixateur**
shampoo and set **un shampooing**
  et une mise en plis
short **court**
sideburns **les favoris** *(pl)*
sides *(of head)* **les côtés** *(m)*
top *(of head)* **le dessus de la tête**
trim **la coupe d'entretien**
I trim **je rafraîchis**
  I trim *(beard)* **je taille**

13a Religious groups

Anglican Church **l'Eglise** *(f)*
  anglicane
French Reformed Church **l'Eglise**
  (f) **réformée de France**
Jehovah's Witnesses **les Témoins**
  (m) **de Jéhovah**
Methodists **les Méthodistes** *(m)*
Mormons **les Mormons** *(f)*
  (l'Eglise *(f)* **de Jésus-Christ des**
  saints des derniers jours)

Old Catholic Church **l'Eglise** *(f)*
  catholique traditionaliste
Pentecostalists **les Eglises** *(f)*
  pentecôtistes
Presbyterians **les Presbytériens**
  (m)
Roman Catholic Church **l'Eglise**
  (f) **catholique**
Quakers/Society of Friends **les**
  Quakers, la Société religieuse
  des Amis
Seventh Day Adventists **les**
  Adventistes *(m)*
Unitarians **les Unitariens** *(m)*

**13b Holidays and religious
festivals**

All Saints (Nov 1) **la Toussaint (le**
  1er nov)
All Souls (Nov 2) **le jour des**
  Morts (le 2 nov)
Ascension Day **l'Ascension** *(f)*
Ash Wednesday **le mercredi des**
  Cendres
Assumption Day (Aug 15)
  l'Assomption *(f)* **(le 15 août)**
bar mitzvah **la bar-mitzva** *(f)*
Boxing Day (Dec 26) **le lendemain**
  de Noël (le 26 déc)
Candlemass **la Chandeleur**
Carnival **le Carnaval** *(m)*
Christmas **Noël** *(m)*
  at Christmas **à Noël**
Christmas Day **le jour de Noël**
Christmas Eve **la veille de Noël**
Corpus Christi **la Fête-Dieu**
Easter **Pâques** *(fpl)*
Easter Monday **le lundi de**
  Pâques
Easter Sunday **le dimanche de**
  Pâques
Feast of the Assumption
  l'Assomption *(f)*
festival **le festival**
Good Friday **le vendredi Saint**

219

Hanukkah **Hanouka /la fête des lumières**
Halloween **la veille de la Toussaint**
Labor Day **la fête du travail**
Lent **le Carême**
New Year's Eve **la Saint-Sylvestre**
New Year's Day **le jour de l'an**
Jewish New Year **le Rosh Haschana**
Palm Sunday **les Rameaux** *(m)*
Passover **la Pâque**
Pentecost, Whitsuntide **la Pentecôte**
Ramadan **le Ramadan**
Sabbath **le Chabbat, le sabbat**
Shrove Tuesday **le Mardi gras**
Yom Kippur **le Yom Kippour**

14b Professions and jobs

The arts

actor/actress **un acteur, une actrice**
announcer **un annonceur, une annonceuse**
architect **un architecte**
artist **un artiste**
bookseller **un libraire**
cameraman **un caméraman**
editor **un rédacteur**
film/movie director **un réalisateur**
film/movie star **une star de cinéma**
journalist **un/une journaliste**
musician **un musicien, une musicienne**
painter (*artist*) **un peintre**
photographer **un photographe**
poet **un poète**
printer **un imprimeur**
producer (theater) **un metteur en scène**
publisher **un éditeur**
reporter **un reporter**

sculptor **un sculpteur**
singer **un chanteur, une chanteuse**
TV announcer **un speaker, une speakerine**
writer **un écrivain, un auteur**

Education and research

lecturer **un professeur**
physicist **un physicien, une physicienne**
primary-school teacher **un instituteur, une institutrice**
principal **un directeur, une directrice, un principal**
pupil (grade school) **un/une élève**
researcher **un chercheur, une chercheuse**
scientist **un/une scientifique**
secondary-school teacher **un professeur**
student **un étudiant, une étudiante**
technician **un technicien, une technicienne**

Food and retail

baker **un boulanger, une boulangère**
brewer **un brasseur**
butcher **un boucher, une bouchère**
buyer **un acheteur, une acheteuse**
caterer (supplying meals) **un traiteur**
cook **un cuisinier, une cuisinière**
farmer **un fermier**
fisherman **un pêcheur**
fishmonger **le poissonnier**
florist **un fleuriste, une fleuriste**
greengrocer **un marchand de fruits et légumes, un primeur**
grocer **un épicier, une épicière**
jeweler **un bijoutier, un bijoutière**

pharmacist   un **pharmacien, une pharmacienne**
pork butcher   un **charcutier**
representative   un **représentant**
sales assistant   un **employé/une employée de magasin**
storekeeper   un **commerçant, une commerçante**
tobacconist   un **marchand de tabac**
waiter   un **garçon (de café), un serveur**
vintner   un **viticulteur, une viticultrice**

Government service

civil servant   un/une **fonctionnaire**
clerk   un **employé, une employée**
customs officer   un **douanier**
firefighter   un **sapeur-pompier**
judge   un **juge**
member of Congress   un **député**
minister   un **ministre**
officer   un **officier**
policeman   un **agent de police**
policewoman   une **femme agent (de police)**
politician   un **homme politique**
sailor   un **marin**
secret agent   un **agent secret**
serviceman   un **militaire**
soldier   un **soldat**

Health care

dentist   un/une **dentiste**
doctor   un **docteur, une femme docteur**
midwife   une **sage-femme**
nurse   un **infirmier, une infirmière**
optician   un **opticien, une opticienne**
physician   un **médecin**
psychiatrist   un/une **psychiatre**
psychologist   un/une **psychologue**
surgeon   un **chirurgien, une femme chirurgien**
vet   un/une **vétérinaire**

Manufacturing and construction

bricklayer   un **maçon**
builder   un **constructeur, un entrepreneur**
carpenter   un **menuisier**
engineer   un **ingénieur**
foreman floor supervisor   un **contremaître**
glazier   un **vitrier**
industrialist   un **industriel, un chef d'industrie**
laborer   un **ouvrier**
manufacturer   un **fabricant**
mechanic   un **mécanicien**
metalworker   un **ferronnier**
miner   un **mineur**
plasterer   un **plâtrier**
stonemason   un **tailleur de pierres, un maçon**

Services

accountant   un **comptable**
actuary   un/une **actuaire**
agent   un **agent**
bank manager   un **directeur de banque**
businessman   un **homme d'affaires**
businesswoman   une **femme d'affaires**
career consultant   un **conseiller, une conseillère d'orientation professionnelle**
caretaker   un/une **concierge**
cleaner   une **femme de ménage, un agent de nettoyage**
computer programmer   un **progammeur, une progammeuse**
counselor   un **conseiller, une conseillère**
draftsman   un **dessinateur, une dessinatrice**
garbage collector   un **éboueur**
electrician   un **électricien**
furniture mover   un **déménageur**
gardener   un **jardinier**

guide **un guide**
hairdresser **un coiffeur, une coiffeuse**
insurance agent **un assureur**
interpreter **un interprète**
lawyer **un avocat**
letter carrier **un facteur**
librarian **un/une bibliothécaire**
meter (gas) reader **un employé du gaz**
office worker **un employé de bureau**
painter-decorator **un peintre décorateur**
plumber **un plombier**
priest **un prêtre**
real estate agent **un agent immobilier**
receptionist **un/une réceptionniste**
servant **un/une domestique, une bonne**
social worker **un assistant/une assistante social**
solicitor **un notaire, un avocat**
stockbroker **un agent de change**
surveyor **un géomètre, un expert**
tax inspector **un percepteur**
trade unionist **un syndicaliste**
translator **un traducteur, une traductrice**
travel agent **un agent touristique**
typist **un/une dactylo**
undertaker **un entrepreneur de pompes funèbres**

Transport

bus driver **un conducteur d'autobus**
driver **un conducteur, une conductrice**
driving instructor **un moniteur/une monitrice d'auto-école**
flight attendant **une hôtesse de l'air, un steward**
pilot **un pilote**
taxi driver **un chauffeur de taxi**
ticket inspector **un contrôleur de billets**
truck driver **un camionneur, un routier**

14c Places of work

blast furnace **le haut-fourneau**
branch office **l'agence** *(f)*, **la succursale**
brewery **la brasserie**
business park **le complexe commercial**
construction site **le chantier de construction**
distillery **la distillerie**
factory **l'usine** *(f)*, **la fabrique**
farm **la ferme**
foundry **la fonderie**
head office **le siège social**
hospital **l'hôpital** *(m)*
limited liability company (ltd.) **la société à responsabilité limité**
mill **l'usine** *(f)*
paper mill **l'usine** *(f)* **de papeterie, la papeterie**
sawmill **la scierie**
spinning mill **la filature**
steel mill **l'aciérie** *(f)*
weaving mill **atelier de tissage**
mine (coal) **la mine (de charbon)**
office **le bureau**
plant **l'usine** *(f)*, **la fabrique**
pub **la brasserie**
shop/store **le magasin**
steel plant **l'aciérie** *(f)*
sweatshop **l'atelier** *(m)* **(où on exploite les ouvriers)**
theme park **le parc d'attractions**
vineyard **le vignoble**
warehouse **l'entrepôt** *(m)*
workshop **l'atelier** *(m)*

15c Letter-writing

Dear **Cher**
Dear Mr. and Mrs. ... **Chers Monsieur et Madame ...**
Dear Peter **Cher Peter**

Dear Sir/Madam   **Cher, Chère Monsieur/Madame**
Madam   **Madame**
greetings from   **salutations de**
I am pleased   **je suis heureux [-se]**
I enclose   **je joins** *(joindre)*
all the best   **Meilleurs vœux**
best wishes from   **amitiés de la part de**
Love and kisses   **bons baisers, grosses bises**
Love from   **affectueusement**
With best wishes   **bien amicalement**
With kind regards   **meilleurs souvenirs**
Yours faithfully   **je vous prie d'agréer mes salutations distinguées**
Yours sincerely   **je vous prie d'agréer l'expression de mes sentiments les meilleurs**

15d Computer hardware

adapter   **l'adaptateur** *(m)*
battery   **la pile**
battery pack   **le paquet de piles**
CD-ROM   **le CD-ROM**
CD-ROM drive   **le lecteur de CD-ROM**
central processing unit   **l'unité** *(f)* **centrale**
charger   **le chargeur**
chip   **la puce**
clone   **le clon**
compatible   **compatible**
computer   **l'ordinateur** *(m)*
computer system   **le système informatique**
desktop   **un PC de bureau**
disk drive   **le lecteur de disque**
diskette   **la disquette**
display   **l'affichage** *(m)*
double density (disk)   **la double**

densité (d'un disque)
drive   **le lecteur**
electric socket   **la prise électrique**
flat screen monitor   **un écran plat**
floppy disk   **la disquette**
floppy drive   **le lecteur de disquette**
front-end processor   **le processeur frontal**
function key   **la touche de fonction**
hard disk   **le disque dur**
hard drive   **le lecteur de disque dur**
hardware   **le hardware, le matériel**
high density (disk)   **la disquette à haute densité**
input device   **l'unité** *(f)* **périphérique d'entrée**
joystick   **la manette de jeu, le joystick**
keyboard   **le clavier**
laptop   **l'ordinateur** *(m)* **portable**
liquid crystal display   **l'affichage** *(m)* **à cristaux liquides**
local area network (LAN)   **le réseau local**
Macintosh   **un mac**
mainframe computer   **l'ordinateur** *(m)* **central**
microprocessor   **le microprocesseur**
mini computer   **le mini-ordinateur**
modem   **le modem**
  dial-up   **une connexion par téléphone**
  DSL   **l'ADSL**
  cable   **le cable**
mouse   **la souris**
network   **le réseau, l'interconnexion** *(f)*
networked   **interconnecté**
notebook   **le PC de poche, un notebook**
on-line   **en ligne**
personal computer/PC   **l'ordinateur** *(m)* **individuel/ le PC**

plug-in drive   **le lecteur à fiche**
port   **le port**
portable   **portable**
processor   **l'unité** *(f)* **centrale**
QWERTY/AZERTY keyboard   **le clavier QWERTY/AZERTY**
random-access memory/RAM   **la mémoire vive/RAM**
resolution   **la résolution**
screen   **l'écran** *(m)*
scroll bar   **la barre de déplacement**
socket/port   **la prise/le port**
storage   **la mémoire**
terminal   **le terminal**
touch screen   **l'écran** *(m)* **tactile**
viewdata system   **le système de vidéographie interactive**
visual display unit, VDU   **la console de visualisation**
wide-area network (WAN)   **le réseau régional**

15d Computer software

algebraic   **algébrique**
algorithm   **l'algorithme** *(m)*
antivirus program   **le programme antivirus**
bug   **le défaut, l'erreur** *(f)*
byte   **l'octet** *(m)*
coded   **codé**
coding   **le codage**
command   **la commande**
compatibility   **la compatibilité**
compatible (in-)   **(in)compatible**
computer-aided design (CAD)   **la conception assistée par ordinateur (CAO)**
computer-aided learning (CAL)   **l'enseignement** *(m)* **assisté par ordinateur**
computer-aided language learning (CALL)   **l'apprentissage** *(m)* **des langues assisté par ordinateur**
computer language   **le langage de**

programmation
copy   **la copie**
data capture   **la saisie des données**
data logging   **l'enregistrement** *(m)* **des données**
data   **les données** *(f)*
databank   **le stockage de données**
data processing   **le traitement des données**
database   **la base de données**
default option   **l'option** *(f)* **implicite**
double clicking   **le double clic**
escape   **(la touche d')** **échappement**
exit   **la touche de sortie**
file   **le fichier**
file management   **la gestion de fichiers**
flowchart   **l'organigramme** *(m)*
format   **le format**
function   **la fonction**
graphic application   **l'application** *(f)* **graphique**
graphics   **les représentations** *(f)* **graphiques**
graphic   **graphique**
graphics accelerator   **l'accélérateur** *(m)* **graphique**
help   **l'aide** *(f)*
help menu   **le menu d'aide**
language   **la langue**
logic circuit   **le circuit logique**
logic gate   **la porte logique**
macro   **macro**
memory   **la mémoire**
menu   **le menu**
operating system   **le système d'exploitation**
output   **la sortie**
output unit   **l'unité** *(f)* **de sortie**
package   **le progiciel**
peripherals   **les périphériques**
password   **le mot de passe**
program   **le programme**
programmable   **programmable**

programmer **le programmeur**
programming **la programmation**
pull-down menu **le menu qui
défile vers le bas**
reference archive **l'archive** *(f)* **de
référence**
return **(la touche) retour**
screen saver **le protecteur
d'écran**
setup **la disposition**
storage **la mémoire**
software **le logiciel**
software package **le progiciel**
space **(la touche d')espacement**
spreadsheet **le tableur**
statistics package **le progiciel de
statistiques**
user-friendly **facile à utiliser**
virus **le virus**

15d Computer printing

continuous *(paper)* **en continu**
dot matrix **la matrice**
font **la police de caractères**
hard copy **la copie sur papier**
ink cartridge **la cartouche d'encre**
inkjet **le jet d'encre**
laser printer **l'imprimante** *(f)* **laser**
low/high density **la basse/haute
densité**
A4 paper **le papier format A4**
paper feed **le système
d'alimentation de papier**
paper tray **le tiroir de papier**
printer **l'imprimante** *(f)*
    bubble printer **l'imprimante** *(f)*
    à jet d'encre
ribbon **le ruban**
roller **le rouleau**
sheet feeder **le chargeur de
papier**
style **le style**
toner **le rouleau d'encre**

16a Hobbies

angling **la pêche (à la ligne)**

bee-keeping **l'apiculture** *(f)*
collecting antiques **faire la
collection des antiquités**
archeology **l'archéologie** *(f)*
archery **le tir à l'arc**
ballroom dancing **la danse de
salon**
birdwatching **l'ornithologie** *(f)*
carpentry **la menuiserie**
chess **les échecs** *(m)*
collecting stamps **faire la
collection de timbres**
dancing **la danse**
fishing **la pêche**
gardening **le jardinage**
gambling **le jeu d'argent**
going to the cinema/movies **aller
au cinéma**
listening to music **écouter de la
musique**
knitting **le tricot**
photography **la photographie**
playing chess **jouer aux échecs**
reading **la lecture**
sewing **la couture**
spinning **le filage**
walking **la marche**
watching television **regarder la
télévision**

16c Photography

automatic **automatique**
cable release **le déclencheur**
camera **l'appareil** *(m)*
camera case **l'étui** *(m)* **(à appareil-
photo)**
I develop **je développe**
developing/processing **la
développement**
I enlarge **j'agrandis**
exposure **la pose**
exposure counter **le compte-
poses**
film **la pellicule**
    black-and-white **en noir et
    blanc**

colour/color **en couleurs**
film winder **le levier d'avancement**
filter **le filtre**
fine grain **à grain fin**
flash **le flash**
flash attachment **la glissière du flash**
home movie **le film d'amateur**
I focus the camera **je fais la mise au point**
in focus **net[te], au point**
out of focus **flou, pas au point**
jammed **bloqué**
lens **l'objectif** *(m)*
   telephoto lens **le téléobjectif**
   wide-angle lens **le grand-angle**
lens cap **le capuchon (d'objectif)**
light **la lumière**
   artificial **artificiel[le]**
   daylight **du jour**
light meter **la cellule photo-électrique**
movie camera **la caméra**
negative **le négatif**
overexposed **surexposé**
overexposure **la surexposition**
picture **l'image** *(f)*
photogenic **photogénique**
photo(graph) **la photo(graphie)**
   holiday/vacation photo **la photo de vacances**
   passport photo **la photo d'identité**
photograph album **l'album** *(m)* **de photos**
roll of film **la bobine**
shutter **l'obturateur** *(m)*
slide **la diapo(sitive)**
I take photos **je prends** *(prendre)* **des photos**
video camera **la caméra vidéo**
videocassette **la vidéocassette**

17b Architectural features

alcove **l'alcôve** *(f)*, **le**
renfoncement
arch **l'arche** *(f)*, **la voûte**
architrave **l'architrave** *(f)*
atrium **l'atrium** *(m)*
bas relief **le bas-relief**
battlement **le créneau**
buttress **le contrefort**
capital **la capitale**
colonnade **la colonnade**
column **la colonne**
   doric **dorique**
   ionic **ionien[ne]**
   corinthian **corinthien[ne]**
concave **concave**
convex **convexe**
cornerstone **la pierre angulaire**
cupola **la coupole**
diptych **le diptyque**
drawbridge **le pont-levis**
eaves **l'avant-toit** *(m)*
embrasure **l'embrasure** *(f)*
façade **la façade**
fanlight **la fenêtre en demi-lune**
gable **le pignon**
gargoyle **la gargouille**
half-timbered **à poutres apparentes, à colombages**
hanging buttress **l'arc-boutant** *(m)*
headstone **la clef de voûte**
herringbone **à chevrons**
high, sharp relief **le haut-relief**
molding **les moulures** *(f)*
nave **la nef** *(f)*
ogive **l'ogive** *(f)*
overhanging **en surplomb, en saillie**
pagoda **la pagode**
pilaster **le pilastre**
pinnacle **le pinacle**
plinth **la plinthe**
porch **le porche**
portico **le portique**
rear arch **l'arc** *(m)* **intérieur**
roof **le toit**
rosette **la rosette**
rotunda **la rotonde**

sacristy   **la sacristie**
spire/steeple   **la flèche**
stained-glass window   **le vitrail, la verrière**
transept   **le transept**
triptych   **le triptyque**
triumphal arch   **l'arc** *(m)* **de triomphe**
vault   **la voûte**
vaulted   **voûté**
vitrail   **le vitrail**
volute   **la volute**
wainscot   **la boiserie, le lambris**

17d Musicians and instruments

accompanist   **un accompagnateur, une accompagnatrice**
accordionist   **l'accordéoniste** *(m)*
alto *(adj)*   **alto**
alto (singer)   **le contralto, (le haute-contre), l'alto** *(f)*
bagpipe   **la cornemuse**
baritone   **le baryton**
bass *(singer)*   **la basse**
bass clarinet   **la clarinette de basse**
bassoon   **le basson**
bassoonist   **le joueur de basson**
bells   **les clochettes**
bugle   **le cor de chasse**
castanets   **les castagnettes** *(f)*
cellist   **le/la violoncelliste**
cello   **le violoncelle**
clarinet   **la clarinette**
clarinettist   **le/la clarinettiste**
classical guitar   **la guitare classique**
clavicord   **le clavicorde**
contralto   **le contralto**
cornet   **le cornet à pistons**
counter-tenor   **le haute-contre**
cymbal   **les cymbales** *(f)*
double bass   **la contrebasse**
double bassoon   **le contrebasson**
drum   **la batterie**
electronic organ   **l'orgue** *(f)*

électronique
euphonium   **la basse**
flautist   **le/la flûtiste**
flute   **la flûte**
French horn   **le cor**
grand piano   **le piano à queue**
guitar   **la guitare**
guitarist   **le/la guitariste**
harmonica   **l'harmonica** *(m)*
harmonium   **l'harmonium** *(m)*
harp   **la harpe**
harpist   **le/la harpiste**
harpsichord   **le clavecin**
harpsichordist   **le/la claveciniste**
horn   **le cor anglais**
Jew's harp   **la guimbarde**
librettist   **le librettiste**
lyre   **la lyre**
mandolin   **la mandoline**
mezzo-soprano   **mezzo-soprano**
oboe player   **le joueur de hautbois**
oboe   **le hautbois**
orchestra leader   **le premier violon**
orchestra players   **les membres** *(m)* **de l'orchestre**
organ   **un orgue**
   church organ   **les grandes orgues** *(m)*
organist   **un/une organiste**
percussion   **les instruments** *(m)* **à percussion**
percussionist   **le percussionniste**
pianist   **le/la pianiste**
piano   **le piano**
pipe   **le flûtiau**
recorder   **la flûte**
saxophone   **le saxophone**
saxophonist   **le/la saxophoniste**
soprano   **le/la soprano**
squeeze-box   **l'accordéon** *(m)*
steel drum   **le tambour de fer**
street singer   **le chanteur de rues**
string instruments   **les instruments** *(m)* **à cordes**
synthesizer   **le synthétiseur**
tenor   **le ténor**
tin whistle   **le flageolet**

triangle **le triangle**
trombone **le trombone**
trombonist **le joueur/la joueuse de trombone**
trumpet **la trompette**
tuba **le tuba**
viol **la viole**
viola player **l'altiste** *(m/f)*
viola **l'alto** *(m)*
violin **le violon**
violinist **le/la violoniste**
violoncello **le violoncelle**
vocalist **le chanteur**
Welsh harp **la harpe galloise**
wind instruments **les instruments à vent**
xylophone **le xylophone**

17d Musical forms

aria **l'aria** *(f)*
ballad **la ballade**
cantata **la cantate**
chamber music **la musique de chambre**
choral music **la musique**
concerto **le concerto**
  oboe concerto **le concerto pour hautbois**
duet **le duo**
fugue **la fugue**
madrigal **le madrigal**
music drama **le drame en musique**
musical (comedy) **la comédie musicale**
nocturne **le nocturne**
octet **l'octuor** *(m)*
opera **l'opéra** *(m)*
operetta **l'opérette** *(f)*
oratorio **l'oratorio** *(m)*
overture **l'ouverture** *(f)*
piano trio **le trio de pianos**
plainsong **le plain-chant**
prelude **le prélude**
quartet **le quatuor**
quintet **le quintette**

requiem mass **la messe de requiem**
sacred music **la musique sacrée**
serenade **la sérénade**
sextet **le sextuor**
septet **le septuor**
sonata **la sonate**
song cycle **le cycle de chansons**
suite **la suite**
symphony **la symphonie**
string quartet **le quatuor d'instruments à corde**
trio **le trio**

17d Musical terms

accompaniment **l'accompagnement** *(m)*
arpeggio **l'arpège** *(m)*
bar **la mesure**
beat **la mesure**
bow **l'archet** *(m)*
bowing **le coup d'archet**
cadence **la cadence**
chord **l'accord** *(m)*
clef **le ton**
  bass **basse**
  treble **soprano**
discord **la dissonance**
first violin **le premier violon**
flat (key) **bémol**
  B flat major **Si bémol**
  flat *(out of tune)* **faux [-se]**
improvisation **l'improvisation** *(f)*
key **le ton**
  major/minor key **le ton majeur/mineur**
C minor **Do mineur**
mute **la sourdine**
note **la note**
  breve **la double rond**
  minim/half note **la blanche**
  crotchet/quarter note **la noire**
  quaver/eighth note **la croche**
  semibreve **la ronde**
  semiquaver/sixteenth note **la double croche**

semitone   **le semiton**
principal (cello)   **le premier
(violoncelle)**
rest   **la pause**
   a minim rest   **la demi-pause**
scale   **la gamme**
score   **la partition, le morceau**
sharp *(key)*   **dièse** *(m)*
   sharp *(out of tune)*   **aigu[ë]**
sheet (of music)   **la partition**

17e Film genres

adventure   **l'aventure** *(f)*
animation   **l'animation** *(f)*
black-and-white   **noir et blanc**
black comedy   **la comédie noire**
cartoons   **les dessins** *(m)* **animés**
comedy   **la comédie**
documentary   **le documentaire**
feature film   **le long métrage**
horror film/movie   **le film d'horreur**
low-budget   **à petit budget**
sci-fi   **de science-fiction**
short film/movie   **le court métrage**
silent cinema/movies   **le cinéma
muet**
tear-jerker   **le mélo**
thriller   **le film à suspense**
video clip   **le clip vidéo**
war film/movie   **le film de guerre**
western   **le western**

19a Means of transport

by air   **par avion**
in an ambulance   **en ambulance**
by bicycle   **à vélo, bicyclette**
by bus   **en bus**
by cablecar   **en téléphérique**
by car   **en voiture**
by coach   **en car**
in a dinghy   **en canot**
by ferry   **en ferry**
by helicopter   **en hélicoptère**
by hovercraft   **en aéroglisseur**
by hydrofoil   **en hydrofoil**

by jumbo jet   **en jumbo-jet, en
gros-porteur**
by plane   **par avion**
by ship   **en bateau**
by subway   **en métro**
by taxi   **en taxi**
by tram   **en tramway**
by trolley   **en trolleybus**
in a truck   **dans un camion**
in a truck/semi   **dans un poids
lourd**

19b Ships and boats

aircraft carrier   **le porte-avions**
canoe   **le canoë**
cargo boat   **le cargo**
dinghy   **le canot**
ferry   **le ferry**
hovercraft   **l'aéroglisseur** *(m)*
hydrofoil   **l'hydrofoil** *(m)*
life boat   **le canot de sauvetage**
merchant ship   **le bateau de
marchandises**
ocean liner   **le paquebot**
petrol tank   **le réservoir d'essence**
rowing boat   **le canot**
sailing boat   **le voilier**
ship   **le bateau**
speedboat   **le bateau à moteur**
submarine   **le sous-marin**
towboat   **le remorqueur**
warship   **le vaisseau de guerre**
yacht   **le yacht**

19c Parts of the car

accelerator   **l'accélérateur** *(m)*
alternator   **l'alternateur** *(m)*
automatic gear   **la boîte de
vitesses automatiques**
back wheel   **la roue arrière**
battery   **la batterie**
bodywork   **la carrosserie**
brake   **le frein**
bumper   **les pare-chocs** *(m)*
carburetor   **le carburateur**

catalytic converter **le pot catalytique**
choke **le starter**
clutch **l'embrayage** *(m)*
dashboard **le tableau de bord**
door **la portière**
    front door **la portière avant**
    passenger door **la portière du passager**
engine **le moteur**
exhaust pipe **le pot d'échappement**
engine **le moteur**
front seats **les sièges** *(m)* **avant**
front wheel **la roue avant**
gearbox **la boîte de vitesses**
headlights **les phares** *(m)*
horn **le klaxon**
hood **la capote**
indicator **le clignotant**
license plate **la plaque d'immatriculation**
lights **les feux** *(m)*
motor **le moteur**
passenger seats **les sièges** *(m)* **de passagers**
pedal **la pédale**
    accelerator **la pédale d'accélérateur**
    brake **la pédale de frein**
    clutch **la pédale d'embrayage** *(m)*
rearview mirror **le rétroviseur**
registration number **le numéro d'immatriculation**
roof **le toit**
roof rack **la galerie**
safety belt, seatbelt **la ceinture de sécurité**
spares **les pièces** *(f)*
    spare wheel **la roue de secours**
sparkplug **la bougie**
speedometer **le compteur**
starter **le démarreur**
steering wheel **le volant**
tank **le réservoir**

throttle valve **l'accélérateur** *(m)*
tire **le pneu**
    back tire **le pneu arrière**
    front tire **le pneu avant**
    spare tire **le pneu de rechange**
tire pressure **la pression des pneus**
tool **l'outil** *(m)*
toolbox **la boîte à outils**
trunk **le coffre**
warning sign **le triangle de présignalisation**
wheel **la roue**
windshield **le pare-brise**
windshieldwiper **un essuie-glace**

19c Road signs

Cross now **Traversez**
Danger! **Attention danger!**
Detour **Déviation**
End of detour **Fin de déviation**
End of roadworks **Fin des travaux**
Enter expressway **Entrée d'autoroute**
Exit expressway **Sortie d'autoroute**
Expressway ends **Fin d'autoroute**
Free parking **Stationnement gratuit**
Keep clear **Interdit**
Maximum speed **Vitesse maximum**
No entry **Entrée interdite**
No parking **Stationnement interdit**
Pedestrian crossing **Passage pour piétons**
Residents only **Sauf riverains**
Road closed **Route barrée**
Roadworks **Travaux**
Toll **Péage**

20a Tourist sights

abbey **l'abbaye** *(f)*

adventure playground   l'aire *(f)* de jeux
amphitheater   l'amphithéâtre *(m)*
aquarium   l'aquarium *(m)*
art gallery   la galerie d'art
battlefield   le champ de bataille
battlements   les remparts *(m)*, les créneaux *(m)*
boulevard   le boulevard
castle   le château
catacombs   les catacombes *(f)*
cathedral   la cathédrale
cave   la grotte
cemetery   le cimetière
city   la cité
chapel   la chapelle
church   l'église *(f)*
concert hall   la salle de concert
convent   le couvent
downtown   le centre-ville
exhibition   le quai
folly   la folie
fortress   le château fort
fountain   la fontaine
gardens   le jardin public
harbor   le port
library   la bibliothèque
mansion   le manoir
market   le marché
monastery   le monastère
monument   le monument
museum   le musée
opera   l'opéra *(m)*
palace   le palais
parliament building   le Parlement
pier   la *(f)* jetée
planetarium   le planétarium
ruins   les ruines *(f)*
shopping area   le quartier commerçant
square   la place
stadium   le stade
statue   la statue
temple   le temple
theater   le théâtre
tomb   la tombe

tower   la tour
town hall   l'hôtel *(m)* de ville
university   l'université *(f)*
zoo   le jardin zoologique

20a On the beach

beach   la plage
beachball   le ballon de plage
bucket and spade/pail and shovel   le seau et la pelle
changing room   la cabine
deckchair   la chaise longue
I dive   je plonge
diver   le plongeur, la plongeuse
sand   le sable
   grain of sand   un grain de sable
sandcastle   le château de sable
sandy *(beach)*   de sable
scuba diving   la plongée sous-marine
sea   le mer
seashore   la grève
snorkel   le tube respiratoire
I snorkel   je nage avec un tube respiratoire
suntan lotion   la lotion *(f)*/ le lait *(m)*
sunshade (umbrella)   le parasol
I surf   je surfe, je pratique le surf
surfboard   la planche de surf
surfboarder   le surfer
surfing   le surf
I swim   je nage
waterskiing   le ski nautique
windsurfing/sailboarding   la planche à voile
I go windsurfing   je fais de la planche à voile

20a Continents and regions

Africa   l'Afrique *(f)*
Antarctica   l'Antarctique *(m)*

APPENDIXES

Arctic **l'Arctique** (m)
Asia **l'Asie** *(f)*
Australia **l'Australie** *(f)*
Balkans **les Balkans** *(m)*
Baltic States **les pays** *(m)* **baltes**
Central America **l'Amérique** *(f)* **centrale**
Eastern Europe **l'Europe** *(f)* **de l'est**
Europe **l'Europe** *(f)*
European Union **l'Union** *(f)* **européenne**
Far East **l'Extrême-Orient** *(m)*
Middle East **le Moyen-Orient**
North America **l'Amérique** *(f)* **du Nord**
Oceania **l'Océanie** *(f)*
Quebec **le Québec**
Scandinavia **la Scandinavie**
South America **l'Amérique** *(f)* **du Sud**
West Indies **les Antilles** *(f)*

20a Countries

Afghanistan **l'Afghanistan** *(m)*
Albania **l'Albanie** *(f)*
Argentina **l'Argentine** *(f)*
Australia **l'Australie** *(f)*
Austria **l'Autriche** *(f)*
Belgium **la Belgique**
Bolivia **la Bolivie**
Bosnia **la Bosnie**
Botswana **le Botswana**
Brazil **le Brésil**
Bulgaria **la Bulgarie**
Burundi **le Burundi**
Cambodia **le Kampuchéa**
Canada **le Canada**
China **la Chine**
Colombia **la Colombie**
Commonwealth of Independent States **Communauté des Etats Indépendants** *(f)*
Croatia **la Croatie**
Cuba **Cuba** *(f)*
Cyprus **Chypre** *(f)*

Czech Republic **la république Tchèque**
Denmark **le Danemark**
Ecuador **l'Equateur** *(m)*
Egypt **l'Egypte** *(f)*
England **l'Angleterre** *(f)*
Estonia **l'Estonie** *(f)*
Finland **la Finlande**
France **la France**
Germany **l'Allemagne** *(f)*
Great Britain **la Grande-Bretagne**
Greece **la Grèce**
Hungary **la Hongrie**
Iceland **l'Islande** *(f)*
India **l'Inde** *(f)*
Indonesia **l'Indonésie** *(f)*
Iran **l'Iran** *(m)*
Iraq **l'Iraq** *(m)*
Ireland **l'Irlande** *(f)*
Israel **d'Israël** *(m)*
Italy **l'Italie** *(f)*
Japan **le Japon**
Jordan **la Jordanie**
Kenya **le Kenya**
Korea (North/South) **la Corée (du Nord/Sud)**
Kuwait **le Koweit**
Latvia **la Lettonie**
Lebanon **le Liban**
Libya **la Libye**
Lithuania **la Lituanie**
Luxemburg **le Luxembourg**
Malaysia **la Malaisie**
Mexico **le Mexique**
Mongolia **la Mongolie**
Morocco **le Maroc**
Netherlands **les Pays-Bas** *(m)*
New Zealand **la Nouvelle-Zélande**
Norway **la Norvège**
Pakistan **le Pakistan**
Peru **le Pérou**
Philippines **les Philippines** *(f)*
Poland **la Pologne**
Portugal **le Portugal**
Romania **la Roumanie**
Russia **la Russie**

Rwanda **le Rwanda**
Saudi Arabia **l'Arabie** *(f)* **Saoudite**
Scotland **l'Ecosse** *(f)*
Serbia **la Serbie**
Slovakia **la Slovaquie**
Slovenia **la Slovénie**
South Africa **l'Afrique** *(f)* **du Sud**
Spain **l'Espagne** *(f)*
Sri Lanka **le Sri Lanka**
Sudan **le Soudan**
Sweden **la Suède**
Switzerland **la Suisse**
Syria **la Syrie**
Taiwan **Taiwan**
Tanzania **la Tanzanie**
Thailand **la Thaïlande**
Tibet **le Tibet**
Tunisia **la Tunisie**
Turkey **la Turquie**
Uganda **l'Ouganda** *(m)*
Ukraine **l'Ukraine**
United States **les Etats-Unis** *(m)*
Uruguay **l'Uruguay** *(m)*
Vietnam **le Vietnam**
Wales **le Pays de Galles**
former Yugoslavia **l'ex-**
   Yougoslavie *(f)*
Congo (former Zaire) **(Congo**
   (l'ex-Zaïre)
Zambia **la Zambie**
Zimbabwe **le Zimbabwe**

20a Oceans and seas

Adriatic Sea **l'Adriatique** *(f)*
Arctic Ocean **l'océan** *(m)* **Arctique**
Atlantic Ocean **l'Atlantique** *(m)*
Baltic Sea **la (mer) Baltique**
Bay of Biscay **le golfe de**
   Gascogne
English Channel **la Manche**
Gulf of Mexico **le golfe du**
   Mexique
Indian Ocean **l'océan** *(m)* **Indien**
Mediterranean Sea **la (mer)**
   Méditerranée

Pacific Ocean **le Pacifique**

21a Main language families

Afro-Asiatic **afro-asiatique**
Altaic **altaïque**
Austronesian **austronésien[ne]**
Australian **australien[ne]**
Caucasian **caucasien[ne]**
Central and South **du Centre et**
   du Sud
Eskimo **esquimau**
Indo **indo-**
indo-European **indo-européen**
   Baltic **balte**
   Celtic **celte**
   Germanic **germanique**
   Hellenic **hellénique**
   Indo-Iranian **indo-iranien**
   Italic **italique**
   Romance **roman**
   Slavic **slave**
independent **indépendant**
Native American **indien**
   d'Amérique du Nord
Paleo-Asiatic **paléo-asiatique**
Papuan **papou**
Sino-Tibetan **sino-tibétain**
Uralic **ouralien[ne]**

21a Languages

Afrikaans **l'afrikaans** *(m)*
Albanian **l'albanais** *(m)*
Arabic **l'arabe** *(m)*
Armenian **l'arménien** *(m)*
Basque **le basque**
Bengali **le bengali**
Breton **le breton**
Bulgarian **le bulgare**
Burmese **le birman**
Chinese **le chinois**
Coptic **le copte**
Czech **le tchèque**
Danish **le danois**
Dutch **le néerlandais**

English **l'anglais** *(m)*
Estonian **l'estonien** *(m)*
Finnish **le finlandais**
Flemish **le flamand**
French **le français**
German **l'allemand** *(m)*
Greek **le grec**
Gujarati **le goujarati**
Hebrew **l'hébreu** *(m)*
Hindi **le hindi**
Hungarian **le hongrois**
Icelandic **l'islandais** *(m)*
Indonesian **l'indonésien** *(m)*
Inuit Eskimo **l'esquimau** *(m)*
Irish Gaelic **le gaélique irlandais**
Italian **l'italien** *(m)*
Japanese **le japonais**
Korean **le coréen**
Kurdish **le kurde**
Latin **le latin**
Mongolian **le mongolien**
Norwegian **le norvégien**
Persian **le perse**
Polish **le polonais**
Portuguese **le portugais**
Punjabi **le panjabi**
Rumanian **le roumain**
Russian **le russe**
Scottish Gaelic **le gaélique
    écossais**
Slovak **le slovaque**
Somali **le somali**
Spanish **l'espagnol** *(m)*
Swahili **le swahili**
Swedish **le suédois**
Thai **le thaïlandais**
Tamil **le tamoul**
Tibetan **le tibétain**
Turkish **le turc**
Urdu **l'ourdou** *(m)*
Vietnamese **le vietnamien**
Welsh **le gallois**

21a Nationalities*

Algerian **algérien[ne]**

American **américain**
American Indian **indien[ne]
    d'Amérique**
Argentinian **argentin**
Australian **australien[ne]**
Austrian **autrichien[ne]**
Belgian **belge**
Brazilian **brésilien[ne]**
Canadian **canadien[ne]**
Egyptian **égyptien[ne]**
Indian **indien[ne]**
Iraqi **irakien[ne]**
Iranian **iranien[ne]**
Irish **irlandais**
Israeli **israélien[ne]**
Lebanese **libanais**
Mexican **mexicain**
Moroccan **marocain**
New Zealander **néo-zélandais**
Pakistani **pakistanais**
Palestinian **palestinien[ne]**
Québécois **Québécois**
Saudi **saoudien[ne]**
Scottish **écossais**
South African **sud-africain**
Swiss **suisse**
    Swiss woman **une Suissesse**
Syrian **syrien[ne]**

21b Grammar

accusative **l'accusatif (**m**)**
accusative *(adj)* **accusatif [-ve]**
adjective **l'adjectif** *(m)*
adverb **l'adverbe** *(m)*
agreement **l'accord** *(m)*
it agrees with **il s'accorde avec**
article **l'article** *(m)*
    definite **défini**
    indefinite **indéfini**
case **le cas**
case ending **la terminaison du
    cas**
clause **la proposition**
comparative **le comparatif**
conjunction **la conjonction**

* Other nationalities are as languages ➤ App.21a above

dative   **le datif**
definite   **défini**
demonstrative   **démonstratif**
direct object   **l'objet** *(m)* **direct**
ending   **la terminaison**
exception   **l'exception** *(f)*
gender   **le genre**
genitive   **le génitif**
indefinite   **indéfini**
indirect object   **l'objet** *(m)* **indirect**
negative   **négatif [-ve]**
nominative   **nominatif [-ve]**
noun   **le nom**
object   **l'objet** *(m)*
phrase   **la locution**
plural   **le pluriel**
   plural *(adj)*   **au pluriel**
possessive   **possessif [-ve]**
preposition   **la préposition**
pronoun   **le pronom**
   demonstrative   **démonstratif [-ve]**
   indefinite   **indéfini**
   interrogative   **interrogatif [-ve]**
   personal   **personnel[le]**
   relative   **relatif [-ve]**
   subject   **sujet**
reflexive   **le réfléchi**
   reflexive *(adj)*   **réfléchi**
rule   **la règle**
sequence   **la concordance**
singular   **singulier [-ère]**
superlative   **le superlatif**
   superlative *(adj)*   **superlatif [-ve]**
word order   **l'ordre** *(m)* **des mots**

Verbs

active voice   **la voix active**
auxiliary   **l'auxiliaire** *(m)*
compound   **composé**
conditional   **le conditionnel**
defective   **défectif [-ve]**
formation   **la formation**
future   **le futur**
gerund   **le nom verbal**
imperative   **l'impératif** *(m)*

imperfect   **l'imparfait** *(m)*
impersonal   **impersonnel**
infinitive   **l'infinitif** *(m)*
interrogative   **l'interrogatif** *(m)*
intransitive   **intransitif**
irregular   **irrégulier [-ère]**
passive voice   **la voix passive**
participle   **le participe**
past   **le passé**
   past *(adj)*   **passé**
perfect   **le parfait**
present   **le présent**
reflexive   **le réfléchi**
   reflexive *(adj)*   **réfléchi**
regular   **régulier [ère]**
sequence   **la concordance**
strong   **fort**
subjunctive   **le subjonctif**
system   **le système**
tense   **le temps**
transitive   **transitif [-ve]**
use   **l'emploi** *(m)*
verb   **le verbe**
weak   **faible**

21b Punctuation

apostrophe   **l'apostrophe** *(f)*
asterisk   **l'astérisque** *(m)*
bracket   **la parenthèse**
colon   **deux points**
comma   **la virgule**
dash   **le tiret**
exclamation mark   **le point d'exclamation**
inverted commas   **les guillemets** *(m)*
parentheses (in)   **(entre) parenthèses** *(f)*
period   **le point**
question mark   **le point d'interrogation**
semicolon   **le point virgule**

22b Stationery

adhesive tape   **le ruban adhésif**

carbon paper   **le papier carbone**
card index   **le fichier**
chalk   **la craie**
clipboard   **le porte-bloc à pince**
compasses, pair of   **le compas**
correction fluid   **le liquide
   correcteur**
datebook   **l'agenda** *(m)*
envelope   **l'enveloppe** *(f)*
eraser   **la gomma**
exercise book   **le cahier
   d'exercices**
felt-tip pen   **le feutre**
file   **le dossier**
filing cabinet   **le classeur**
fountain pen   **le stylo (à encre)**
glue   **la colle**
highlighter   **le surligneur**
hole punch   **la perforeuse**
ink   **l'encre** *(f)*
ink refill   **la cartouche d'encre**
in-tray/out-tray   **la corbeille
   arrivée/départ**
label   **l'étiquette** *(f)*
marker   **le marqueur**
notebook   **le calepin**
overhead projector   **le
   rétroprojecteur**
paper   **le papier**
paper clip   **le trombone**
paper knife   **le coupe-papier**
pen   **le stylo**
pencil   **le stylo à bille**
photocopier   **la photocopieuse**
pocket calculator   **la calculette, la
   calculatrice**
protractor   **le rapporteur**
push pin   **la punaise**
ring binder   **le classeur à
   anneaux**
rubber band/elastic band
   un élastique
ruler   **la règle**
scalpel   **le scalpel**
scissors   **les ciseaux** *(m)*
screen   **l'écran** *(m)*
set square   **l'équerre** *(f)*

sheet of paper   **la feuille de papier**
shredder   **la déchiqueteuse**
stamp   **le timbre**
stapler   **l'agrafe** *(f)*
staple remover   **l'otagraf®** *(m)*
stationery   **la papeterie**
textbook   **le livre scolaire**
typewriter   **la machine à écrire**
typewriter ribbon   **le ruban de la
   machine à écrire**
transparency (for OHP)   **le
   transparent**
wastepaper basket   **la corbeille à
   papiers**
whiteboard   **le tableau blanc**

23a Scientific disciplines

applied sciences   **les sciences** *(f)*
   appliquées
anthropology   **l'anthropologie** *(f)*
astronomy   **l'astronomie** *(f)*
astrophysics   **l'astrophysique** *(f)*
biochemistry   **la biochimie**
biology   **la biologie**
botany   **la botanique**
chemistry   **la chimie**
geology   **la géologie**
medicine   **la médecine**
microbiology   **la microbiologie**
physics   **la physique**
physiology   **la physiologie**
psychology   **la psychologie**
social sciences   **les sciences** *(f)*
   humaines
technology   **la technologie**
zoology   **la zoologie**

23b Chemical elements

aluminum   **l'aluminium** *(m)*
arsenic   **l'arsenic** *(m)*
calcium   **le calcium**
carbon   **le carbone**
chlorine   **le chlore**
copper   **le cuivre**

gold l'or *(m)*
hydrogen l'hydrogène *(m)*
iodine l'iode *(m)*
iron le fer
lead le plomb
magnesium le magnésium
mercury le mercure
nitrogen l'azote *(m)*
oxygen l'oxygène *(m)*
phosphorus le phosphore
platinum le platine
plutonium le plutonium
potassium le potassium
silver l'argent *(m)*
sodium le sodium
sulphur le soufre
uranium l'uranium *(m)*
zinc le zinc

23b Compounds and alloys

acetic acid l'acide *(m)* acétique
alloy l'alliage *(m)*
ammonia l'ammoniac *(m)*,
  l'ammoniaque *(f)*
asbestos l'amiante *(f)*
brass le cuivre
carbon dioxide le gaz carbonique
carbon monoxide l'oxyde *(m)* de
  carbone
copper oxide l'oxyde *(m)* de
  cuivre
hydrochloric acid l'acide *(m)*
  chlorhydrique
iron oxide l'oxyde *(m)* de fer
lead oxide l'oxyde *(m)* de plomb
nickel le nickel
nitric acid l'acide *(m)* nitrique
it oxidizes il s'oxyde
ozone l'ozone *(m)*
propane le propane
silver nitrate le nitrate d'argent
sodium bicarbonate le
  bicarbonate de soude
sodium carbonate le carbonate de
  sodium
sodium chloride le chlorure de

sodium
sulphuric acid l'acide *(m)*
  sulfurique
tin l'étain *(m)*

23c The zodiac

Aries Bélier
Taurus Taureau
Gemini Gémeaux
Cancer Cancer
Leo Lion
Virgo Vierge
Libra Balance
Scorpio Scorpion
Sagittarius Sagittaire
Capricorn Capricorne
Aquarius Verseau
Pisces Poisson
zodiac le zodiaque

23c Planets and stars

Earth la Terre *(f)*
Venus Vénus *(f)*
Mercury Mercure *(f)*
Pluto Pluton *(m)*
Mars Mars *(f)*
Jupiter Jupiter *(m)*
Saturn Saturne *(f)*
Uranus Uranus *(f)*
Neptune Neptune *(m)*
Pole star l'étoile *(f)* polaire
Halley's comet la comète de
  Halley
Southern cross la croix du Sud
Great Bear la grande Ourse

24b Wild animals

baboon le babouin
badger le blaireau
bear l'ours *(m)*
beaver le castor
bison/buffalo le bison
camel le chameau

cheetah   **le guépard**
chimpanzee   **le chimpanzé**
cougar   **le couguar**
coyote   **le coyote**
deer   **le cerf** *(invar)*, **le chevreuil**
elephant   **l'éléphant** *(m)*
elk   **l'élan** *(m)*
fox   **le renard**
frog   **la grenouille**
giraffe   **la girafe**
gorilla   **le gorille**
grizzly bear   **le grizzly, le grizzui**
hedgehog   **le hérisson**
hippopotamus   **l'hippopotame** *(m)*
hyena   **l'hyène** *(f)*
jaguar   **le jaguar**
lion   **le lion**
lynx   **le lynx**
mink   **le vison**
mole   **la taupe**
mongoose   **la mangouste** *(f)*
monkey   **le singe**
moose   **l'élan** *(m)*
mouse   **la souris**
otter   **la loutre**
panther   **la panthère**
polar bear   **l'ours** *(m)* **polaire**
puma   **le puma**
rat   **le rat**
reindeer   **le renne**
rhinoceros   **le rhinocéros**
squirrel   **l'écureuil** *(m)*
tiger   **le tigre**
vole   **le campagnol**
whale   **la baleine**
wolf   **le loup**
zebra   **le zèbre**

24b Birds

albatross   **l'albatros** *(m)*
blackbird   **le merle**
bluetit   **la mésange bleue**
budgerigar   **la perruche**
buzzard   **la buse**
crow   **la corneille, le corbeau**
dove   **la colombe**

eagle   **l'aigle** *(m)*
  golden eagle   **l'aigle** *(m)* **royal**
emu   **l'émeu** *(m)*
finch   **le pinson**
hawk/falcon   **le faucon**
heron   **le héron**
hummingbird   **l'oiseau-mouche**
  (m), **le colibri**
kingfisher   **le martin-pêcheur**
magpie   **la pie**
ostrich   **l'autruche** *(f)*
owl   **le hibou, la chouette**
parrot   **le perroquet**
peacock/hen   **le paon, la paonne**
pelican   **le pélican**
penguin   **le pingouin**
pigeon   **le pigeon**
puffin   **le macareux**
robin   **le rouge-gorge**
seagull   **la mouette**
sparrow   **le moineau**
starling   **l'étourneau** *(m)*, **le**
  sansonnet
swallow   **l'hirondelle** *(m)*
swan   **le cygne**
swift   **le martinet**
thrush   **la grive**
woodpecker   **le pic**
wren   **le roitelet**

24b Parts of the animal body

beak   **le bec**
claw   **la griffe**
comb   **la crête**
feather   **la plume**
fin   **la nageoire**
fleece   **la toison**
fur   **la fourrure**
gills   **les ouïes**
hide   **la peau**
hoof   **le sabot**
mane   **la crinière**
paw   **la patte**
pelt   **la peau**
scale   **l'écaille** *(f)*
shell *(oyster, snail)*   **la coquille**

(tortoise, crab) **la carapace**
tail **la queue**
trunk **la trompe**
tusk **la défense**
udder **le pis, la mamelle**
wing **l'aile** *(f)*

24c Trees

apple tree **le pommier**
ash **le frêne**
beech **le hêtre**
cherry tree **le cerisier**
chestnut **le marronnier**
cypress **le cyprès**
eucalyptus **l'eucalyptus** *(m)*
fig tree **le figuier**
fir tree **le sapin**
fruit tree **l'arbre** *(m)* **fruitier**
holly **le houx**
maple **l'érable** *(m)*
oak **le chêne**
olive tree **l'olivier** *(m)*
palm **le palmier**
peach tree **le pêcher**
pear tree **le poirier**
pine **le pin**
plum tree **le prunier**
poplar **le peuplier**
redwood **le séquoia**
rhododendron **le rhododendron**
walnut tree **le noyer**
willow **le saule**
yew **l'if** *(m)*

24c Flowers and weeds

azalia **l'azalée** *(f)*
carnation **l'œillet** *(m)*
chrysanthemum **le chrysanthème**
clover **le trèfle**
crocus **le crocus**
daffodil **la jonquille**
dahlia **le dahlia**
daisy **la pâquerette**
dandelion **le pissenlit**
foxglove **la digitale**

geranium **le géranium**
hydrangea **l'hortensia** *(m)*
lily **le lys/lis**
nettle (stinging) **l'ortie** *(f)*
orchid **l'orchidée** *(f)*
pansy **la pensée**
poppy **le coquelicot**
primrose **la primevère**
rose **la rose**
snowdrop **le perce-neige** *(inv)*
sunflower **le tournesol**
thistle **le chardon**
tulip **la tulipe**
violet **la violette**

25a Political institutions

assembly **l'assemblée** *(f)*
association **l'association** *(f)*
cabinet **le conseil des ministres**
committee **la commission, le comité**
confederation **la confédération**
congress **le congrès**
council **le conseil**
federation **la fédération**
House of Representatives **la Chambre des Députés, l'Assemblée** *(f)* **nationale**
local authority **la municipalité**
Lower House/Lower Chamber **la Chambre des Députés**
parliament **le parlement**
party **le parti**
Senate **le Sénat**
town council **la municipalité, le conseil municipal**
town hall **la mairie**
Upper House **la Chambre haute**

25a Representatives and politicians

Chancellor **le Chancelier**
congressman/woman **le député**

elected representative **l'élu** *(m)*
Foreign Minister/Secretary of State **le ministre des Affaires Etrangères**
head of state **le chef d'Etat**
Home Secretary/Minister of the Interior **le ministre de l'Intérieur**
leader **le chef, le leader**
leader of the party/party leader **le chef du parti**
mayor **le maire**
Minister/Secretary of **le ministre**
Arts/Culture **de la Culture**
Defense **de la Défense**
Education **de l'Education nationale**
Employment/Labor **du Travail et de l'Emploi**
Health **de la Santé**
Trade/Commerce **du Commerce**
Transport/Transportation **des Transports**
politician **l'homme** *(m)* **politique**
Prefect (Chief Executive of a département) **le Préfet**
President **le Président**
Prime Minister **le Premier Ministre**
representative **le député**
senator **le sénateur**
Speaker (UK) **le Président/la Présidente des communes**

27b Military ranks

---

admiral **l'amiral** *(m)*
airman first class (US)
marshal **le géneral de corps aérien**
brigadier **le général de brigade**
captain **le capitaine**
commodore **le contre-amiral**
corporal **le caporal-chef**

fieldmarshal **le maréchal (de France)**
general **le général**
lieutenant **le lieutenant**
major **le major**
private **le soldat (de deuxième classe), le simple sodat**
Private Smith **soldat Smith**
rear-admiral **le contre-amiral**
sergeant **le sergent**
sergeant-major **l'adjudant** *(m)*
sergeant-major (US) **l'adjudant-chef** *(m)*

27c International organizations

Council of Europe **le Conseil de l'Europe**
Council of Ministers **le Conseil des Ministres**
EC/European Community **la Communauté Européenne /CE**
EU/European Union **l'Union** *(f)* **Européenne/UE**
NATO/North Atlantic Treaty Organization **l'Organisation** *(f)* **du Traité de l'Atlantique Nord/OTAN**
OPEC/Organization of Oil Exporting Countries **l'Organisation** *(f)* **des Pays Exportateurs de Pétrole/OPEP**
Security Council **le Conseil de Sécurité**
UNO/United Nations Organization **l'Organisation** *(f)* **des Nations Unies /ONU**
WHO/World Health Organization **l'Organisation** *(f)* **mondiale de la Santé/OMS**
World Bank **la Banque mondiale**

D
SUBJECT INDEX

Subject index

Numbers refer to Vocabularies